Heartland TV

*Prime Time Television and the
Struggle for U.S. Identity*

Victoria E. Johnson

NEW YORK UNIVERSITY PRESS
New York and London

NEW YORK UNIVERSITY PRESS
New York and London
www.nyupress.org

Library of Congress Cataloging-in-Publication Data
Johnson, Victoria E.
Heartland TV : prime time television and the struggle for U.S.
identity / Victoria E. Johnson.
p.   cm.
Includes bibliographical references and index.
ISBN-13: 978-0-8147-4292-1 (cloth : alk. paper)
ISBN-10: 0-8147-4292-0 (cloth : alk. paper)
ISBN-13: 978-0-8147-4293-8 (pbk. : alk. paper)
ISBN-10: 0-8147-4293-9 (pbk. : alk. paper)
  1. Middle West—On television. 2. Middle West—Press coverage—
United States. 3. Television broadcasting of news—United States.
I. Title.
PN1992.8.M52J64 2007
791.43'6277—dc22   2007028429

New York University Press books are printed on acid-free paper,
and their binding materials are chosen for strength and durability.

Manufactured in the United States of America

c 10 9 8 7 6 5 4 3 2 1
p 10 9 8 7 6 5 4 3 2 1

Contents

Acknowledgments

I would like to extend my deepest thanks to Lynn Spigel for her mentorship as my advisor during my graduate study at the University of Southern California's School of Cinema-TV and, even more, for her invaluable encouragement, guidance, and friendship since. I have always been grateful to have attended USC, where I was privileged to work with tremendously supportive faculty and to develop lasting friendships with an outstanding group of colleagues. In this regard, I would especially like to thank Marsha Kinder, Rick Jewell, Michael Renov, David James, and Todd Boyd as well as my graduate cohort, including Mary Kearney, Janice Gore, Angelo Restivo, Bhaskar Sarkar, Eric Freedman, Harry Benshoff, and Sean Griffin.

The conceptualization of *Heartland TV* in its current form developed, primarily, through talks delivered at the annual Society for Cinema and Media Studies Conferences or at the Console-ing Passions Conferences. For their earliest and continued support of such talks, and for conversations about my written work as it evolved, I would particularly like to thank Anna McCarthy, Lisa Parks, Michael Curtin, Mark Williams, Mary Desjardins, Ed Linenthal, Mimi White, Heather Hendershot, Tara McPherson, and Jeff Sconce. In the last few years, with the development and expansion of the SCMS-TV Studies Interest Group and the initiation of the Flow Conference, I have been particularly energized by extended conversations and collaborations with colleagues including, especially, Michael Kackman, Jason Mittell, Jon Kraszewski, Amanda Lotz, Norma Coates, Cyndi Fuchs, Ron Becker, Alex Russo, Derek Kompare, Marsha Cassidy, and Jeffrey Miller.

I became fascinated with research as an undergraduate, taking refuge from the prairie winds and cold by retreating to the University of Illinois library when I was not otherwise attending classes taught by James Hay, David Desser, and Kim Worthy—my first mentors within the field of Film and TV Studies, and each of whose passionate dedication to teaching has been an inspiration since. For recognizing my scholarly interests and enthusiastically encouraging their development—and, further, for exemplifying that every opportunity to teach and to do academic research is, indeed, joyful and a privilege—I am in debt to these mentors, as well as to Pat Sheehan and Sam Brylawski at the Library of Congress Motion Picture and Recorded Sound Division, who offered me an internship the summer before my senior year in college. In graduate school I was fortunate to continue to have outstanding archive mentors as a student staff member at the University of Southern California School of Cinema-Television Library and Archive of Performing Arts, where I worked with Steve Hanson and Ned Comstock. For work critical to *Heartland TV,* I extend thanks to each of the exceptional staff members at: The State Historical Society of Wisconsin (SHSW), in Madison; the UCLA Microfilm Library and the UCLA Film and Television Archive and Archive Research and Study Center, in Los Angeles; the Museum of Television and Radio, in both New York and in Beverly Hills; and the Municipal Information Library of Minneapolis, Minnesota. I am particularly grateful to Gary Browning at the Museum of TV and Radio in Beverly Hills, Mary Jo Laakso, in Minneapolis, and Mark Quigley at the UCLA Film and Television Archive for their kindness and enthusiasm for this project.

In my first full-time faculty appointment I was privileged to work at the University of North Carolina in Chapel Hill. While at UNC, I developed the working contours of *Heartland TV* inspired, in part, by research on a different project entirely. Appointed as the Kenan Fellow to the Institute for the Arts and Humanities in Spring 2000, I conducted research examining the introduction of television to the state of North Carolina. That work sparked my interest in the cultural and geographic analysis of broadcast policy that is central to chapter 1. David Sontag is owed special thanks for inviting television industry leaders such as Les Moonves to Chapel Hill for his "Business of the Business" class, and then graciously allowing me to pepper them with questions. I would like to thank Les Moonves and Jeff Sagansky, in particular, for their willingness to be interviewed for this project. For their support I thank each of the faculty in the Department of Communication Studies and, particularly, Lawrence Rosenfeld, Bill Balthrop, Lawrence Grossberg, Ken Hillis, Gerald Horne, and Francesca Talenti. Beyond the department's walls, my thanks go to Robert Allen, Thomas Fahy, Ferrel Guillory, and each of my fellow "Bus Tour" alumni. Additionally, I would like to thank Joanne Hershfield and Jim Fink for their abiding friendship.

Heartland TV reached its final development and completion after I moved to the University of California, Irvine. For support of one quarter's teaching release, which allowed me to finish necessary archival research, I am grateful to have received a Career Development Grant from UCI. I would like to extend thanks to the faculty, staff, and students at UCI for their genuine support, exceptional collegiality and, not least, for their incredibly good company. I owe particular thanks to *each* of the faculty of the Department of Film and Media Studies, of the Program in Visual Studies, and of the Program in African American Studies. I would especially like to note the support of the Chairs of the Department of Film and Media Studies, Mark Poster, Akira Lippit, and Fatimah Tobing Rony, and of the Director of African American Studies, Lindon Barrett, as well as Dean Karen Lawrence, and Associate Deans Cecile Whiting and Linda Bauer. Additional thanks to Vikki Duncan, Virak Seng, and Donna Iliescu for the crucial day-to-day institutional support that keeps everything running. And, to Bliss Lim, Glen Mimura, Michelle Montague, Philip Nickle, Doug Haynes, Jenny Terry, and Kristen Hatch, thank you for the wonderfully supportive and productive conversations and encouragement.

Portions of chapter 2 pertaining to *The Lawrence Welk Show* were published in an earlier form, copyright 1997 from "Citizen Welk: Bubbles, Blue Hair, and Middle America," in *The Revolution Wasn't Televised: Sixties Television and Social Conflict,* eds. Lynn Spigel and Michael Curtin (New York: Routledge, 1997): 265–285, and are reproduced here by permission of Routledge/Taylor & Francis Group, LLC. Portions of chapter 6 were published in an earlier, pre-9/11 version, as "Fertility Among the Ruins: The 'Heartland,' Maternity, and the Oklahoma City Bombing," *Continuum: Journal of Media & Cultural Studies* 13.1 (1999): 57–75, and are reproduced by permission of Taylor & Francis (UK) Journals, http://www.tandf.co.uk/journals. I would like to thank Felicidad Lim, William Alvarez, Karen E. Johnson, the Haakenson family, Maritess Santiago, and Kim Waldman at AP Wide World Photos for assistance with illustrations and permissions. Support for illustration permissions and indexing by Martin Tulic was provided by a grant from the University of California, Irvine Humanities Center.

I thank Eric Zinner and Emily Park, as well as the Editorial Board and staff at New York University Press and the anonymous readers whose support and suggestions for *Heartland TV* were tremendously helpful. Eric's early enthusiasm and his commitment to the project as it developed have been inspiring. Emily's support and guidance have been invaluable as the book reached completion.

All writing is, in some sense, autobiographical and much of this work likely stems from the fact that, while I now call California home, I grew up in Carbondale, Illinois, with much summer time spent in North Dakota. I would thus like to thank the cousins with whom I grew up and friends from "C'Dale" who have known me since *The Mary Tyler Moore Show* was on the air and whose friendship continues to this day. Particular thanks go to Laurie Johnson, Katy Hughes, Jack Harris, Jill Mallin, Teryl Franklin and Brian Mattmiller (who together also fed and housed me during my archival labors in Madison, Wisconsin), Tricia Flejter, Jenny Sykes, Laura Fudacz, Sue Misner, and Beth Lepard. I couldn't ask for better friends or memories. From my Urbana days to the present, special thanks go to Kym Nelson, Scott Wylie, and to Stacy VanDeveer. From my first days in Los Angeles, I have been privileged to be friends with Anne Bergman, whose writing, family, perspective, humor, and kindness I deeply admire and dearly treasure. Thanks also to Rich Cante, whose friendship and shared professional and personal travels have encouraged me in both work and play, every step of the way.

This book is dedicated to my parents, Karen and David C. Johnson, and to the memory of my grandfather, farmer and statesman, Walter C. Erdman.

Introduction

TV, *the Heartland Myth, and the* *Value of Cultural Populism*

In 1939, Westinghouse sponsored the production of a film promoting the marvels of modern technology on display at the New York World's Fair "World of Tomorrow" Pavilion. *The Middleton Family at the New York World's Fair* allowed movie-going audiences from across the United States to "travel" to the fair and to explore the Pavilion's wonders alongside its fictional featured family, the Middletons from central Indiana. Though the Middletons are thrilled by a series of electrical wonders housed in the fair's "Playground of Science"—including the "Electro the Westinghouse Moto Man" robot who smokes cigarettes and responds to human commands and the electric dishwasher admired by Grandma and Mother—television is the technology that uniformly captivates each member of the family's multiple generations. Television holds great promise in its newness—its ability to transcend and bind great reaches of space with sound and picture—and yet its adoption is simultaneously made non-threatening, consistent as it is with already-familiar media and modes of communicating. When Jim Treadway, an electrical engineer from "back home" introduces the Middleton's youngest son, Bud, to the Pavilion's TV studio, for example, the youth's first response is that the camera reminds him of Riverdale's portrait photographer's studio. "Ah, looks like the shop of old 'Watch the birdie' Schultz. Remember him, Jim? Six deluxe portraits for a buck." Once Jim corrects him, pointing out that *this* camera enables television broadcasts, Bud immediately takes to the new medium, addressing fairgoers in a closed-circuit telecast with the chummy, "Hiya folks! This is Clark Gable Middleton speaking, as you can see if you've got your television sets turned on!" Bud's amazement at TV's technical capability is thus accompanied by familiarizing references to pre-televisual media,

Bud Middleton and Jim Treadway in the "World of Tomorrow" TV studio.

each of which is seamlessly incorporated into his understanding and use of TV.

Strategically, Westinghouse used *The Middleton Family at the New York World's Fair* to encourage audiences across the United States to apprehend the Pavilion's wonders through the eyes of midwesterners and their presumed "common sense" Heartland values. Midwesternness was the frame through which television was introduced, through which its uses were imagined, and through which its ideal audience was represented. Regional appeals were invoked to ally television and its uses with national, consensual ideals and values. Specifically, midwesterners represent the "all-American" cultural values of populism, here allied with the political ideology of New Deal-era liberalism. The Middletons embody these values through a commitment to family, a belief in free enterprise and progress within tradition, and an aesthetic sensibility that values regionalist expression and representational art. Within the larger narrative of *The Middleton Family at the New York World's Fair,* for example, Bud's eager embrace of a productive future through TV is mirrored by elder sister Babs's romantic redirection to a "proper" domestic life with Jim. As an art major at an eastern university, Babs has grown away from her Indiana roots in directions that concern her family and seem out of step with the film's broader imagination of national ideals of the period. Grandma comments to Middleton patriarch, Tom, that Babs's conversations and pronouncements are "over my head. I gave up when she told me pictures on calendars weren't art."

Babs's embrace of aesthetic abstraction over easily understood, familiar "pictures of people and objects" is made more worrisome by the fact that she is enamored with her art teacher, Nicholas Makaroff, a vaguely Russian, self-proclaimed genius whose passionate appreciation of abstract expressionism is paralleled only by his virulent anti-Americanism. Although Babs is initially smitten by Makaroff's book-smart intellectualism, political sloganeering, and wide-ranging travels (he knows "the world like we know Main Street!" she exclaims), she is gradually won over by the Westinghouse engineer's home-grown, pragmatic, can-do-ism. When Makaroff denounces all of the Middletons as "provincial," Babs embraces Jim, who claims that "nothing is impossible under the American system of private enterprise," newly symbolized by television.

If *The Middleton Family at the New York World's Fair* at first appears to be a distant example of corporate propaganda—a clumsily obvious, if endearing appeal to "Middletons" throughout the country to welcome the pending technological transition through screens of nostalgic familiarity—it should also be considered a prominent early example of the common and recurring tensions that accompanied television's introduction and standardization and the historic assumptions regarding its purpose and identity that are still actively engaged and struggled over today. Though television has been generally theorized as a space-binding medium, uniquely capable of addressing a national audience from a unified, centralized point of transmission (and, by extension, point-of-view), from its inception to the present, TV has been a rather more contentious entity—a site of ongoing struggle over the expression and importance of imagined *place*-bound ideals within this overarching national venue. As television enters the twenty-first century firm in its position as the central medium of information and entertainment in everyday American life,[1] the Midwest imagined as the United States's culturally and ideologically populist "Heartland" remains a remarkably consistent and provocative reference point in national media.

Indeed, the broadcast era is marked by a transition from popular representations of the Midwest as home to a radical populist political tradition to a "Heartland" characterized by centrist—and, increasingly, post-1960s, neoconservative—traditional cultural values and "mass," "low" market dispositions. National networking and the emergence and solidification of national markets reimagined U.S. populism (from its rise in the late 1800s through Farmers' Cooperative organizations or movements such as Abolitionism) as *cultural* ethos at "home" in the Heartland. It is important to emphasize here, as media theorist David Morley has noted, that while "it is sometimes hard to resist the idea that the very idea of home is itself reactionary and should simply be ceded to the political Right,"[2] the Heartland myth is not only representative of neoconservative political trends in U.S. culture. In fact, the productivity and richness of the myth is rooted also in its availability for recuperation and appropriation as a mainstream consensus site of shared cultural values and national ideals. This is why examining key moments in which the myth has been significantly taken up and revalued in broader popular discourse becomes particularly important.

Most recently, representations of the Midwest as Heartland have been energized following a series of traumas, from the 1995 bombing of the Alfred P. Murrah Federal Building in Oklahoma City to the contentious 2000 presidential election, 9/11, the war in Iraq, and the presidential campaign and election of 2004. Indeed, *USA Today*'s November 6, 2000 publication of the now-canonical "red state, blue state" map—an image immediately, surprisingly, and unproblematically taken up by television news shows—serves as a vivid contemporary example wherein television programming and broader public debates regarding place-identity, nationally representative ideals, and social power have been troubled over (and also, I will argue, significantly, simultaneously *un*troubled in their rapid adoption as the presumptive socio-political "common sense"). However, such regional mythologies are also integral to non-traumatic, everyday understandings of television and broader U.S. culture. With regard to the development of new entertainment series, for example, network executives have recently spoken of "not wanting shows that are aimed at people within 10 miles of the Atlantic and the Pacific,"[3] and of imagining their core audience as "the 37-year-old woman from Topeka, Kansas."[4] While the context in which such proclamations were made—as well as resulting development, marketing, and programming decisions based on those proclamations—was specific to a post-9/11 assumption that television audiences were seeking less "edgy" and "urban" fare allied with presumptively more conservative, rural "red state" values, the Middletons encourage us to consider: Rather than representing a *new* way of thinking about region, nation, and the politics of identity, the red and blue maps and their accompanying industrial and popular discourses should instead be thought of as part of a much longer trajectory of historic investments in and reiterations of this perceived cultural "divide" and its presumptively opposed audiences, tastes, and values.

Heartland TV: Prime Time Television and the Struggle for U.S. Identity examines the ways that presumed midwestern ideals and the Midwest as imagined, symbolic Heartland have been central to television's promotion and development and to the broader critical and public discourse regarding the medium's value and cultural worth. It interrogates the paradoxical ways that the Heartland historically has been a central site of desire and fantasy in American popular culture as seen on TV and in dialogue with other everyday media discourse. Energized particularly in times of cultural transition or perceived cultural threat or tension, the Heartland myth provides a short-hand cultural common sense framework for "all-American" identification, redeeming goodness, face-to-face community, sanctity, and emplaced ideals to which a desirous and nostalgic public discourse repeatedly returns. Positively embraced as the locus of solid dependability, cultural populism, and producerist, "plain folks" independence, the Midwest as Heartland, in this iteration, symbolizes the ideal nation (in other words, "We the People" are, ideally, midwesterners). Conversely, the Midwest Heartland also functions as an object of derision—condemned for its perceived naiveté and lack of mobility as a site of hopelessly rooted, outdated American past life and values, entrenched political and social conservatism, and bastion of the "mass," undifferentiated, un-hip people and perspectives—and in this iteration, the Midwest becomes the "other" against which the ideal nation is defined by relief ("We the People" are *not* midwestern, in principle). In short, the Midwest as Heartland, with its attendant ascribed values, is a key prism through and against which "common sense" ideals regarding citizenship, national identity, and cultural worth have been variously debated and understood in critical moments in television and broader U.S. social history.

Geography as Capital: Rethinking National TV's Regionalism

Heartland TV writes regionalism back into *national* network television history by examining its role as: a network infrastructure and market development strategy; a network promotional, branding appeal; a key consideration in broadcast regulatory policy; an aesthetic style and mode of address evidenced in programs; and a critical element in the imagination and judgment of television's audience. Television's role in constructing and reimagining the Heartland is thus a historical, technological, economic, cultural, and political phenomenon. At each of these sites, and at the core of this myth, is the idea that geography—both real and symbolic—is capital. Indeed, the foundational concept that energizes the Heartland myth's historic revisiting *and* sets an apparent limit to its actual *revision* is the persistent definition of the Midwest as home of the populist, rural, pastoral American "middle." This "middle" is both structural and imagined. It is structural as a capital relation expressed through strategic market expansion and development and definitions of consumer demography. Pierre Bourdieu speaks of geography as capital in this sense, describing a region's "distribution in socially ranked geographical space."[5] Geography is also symbolic capital, expressed through aesthetic distinctions and presumptions regarding audience disposition or "tastes." As Jan Radway notes, a disposition operates "as a 'predisposition, tendency, propensity, or inclination' to order the world . . . in a familiarly structured way. Dispositions, then, are exhibited partly as subsequent patterns of cultural consumption, appreciation, and appropriation."[6] The invocation and broader social value of the Heartland as capital is variable, however. While the core mythology that has defined the region within popular culture has remained remarkably stable since its inception, the broader social power and cultural worth of that myth has consistently shifted in relation to different historical contexts and political imperatives.

Television's regional imaginaries thus engage and inform national identities in different, critical historical moments. Particularly in times of social transition or cultural upheaval, these values are revisited to be energized as an ideal or disdained within broader popular discourse as best suits or functions in relation to broader national hegemonic "common sense." The subsequent chapters thus examine the relative value of the Heartland to prevailing understandings or constructions of the national in different, critical moments in postwar U.S. history. These examples significantly complicate and revise several of the most familiar narratives of U.S. television history—narratives that tend to efface regional concerns from national networking, programming, and audience address. For example, although many survey histories of network development often imply that television followed a smoothly standardized path, paved by radio and leading toward immediate network connection and universal service from coast-to-coast, television's development was notably staggered and uneven.[7] Struggles over how television networking should expand across the nation, what type of service TV might provide, and to whom infrastructural and economic concerns were to be addressed were radically informed by existing technological realities and debates over electrification. Broadcast executives thus balanced public rhetorical appeals to "universal" service and "national" networking with internal strategic plans that encouraged network expansion only into markets with enough population density to rationalize the investment, thus reinforcing the uneven access to rural consumers already mapped by transportation, telephone, and power lines.

Considering national network development in relation to these legacies reveals the literal and figurative power with which government regulators and broadcast industry executives, among others, imagined the medium and its audiences in relation to existing regional mythologies widely circulating within the broader U.S. culture of the late-nineteenth and early-twentieth centuries. In this respect, the Midwest has been a particularly problematic region in network history. It is simultaneously understood to be the most reliable, "mass," "all-American" market—as an aggregate class of consumers with presumptively popular, commercial tastes—*and* to be a risky investment, considering its lower population density and weaker, more rural market strength compared to coastal, more thoroughly urban market areas.

Even a cursory review of contemporary television trade industry publications and popular press features about the Midwest make clear that market identity inflects broader cultural and political conceptualizations —and vice-versa—each of which reinforces this ambivalent Heartland myth:

> If you want to follow the money, get on a plane. Forty-five of the nation's 50 most affluent ZIP codes hug the East and West coasts.

Fly-Over Land has just three, all on the North Shore of Chicago. . . .
This elite group . . . watch far less prime-time TV and read more news
magazines. . . .[8]

Or, in describing IKEA's choice of store placement, targeting "people
who had traveled abroad, who considered themselves risk takers who
liked fine food and wine, who were early-adopters of technologies."

The company then chose sites for new stores based on the distribution
of such values. The results looked like the red and blue maps . . . [ac-
cording to] Kent Nordin, until recently IKEA's sales and marketing
manager for North America, ... "There's more Buicks driven in the
middle than on the coasts." The company went to the coasts.[9]

Economic conceptualizations of the region as being both "mass," populist, consumer-class home *and* at a geographic remove from market currents do not determine the broader cultural and political myths of the
region but, instead, together with policy, programming, and larger popular discourses, help to form a "unity" of regional representations that
"are mutually reinforcing" and whose "fractured and selective status allows them to be continually renewed and secured,"[10] positioning the
Midwest as locus of American "populist" tastes and values.

Though excellent histories and analyses of local television have examined specificities of regional identity,[11] this project focuses exclusively
on images and broader industrial and public discourse that presume to
speak from a "national" perspective in address to an audience imagined
to *be* broadly national. Since television policy and programming em-
anate from specific locales and, considering that all television viewing
takes place at particular sites by variegated groups or individual viewers, this notion of a "national" perspective and a broadly "national"
audience is already mythological. However, the investment in the myth
of national community, made knowable only as conjoined via mass media, remains conceptually, ideologically critical—girding expectations
for television's broader socio-cultural and political importance within
U.S. culture, as well as informing daily engagement with the medium.[12]

Whereas, from the 1940s through the mid-1970s, the "Big Three"
television networks (NBC, CBS, and ABC) gained market and cultural
dominance, becoming iconographic of a general postwar encouragement of national integration in industry (through governmental policy

and regulation), it has been wisely argued that American television networks have lost their primacy in the shift from the network era to the late 1990s "neo-network" period.[13] Proliferating after the Telecommunications Act of 1996, the "neo-network" era describes the contemporary TV industry's attempt to maximize profit from a smaller viewing audience by reaching narrower and narrower demographics through "niche" network branding. As John Caldwell points out, narrowcasting reconfigures the audience in ways that appeal to cultural diversification.[14] In the current multi-media era, one appeal to diversification is through regionalism. The Heartland—imagined as a midwestern "home" for viewers, regardless of their actual, physical location—has recently been re-energized as just such a strategic appeal. Within the U.S. context, then, I consider the ways in which "globalization seems also to have led to a strengthening of 'local' allegiances and identities *within* nation-states."[15]

Although broadcast network singularity as the key, shared site of "mass-mediated theater and performance of nation, where national identity . . . is produced, secured, and maintained through crafting homogeneity and difference"[16] has, arguably, shifted ground in its primacy and function, I maintain that it remains *ideologically* central, particularly in the intersection between television and broader popular discourses that engage, contest, and/or affirm the representations, debates, and struggles therein. Attention to network TV is also important when considering the specificity of the U.S. media context. U.S. commercial television is uniquely parochial, remaining more "traditional" in its scope and use than in most advanced western contexts in ways that, arguably, actively discourage thinking differently about television and its daily use now than at its introduction. For example, the relative isolationism of domestic U.S. television has, arguably, encouraged the system's ongoing negotiation of local-region-nation dilemmas in ways that resist or at least qualify many contemporary critical conceptions of media, spatial transcendence, and de-territorialization.

Overall, *Heartland TV* argues for commercial television's continued significance and primacy as a critically important site of analysis because it remains the primary communications medium within everyday life for the majority of the U.S. population. In this respect—its continued centrality, "mass" accessibility, and "democratic" level of distribution and access across the nation—television remains unlike any other communications medium in its capacity to serve as a site of shared, national culture. While changes in business practices and the competitive media environment have undeniably altered the nature of television's cultural significance from the zenith of the three-network era—a period in which, on any given evening, one-quarter of the national viewing audience was often tuned in to the same program at the same time—the continued engagement with TV by the U.S. public (regardless of race, class, gender, generation, geographic, and educational lines) points to its continued significance as a shared site of cultural production *and* the apparent, lingering, felt need for television in these terms. *Heartland TV* thus examines network appeals to the continued investment in television's centrality for the imagination of national community, simultaneous with industrial strategies for further "niche-ing" the audience through overt appeals to Heartland programming, aesthetics, and address. I focus on prime time, commercial, network programming because of its popularity as the most watched, discussed, and debated site of television culture, shared by a more broadly diversified audience than any other "daypart" in the television schedule.

Historically, formal, textual analysis of television programming and promotion has focused on the genre or aesthetic that is considered critically and artistically distinctive within a given period in the medium's development (for example the "golden age" anthology drama or suburban sitcom of the 1950s, the politically engaged documentary series of the 1960s, the socially relevant sitcom of the 1970s, the auteur drama of the 1980s, etc.). While the importance of these program forms cannot be underestimated, *Heartland TV* extends this field of scholarship to also analyze programs that have generally been written *out* of scholarly histories of TV because of their "mass" audience and "low" appeal—programs whose aesthetic characteristics and presumed audience seemed to run counter to, but coexisted with, historically hailed and critically valued iconic genres. Additionally, *Heartland TV* revisits these iconic genres in order to interrogate the ways that their regional invocations, appeals, and, at times, counterintuitive evocations of midwesternness significantly informed critical apprehensions of their social value and cultural worth. In this respect, *Heartland TV* uses formal analysis of program aesthetics and address—in dialogue with institutional and popular discourses about them—both to reconsider "totally typical" popular program forms and to reread "quality" television genres and series in terms of their historic *dependence* upon regional mythology to stake and shore up these genre's positions within the historical canon.[17]

Indeed, while critically revered for its ability to "transport" audience members to new locales featuring diverse cultural expertise from across the nation, television simultaneously allows its viewers to settle in with familiar, "vernacular" cultural expressions associated with emplaced, regional traditions. Midwesternness-as-seen-on-TV has often been perceived, in this sense, to be a potential threat to "national purpose." Televised regional appeals, it has been feared, might "create a permeable space between regions and forces otherwise kept conceptually distinct" failing "to maintain the fences cordoning off culture from commerce, the sacred from the profane, and the low from the high."[18] The chapters that follow analyze and exemplify regional aesthetics in programming through reference to scholarly work from television studies and art history that interrogates theories of value, particularly as articulated by Erika Doss, Jan Radway, Lynn Spigel, and John Caldwell.[19] *Heartland TV* thus traces television's role in broader postwar transformations and revaluation of the regional within the nation, and in the linking of regionalist aesthetics to *political* ideology. Several chapters here focus on programs and branding appeals that were strategically used to attract a broad, "populist" audience through the explicit promotion of Heartland ideals. Television programming that appealed to imagined Heartland ideals and/or presumed to speak to a Heartland audience was (and often continues to be) read through critical apprehensions developed for understanding and reassessing regionalist art practice. When praised, regionalist art and television are hailed for their accessibility and populist appeals; when disdained, both are considered culturally suspect by making "connections between culture and the market" and threatening to "obliterate the distinction between those who were cultured and those who were not."[20]

Examining this last point in detail, *Heartland TV* considers regionalism in regard to the conceptualization of television's *audience,* and interrogates the critical valuation of the imagined Heartland audience as crucially bound up with broader discourses regarding taste, market differentiation, and the politics of social value. Of particular interest here is the rise of public discourse identifying the Heartland as an ideological "middle"-ground within postwar culture simultaneous to growing criticisms of television's "middlebrow" cultural status. Throughout *Heartland TV,* I interrogate the persistent association of midwesternness with "mass," undifferentiated taste and midwestern audiences with a "natural" affinity for middlebrow and "low" TV programming. The fear of national culture "down-classed" by television programming extends to critical perceptions of the medium's purpose and the identity and value of the audience it serves. As Laurie Ouellette's critical history of public broadcasting in the United States details, from its inception television has struggled to strike a balance between mass-audience entertainment appeals to "the people" and program service that is expressly pedagogical, situated "above popular culture."[21] As exemplified above, this imagined idea of the "indiscriminate mass audience" naturally gravitating toward populist offerings is discursively linked to a *specifically* midwestern audience. The Heartland audience is presumed to appreciate the popular rather than the educational, the "lowest common denominator" rather than minoritarian, "high," "class," "elite," cultural programming, the anti-aesthetic versus the auteurist, the average versus the exceptional. There is a doubled sensibility here: While the midwestern audience is imagined to be "low" in terms of taste and cultural sensibilities, its "averageness" is also periodically invoked in ideal terms—as reliably majoritarian, unswayed by fads, and, therefore, allied with stability, traditional values, and the smooth functioning of representative democracy (reflected in an oft-repeated TV industry argument that what is popular with the majority audience succeeds in the ratings, thus positioning TV as analogous to a voting booth).

But, how, explicitly, *is* a region "imagined"? What does it "look" like? How has regional mythology significantly influenced broadcast policy, network television's promotion and development, prime time program aesthetics and address, and public debates over the medium's cultural value (debates that are, largely, about the *audience's* presumed market value and cultural worth)? And, what is at stake in thinking about television history in these ways?

The Heartland Myth as Selective Tradition

Methodologically, *Heartland TV* is indebted to cultural studies' conceptualization of popular culture as a key site in the imagination, struggle over, reiteration, and social production of prevailing cultural "common sense." The chapters that follow are informed, particularly, by work from British and American Cultural Studies that theorizes media's relation to and importance in the imagination of place and national identity, and the role of the popular in struggles over social meaning and value in daily life.

While the chapters proceed chronologically in terms of the key text or problematic through which each is focused, *Heartland TV* does not propose a teleological progression or development of the Heartland myth over time. Instead, I am interested in the consistency across time of particularly charged elements of the Heartland myth and the critical ways in which those elements assume "relative weight" as explanatory narratives regarding citizenship ideals and values within "the forces in balance at any historical moment."[22] Sociologist Herman Gray has argued that U.S. popular media are characterized by a "continuing press towards an imaginary middle."[23] *Heartland TV* argues that, in such representation, this "middle" is often imagined to be *located* in a Midwest whose Heartlander values appear "to popular experience as transhistorical—the bedrock, universal wisdom of the ages . . . the terrain of what is 'taken for granted' in social and political thought," when, in fact, this myth is "thoroughly formed as a 'product of history' " within which "different forces come together, conjuncturally, to create the new terrain on which different politics must firm up."[24]

Though historically responsive and adaptive to social influence and change, the core mythologies through which the Heartland Midwest is imagined have remained remarkably stable since their emergence and solidification at the beginning of the broadcast era. Thomas Frank has recently remarked that this modern reimagining of the Midwest from its nineteenth-century and early-twentieth-century associations with radicalism to its contemporary image as traditional "home" "has to stand as one of the great reversals of American history."[25] *Heartland TV* argues that this reversal was critical to the successful foundation of national market culture and integral to forging consensus ideology of the "nation" in post-1920s America. The Heartland myth, in these respects, exemplifies "selective tradition," as theorized by Raymond Williams. Selective tradition describes

> an intentionally selective version of a shaping past and a pre-shaped present, which is then powerfully operative in the process of social and cultural definition and identification. From a whole possible area of past and present, in a particular culture, certain meanings and practices are neglected or excluded. . . . This selection is presented and usually

successfully passed off as "*the* tradition," "*the* significant past." . . . It is a version of the past which is intended to connect with and ratify the present. . . . It is a very powerful process, . . . It is also at the same time, a vulnerable process, since it has in practice to discard whole areas of significance, or reinterpret or dilute them, or convert them into forms which support or at least do not contradict the really important elements of the current hegemony.[26]

"Hegemony," as Williams reminds readers, is not simply the "dominant" within culture but is instead also descriptive of a process by which "otherwise disparate meanings, values, and practices" are organized into coherent clusters of meaning and articulated, interconnected values. Selective tradition, in this sense, describes a set of relations or associations that function within a broader discursive field within and against which cultural common sense is forged.[27]

The chapters that follow thus reconstruct a dialogue between television industry policy, regulatory statements, television programming, and popular press sources, in key, critical, historical conjunctures in prime time television and broader U.S. social history. These are moments of conjuncture in which the symbolic function of the Heartland Midwest has been explicitly and strategically engaged in the process of revaluing regionalism in relation to "national" identity—moments when the region's imagined, *culturally* based identity is politicized in contrast to, or as representative of, national values. Across these sites, the imagination of the Midwest as Heartland emerges as a discursive field within which "certain ways of talking about" the Midwest and regional identity are "ruled in" while selective tradition " 'rules out,' limits and restricts other ways of talking, . . . in relation to the topic or constructing knowledge about it." [28] Across each of these different sites, a "characteristic way of thinking" appears, encouraging a particular common sense framework through which midwestern identity and its presumed value are both communicated and by which a range of understandings are circumscribed.[29] These discursive networks and sites of conjuncture invoke past understandings of the region and its significance while engaging contemporary debates over national identity and regional representation that have continued relevance in the present.

The regional borders of the Midwest solidified by the 1920s concurrent with the rise of broadcast media and mass-market culture. The regional parameters have, from this period on, been understood to include a twelve-state region bordered by Ohio on the East across to the Dakotas at the region's Northwest, all the way down in a straight line south to Oklahoma at its southern edge.[30] As a perceptual or symbolic region, however, the Heartland is both a more limited *and* a more expansive regional idea. As analyzed in the following chapters, the "Heartland" myth—while understood to be thoroughly midwestern and located within the parameters of this region—is more *limited* in that it excludes certain spaces, people, and practices within its borders. Popular appeals to the Heartland are also more *expansive* when they invoke imagined Heartland "sensibilities" transcendent of geographic location. Geographer James R. Shortridge's *The Middle West: Its Meaning in American Culture* argues that the concept of *pastoral* life and culture is the trope through which the symbolic limits and expansiveness of the Midwest are conjoined and imagined as a unified mythology.[31] Rural, pastoral populism is, in this respect, the selective tradition through which cultural common sense regarding the region is filtered, and by which exceptions to such thinking are "ruled out" or excised from popular discourse.

An early entry in the now burgeoning field of cultural geography, Shortridge's work remains the only single-authored, book-length study to theorize the evolution within U.S. history of the Midwest as *cultural* symbol, established across a body of academic and popular discourses from the nation's founder's period to the contemporary era. Shortridge isolates the emergence of the "Midwest" as the key place-holder for the pastoral within U.S. culture, carefully assessing how the valuation of that myth has shifted in different historical moments. He identifies the first use of the term "Middle West" to date from 1827 in reference to a cartographic ordering of U.S. space, from north to south, wherein "Tennessee was middle-western in contrast, not with Missouri . . . but with the Northwest (e.g., Ohio and Indiana) and the Southwest (e.g., Alabama and Mississippi)."[32] By the mid-1800s, the region's association with agriculture was solidified and aligned with values of vigor and morality via a producerist work ethic. Hence, President Lincoln's 1862 pronouncement that "the great interior region . . . is the great body of the republic."[33] By the end of the 1800s, the concept of the Middle West shifted cartographically to the plains frontier, centered upon the "comparatively settled and stable 'middle' states of Kansas and Nebraska."[34] In this period, the central cultural traits associated with the Midwest became standardized in popular representations of the region as rural, pastoral, and home to national values of self-reliance, independence, kindness, pragmatism, industry, and humility. In the early 1900s, the term "Midwest" begins to be used frequently and the area described as "midwestern" grows, indicative of the widely admired aspects of pastoralism within the national culture.

According to Shortridge's account, the 1920s represent a key moment in shifting the valuation of the Midwest within American ideology. I argue that this shift is particularly significant because it is coincident with the rise of broadcasting and the growth of mass-market culture. Even though from the 1920s on, the Midwest was no longer a predominantly rural society—having become more urban than rural and more industrial than agricultural—popular discourses about the Midwest continued to define the region through reference to pastoralism. Thus, central to *Heartland TV*'s analysis of the circulation and significance of midwestern mythology is Shortridge's suggestion that the "failure . . . to incorporate the new" realities of midwestern life and culture "into the established view of the Middle West" as pastoral, "is an example of what may be a general need for Americans to regionalize—that is, compartmentalize—national myths in order to avoid a confrontation with the contradictions inherent in these myths."[35] While Shortridge's analysis of the Midwest as pastoral is a critical starting-point to any analysis of the Midwest as regional mythology, I extend this analysis to interrogate the broader cultural politics and apparent social value of this mythology, specifically as it is articulated to struggles over cultural capital through race, gender, sex, and class identity at critical intersections of U.S. social and prime time TV history.

As noted by Gilbert B. Rodman, articulation describes "the process by which otherwise unrelated cultural phenomena—practices, beliefs, texts, social groups, etc.—come to be linked together in a meaningful . . . and seemingly natural way."[36] The following chapters argue that, while pastoral populism is key to understanding the Midwest in the cultural imagination of the United States, this foundational mythology has its longevity—in the face of changing historic, demographic, economic, and cultural realities—due to the articulation of the Midwest to "practices, beliefs, texts, and social groups" that are imagined as, fundamentally, "square." Discursive constructions of the social capital and political worth of the Heartland, conceived *as* midwestern, are activated through the articulation of imagined "square" sensibilities to the pastoral myth. "Squareness" is the link between the presumed rural geographic remove of the Heartland and the Midwest's imagined *cultural* distance from progressive social currents and conversance. [37]

Hip to Be Square? "Possessive Investments" at Home in the Heartland

Heartland TV unpacks and examines the ways in which the Heartland Midwest has been imagined to be the common sense locus of the square, populist American dream—unquestioned home of square people, culture, and values. While hipsters represent all that is bright, new, and modern in culture, they are also simultaneously criticized as inauthentic and conformist in their slavish attention to consumer trends—icons of misplaced energy and non-productive labor.[38] Thus, the squareness of the Midwest is *idealized* in different historical moments, as the site of "authentic" culture—a region marked by stability and producerist energy. The ideal square is iconic of American populism, endearingly amateurish, ordinary, non-threatening, unswayed by fads and materialism, devout, hard-working, simple, and at the center of U.S. culture both figuratively and geographically.

At root, this aspect of the Heartland myth plugs into the long-standing debate over cultural populism and cultural elitism wherein "square" is associated with the "common," "ordinary" person pitted against the "elitist" snob. While the "red and blue" maps encourage us to think of this as a contemporary route to understanding a "divided nation," populated by squares in the middle and steeled against hipster elites from either coast, this conception of populist v. elite, square v. hip has been central to the imagination of the Heartland from the inception of the regional myth. However, the square is also a figure available for disdain and rejection as an out-of-touch, isolationist, plain figure threatening to pull down the rest of the nation with "low" tastes and comprehension, conservative narrow-mindedness, and naïve lack of sophistication. This is the square perceived as dangerously backward, on the fringe of U.S. culture, an embarrassment to the nation's image and progress. Significantly, while historically "hip" has been associated with progressivism, rebelliousness, outsiderness, bohemian expression, youth, urbanity, African American culture, gay culture, and queered perspective,[39] the counter-posed "square" is traditionally understood to be mainstream, majoritarian, conservative, rural, old-fashioned, and rooted in past life and culture. Further, the square is characterized by a "straight" heteronormativity (embodied, particularly, by the patriarchal, nuclear family ideal) and, crucially, imagined as "white."

Regarding the construction of "whiteness" and the resultant resources, power, and opportunity allied with investment in whiteness within U.S. culture, George Lipsitz states, "whiteness never works in isolation; it functions as part of a broader dynamic grid created through intersections of race, gender, class, and sexuality."[40] I argue that geography must be added to this matrix, and that the persistent association of "midwesternness" *as* "white" is critical to the region's revaluation—particularly in moments of social upheaval and trauma—as "home" of "authentic" cultural populism and traditional U.S. values. In such moments, the Midwest is recuperated *as* a "white," heteronormative, familial space, in "a strategic deployment of power" that invests the region with identifications that have functioned historically to "universalize [the region] into Americanness."[41] *Heartland TV* thus argues that, while the Heartland is often disdained in popular discourse for its perceived "square" lack of cultural capital, its ongoing social and political relevance is *secured* via the articulation of "squareness" to the imagination of the region as almost exclusively patriarchal, "straight," and white. Through this highly selective and partial imagination of the Midwest as affiliated—in raced, gendered, and sexed terms—with dominant cultural identifications, the Heartland remains powerful, in spite of its square "vulnerability" in other respects. This imagination of the Heartland as an essentially "straight," white space places it at the center of a "culture that still holds real power."[42] Imagined in this way, the Heartland Midwest underscores the nation's historic and ongoing, systemic racism while also functioning as the site upon which to transfer or "locate" the culture's possessive investment in whiteness. The Heartland thus offers a myth through which the nation reifies racism as the status-quo, *and* by which national discourse disavows racism, proclaiming enlightened ideals that stand in direct contrast to those imagined to inhere in the region.

Consequently, *Heartland TV* interrogates the ways in which the Heartland is energized as a primary site "where whiteness rushe(s) to reconstitute itself and rebuild its defenses."[43] Arguably, this reconstitution is all the more politically powerful for the fact that it is *not* couched in overtly raced terms, but, rather through a spatial imaginary that posits the Heartland Midwest as shared, national "home" wherein the presumptive "invisibility" of race implies "universal" value. Geographic identity thus becomes "visible" through the iconography of race, gender, sexuality, and landscape. While "whiteness" is not monolithic or homogeneous, it is imagined and mobilized as such in articulation to place as a social category. As Ian Haney López notes, "consider the ease with which we assign racial identities knowing only that someone is from Santa Monica or South Central, Greenwich Village or Harlem." And, moreover, that "this link between space and race functions as a matter of what others *believe* of our identity and how we think of ourselves" and imagine—or limit the imagination of—other possibilities. [44]

Heartland TV thus raises questions and provides theoretical analyses regarding how "whiteness" and heteronormativity are routinely mobilized as *belonging* in the Midwest, particularly in ways that have actively rewritten the physical and imagined borders of the region through the elision of urbanity, people of color, and non-agrarian industry. At stake, here, are broader questions regarding how the Midwest functions as a site of transference and disavowal for the broader nation, with regard to race, sexuality, and citizenship ideals. Thus, popular imaginations of the Midwest as Heartland are public engagements and struggles over questions of citizenship and value. As Lauren Berlant has stated, "Americans experience themselves as national through public accounts of what is important about them." [45] Citizenship, writes Berlant, is "always in process. It is continually being produced out of a political, rhetorical, and economic struggle over who will count as 'the people' and how social membership will be measured and valued." [46] Moments of historical transition "make more, not less central the work of media in redefining citizenship and framing what can legitimately be read as national pedagogy." [47] The common sense myth of the Midwest as pastoral Heartland thus has broader *political* resonance as regards who "counts" within the framework of both regional and national understandings.

Methodology and Chapter Summaries

While *Heartland TV* cannot reconstitute the specific ways in which individual viewers and groups interpreted discourses about the Heartland analyzed here, by marshalling television industry policy and governmental regulatory statements, television program address and aesthetics, and popular press sources, and reading them as an intertextual network of meanings, a "common sense" way of imagining the Heartland and of struggling over postwar ideals regarding regional and national identity emerges. It then becomes possible to trace, contextually, shifts, reiterations, and reinterpretations of this common sense to explore specifically how, in key historical moments and in strategic programming and promotional appeals *in* those moments, television has been a central site for imagining and struggling over ideals of national identity through regionalism.

In considering questions of symbolic representation and cultural value, *Heartland TV* revisits U.S. television history through cultural studies approaches to television studies, cultural geography, critical theory of space and place, critical race theory, feminist theory, art history, and related histories and theories of cultural value. *Heartland TV* thus enters into dialogue with and extends critical histories of television that consider popular television in relation to domestic communication policy and acknowledge that networking as a practice, and programming as a textual field, are historically engaged in dialogue and tension with larger social forces. Important here as well are contemporary and historical theories regarding the nation, space, place, and communications technology, particularly as related to the unevenness of technological development in the United States and to understandings of citizenship based, in part, on such access and connection.

The core historical evidence marshaled here to reconstruct discursive networks of the Heartland consists of popularly, publicly available materials. Popular press, archival documents, and government documents and speeches that are often not easily accessible are here compiled together for ease of reference and study. Analysis of program texts is here also focused on programs that are widely available for review, study, or classroom use. I have attempted to reconstruct the larger social context of broadcasting and Heartland mythology in history through reference to television industry trade periodicals, government documents, newspapers, and popular press periodicals, as well as network television programming and promotional appeals. I have focused on mass-market periodicals because of their presumed address to an imagined, unified, national audience having wide demographic appeal. These media venues thus share television's "national" appeal and audience concerns, but, poised as competing media within the consumer market, also serve as venues for criticism and debate regarding television's role in everyday American life. The limits and significance of the presumed, shared, "national" audience addressed by popular press sources and television programming is interrogated in the following chapters. Overall, however, it is clear that the audience appealed to across these venues is largely and presumptively white and middle class. Of particular interest in *Heartland TV,* then, is the articulation of "white middle class" to an imagined *midwestern* family mythology as it shifts historically in relation to the Heartland as imagined home to such an "ideal."[48]

Heartland TV also offers a reading of the ways in which television industry policy, regulatory statements, network development, and promotional plans and programming have *strategically* engaged regional mythology to define and meet "public interest" standards, to attract a broad, "populist" audience, and to appeal to audiences through the promotion of Heartland ideals. Across these sites, the Heartland has been imagined and invoked as both representative of television's "universal" promise and popular possibilities, and as a challenge or field of resistance to TV's technological, aesthetic, and commercial potential. As historical evidence and support in considering these issues, I have turned to archival collections of the NBC network and network executives from NBC, ABC, and CBS, as well as to the collections of members of the Federal Communications Commission and television producers and journalists.[49] Also included in both popular references and in archival documents are examples of public responses regarding television. Such documents are included not to offer a generalized understanding of popular reception of Heartlander appeals, but, rather, to suggest the relative intensity with which issues regarding place and nation on TV were felt and engaged at different historical moments by the larger public.

I had several criteria when considering whether a site—particularly a program text or set of programs—constituted a critical "conjuncture." Stuart Hall defines a conjuncture as a historically specific moment within which a critical network of discourses forms across political, institutional, and popular sites, engaged in working through a broader social dilemma.[50] Each of the chapters that follow examines a particularly energized moment in postwar U.S. history within which the Heartland myth was explicitly interrogated in relation to "national" ideals and values. While the myth of the Heartland is an ongoing one, the sites studied here are unique as catalysts that clearly provoked or were meaningfully central to a broader national debate regarding middlewesternness, national "purpose," and cultural value during key moments in television and broader U.S. social history. Each of these sites—in policy, strategic use of promotions and programming, and critical apprehensions of TV's audience and purpose—represented a central matrix for working through the cultural and political worth of populist, midwestern values for the nation. Each explicitly emphasize, express, and engage the "Heartland" as a "keyword" that energized struggles over the text (whether it be policy, program, network branding appeal, star persona, presumed audience, or, generally, a combination of each of the above). These texts and the debates into which they entered are each significant interrogations of the broader construction and public refashioning of a "populist" American "mass" "middle" in relation to an imagined coastal "elite." At each of these featured sites, more than at any other on TV in that postwar historical moment, the Heartland and its imagination in terms of national value and American identity was centrally at stake. And, as indicated above, each of the critical sites here also significantly interrogates and revises "given," "common sense" understandings of TV history *through* cultural geography.

This explains why, for example, *Good Times* (CBS, 1974–1979), set in Chicago, is not the key text from the 1970s here. As chapters 3 and 4 outline, Chicago and its African American populations were effectively excised from popular discourse regarding the Heartland in this period. I have also not discussed the Garry Marshall-produced programs *Happy Days* (1974–1984) or *Laverne and Shirley* (1976–1983)—both hugely popular for ABC during the 1970s and both set in a nostalgically imagined 1950s Milwaukee (though in its last three seasons *Laverne and Shirley* had moved to Los Angeles). These series are addressed in Daniel Marcus' *Happy Days and Wonder Years: The Fifties and Sixties in Contemporary Cultural Politics* and in Janet Staiger's *Blockbuster TV: Must-See Sitcoms in the Network Era*. Marcus' theorization of nostalgia and political conservatism and Staiger's analysis of the critical judgment (read: disdain) visited upon these programs resonate with *Heartland TV*'s focus on the cultural imagination of a "populist" American "middle," but the programs themselves were not discussed as "Heartland" texts or as indicative of a broader shift or interrogation of the myth. However, during much of this same period, MTM Productions of the 1970s *were* discussed in these terms via analyses of their settings, star personae, and "work family" cultures. *Heartland TV* also does not examine the long-running pastoral family drama, *Little House on the Prairie* (NBC, 1974–1982) in order that I might focus instead on MTM

Productions' comedies in terms of "quality," race, urbanity, and the "middle-ethic" ideal. However, forthcoming work by Anna Thompson-Hajdik on the relationship between *Little House on the Prairie* and Walnut Grove, Minnesota does address this series and also dovetails with my chapter 4 discussion of Heartland tourism via MTM icons as they have functioned in the promotion of Minneapolis and Chicago. Finally, in my readings of both the programs themselves and the popular press responses to them, I interpret *The Beverly Hillbillies* (CBS, 1962–1971), *The Andy Griffith Show* (CBS, 1960–1968) and *Mayberry, RFD* (CBS, 1968–1971) to be understood as more southern than midwestern. Though *Green Acres'* (CBS, 1965–1971) fantastic pastoral universe suggests, potentially, an uncanny, science-fiction Heartland, in this study I choose to focus for that period on the unmatched popularity of *The Lawrence Welk Show,* which was always identified as midwestern in popular and critical discourse and by the judgments of its audience. [51]

While there are overlaps and contemporary connections made in each of the following chapters, the studies featured in *Heartland TV* proceed chronologically, from the origination of broadcasting to the contemporary, "neo-network" era. The first three chapters focus on key debates and texts during the period from the 1920s through the 1960s. This era is characterized by a systematic revaluing of the region *toward* the nation and national ideals in relation to cultural expression, markets, and political ideology. In this period, the Heartland myth is significantly revised and stabilized, moving from its place as idealized "center" of representative U.S. identity to its conceptualization as a potentially resistant site characterized by isolationist conservatism mired in the past. Chapters 4 through the epilogue focus on the period from 1970 to the present, which can be characterized by a revaluing of the "niche" within the nation and, therefore, of the populist possibilities represented by the Heartland in relation to cultural production, markets, and political ideology. This chronological approach is intended to underscore the tenacity of the Heartland myth—its powerful "residue" in times of progress and change—as well as to throw into relief powerful challenges to or reimaginations of this mythology, emphasizing why such moments are perceived as exceptional and, even, intensely threatening. Each chapter thus charts the shifting articulation of the pastoral-populist myth, regional aesthetics, and the relative value of "squareness" as capital to prevailing cultural ideals at key sites of conjuncture between television and broader socio-political discourse.

One of the key interventions that *Heartland TV* makes is to read broadcast policy through cultural geography in order to examine how regional mythologies were actually written into regulatory definitions and standards regarding public interest and audience differentiation. Because the policies closely analyzed in chapter 1 remained fundamentally unchanged from their inception in the 1930s until 1996's revision of the Telecommunications Act, the *structural* impact of these policies becomes "visible" as it then informs strategies of network promotion, identification, and conceptualization of audience address through the network era (through chapter 4 here in particular). Thus, *Heartland TV* opens with a chapter that focuses on the revaluing of post-1930s U.S. culture *from* regionalism to nationalism through networking, and concludes with the epilogue's analysis of the transition to a "neo-network" era which is currently revaluing regional appeals as network branding strategies. However, each chapter significantly interrogates the ways in which regulatory expectations (for service in the "public interest"), as well as market imperatives, contribute to "regional" modes of network programming, promotion, and audience appeal.

Chapter 1, " 'Essential, Desirable, and *Possible* Markets': Broadcasting Midwestern Tastes and Values" charts historic struggles between the expressed, rhetorical ideals of "universal," national networking and the rather more uneven realities of local service. This chapter focuses on institutional/network and regulatory/policy expectations for regional expression, understandings of national service obligations, and the imagined limits of each, from the pre-broadcast era through the 1940s. Specifically, chapter 1 interrogates the role of Heartland mythology in structuring network development rationales, broadcast law, and regulatory policy. It traces, in particular, the ways in which "service in the public interest" was codified as a geographically differentiated standard. This chapter thus offers a critical rhetorical analysis of network development rationales and strategic plans, communications law, and regulatory statements in relation to or as informed by changing cultural mythologies of region and nation. To analyze the development of network infrastructure and promotion, I focus on archival accounts of NBC's plans for the physical expansion of television networking in ways that might balance economy of scale with the expressed promise of genuinely national service (at least rhetorically). The chapter examines regulatory statements and guiding principles of the period, including analysis of *The Blue Book* (1946), which codified the Federal Communications Commission's assertion that American tastes and values were differentiated according to geographic region or "zone." Subsequent chapters offer evidence that the principles of geographic differentiation established in *The Blue Book*—as a standard for public service, program types, and presumed audience reflecting different tastes and necessitating different market appeals—set the precedent for ongoing debates regarding regionalism and TV as a market and cultural forum to this day. Indeed, such debates have, arguably, been energized in the context of multiple-platform TV delivery and new media outlets.

The interrogation in chapter 1 of the role of Heartland mythology in structuring network development rationales, broadcast law, and regulatory policy leads to an analysis of early network programming and promotions that strategically appealed to Heartland values and "populist" audiences through regional, "pre-televisual" expressive forms from American arts, folk culture, and everyday life. Chapter 2, "Square Dancing and Champagne Music: Regional Aesthetics and Middle America," focuses on the specific examples of *Jubilee, U.S.A.* (ABC, 1955–1961) and *The Lawrence Welk Show* (ABC, 1955–1971) to examine the paradox that, while most histories of American network television propose that the medium rose to prominence due to promotional rhetoric and "Golden Age" programming that promised unprecedented enlightenment through the transmission of urban, "high" cultural ideals, the network promotions and programs of the 1950s and beyond also overtly appealed to "populist" and expressly rural traditions.[52] In promoting itself as America's new, uniquely *national* medium, network executives and program producers presented *both* the "high" urban ideals particularly associated with the American East (especially New York City) and populist, vernacular traditions and values that were historically associated with the broader American Heartland. Popular critics and scholars have tended to embrace television in its "high" appeals and generic forms while puzzling over the popularity of "populist" programs. This puzzlement played itself out in contemporary debates over the medium's purpose and cultural worth, as examined here through a close reading of these programs' aesthetics and content and through an analysis of related critical valuations of their audiences' tastes and presumed politics.

The dual "mass" audience popularity and vehement critical disdain of "populist" programs through the 1960s underscores the paradoxical nature of television and points to a relatively effaced aspect of prime time history. Though television industry rhetoric, programming, and space-age broadcast technologies positioned 1960s America as the leading symbol of a reinvigorated New York- and Washington, D.C.-centered cosmopolitan, worldly culture, there simultaneously remained vigorous, competing tensions and ambivalence in postwar American life that held fast to residual ideals of pre-war, place-bound tradition and "knowable" community, and that challenged the very desirability of a national identity shared in common.[53] However, while prestige network documentary series such as *CBS Reports* defined 1960s America according to New Frontier ideals of progress and mobility, such programs also reinforced and perpetuated rather *fantastic* elements of the Heartland myth as, particularly, African Americans, the working-class, urban centers, and political activism were increasingly written out of these programs' representations of the U.S. Midwest. This excision of racial diversity and sexual "difference" is the focus of chapters 4 and 5, respectively. Chapter 3, however, extends Michael Curtin's groundbreaking work on the "international" look of 1960s documentary to focus on the domestic documentary's portrayal of the Midwest Heartland as a particular kind of "resistant" and residual site within the New Frontier.

Chapter 3, " 'Strictly Conventional and Moral': *CBS Reports* in Webster Groves," also connects documentary programming with the governmental and popular press rhetoric that increasingly defined the region as home to what, by the 1970s, would be defined as an emerging "Silent Majority," in ways that significantly revalued "traditional" Heartland mythologies to appear threateningly out-of-touch, retrogressive, and divisive in the face of national progress in civil rights and the Cold War. This chapter focuses solely on two key sites through which TV viewers "talked back" to regulators and documentary producers and journalists in the 1960s. In particular, responses to Newton Minow's "Vast Wasteland" speech and to *CBS Reports* journalists and producers pertaining to two documentaries about Webster Groves, Missouri indicate the unresolved and, frequently, quite raw tensions regarding television and capital relations in the 1960s. "Talking back" to the television set by midwestern viewers, in particular here, reveals a desire to be identified with and to claim the "elite" values promoted and embodied by reformers such as Minow and CBS News' Fred Friendly. However, there is also here a felt threat that "outsider" perspectives of the local might be detrimental to the region's image when viewed by the nation-at-large.

Popular representations of the Midwest as home to residual, traditional values and past life and culture, as seen in chapters 2 and 3, establish the field within which MTM Productions' 1970s comedy series were interpreted, critically, as counterintuitive portrayals of the Midwest as "newly" urbane consumer spaces, home to hip (if understated) sexuality and bourgeois feminism. Chapter 4, " 'You're Gonna Make It After All!' The Urbane Midwest in MTM Productions' 'Quality' Comedies," writes geography back into the narrative of MTM Productions' historic position as a "quality" production company—a significant element of the creators' pitch and an inherent marker of the programs' distinctiveness within the 1970s TV landscape, but also an element that has been absent from existing analyses of the series. This chapter thus interrogates MTM Productions' *The Mary Tyler Moore Show* (CBS, 1970–1977), *The Bob Newhart Show* (CBS, 1972–1978), and *WKRP in Cincinnati* (CBS, 1978–1982) specifically as regards the programs' imagination of the American Middle West in a fundamentally new, perceptually counterintuitive way—a progressive portrayal that was distinctive in post-1960s representations of the U.S. Heartland. Simultaneous with Nixon's proclamations of a "Silent Majority" downtrodden by the coastal media elite and coincident with Spiro Agnew's condemnation of media producers as out-of-step with Heartland values, MTM Productions pointed to newly urbane understandings of regional identity and political identification while simultaneously positioning the Midwest as the lone U.S. region to have "survived the 1960s" with "untroubled" stability. These programs served as sites for battles over taste through place, positing that the Middle West was a region where urban life, feminism, progressive politics, and national conversance were, indeed, imaginable, if in circumscribed ways (particularly with regard to race). Such battles took place in and around these programs at the intersection of the relation between celebrity personae, popular entertainment, and civic activism and ideals.

Chapter 5 extends the analysis of counterintuitive representations of the Midwest in "There *Is* No 'Dayton Chic': Queering the Midwest in *Roseanne, Ellen,* and *The Ellen Show*." This chapter examines key episodes of the situation comedies *Roseanne* (ABC, 1988–1997), *Ellen* (ABC, 1994–1997), and *The Ellen Show* (CBS, 2001–2002) to assess each program's construction and use of the Midwest and midwesternness as *abject* in relation to the series' comparatively mobile, cosmopolitan, place-transcendent portrayal of lesbian identity. This chapter

examines the ways in which potentially progressive portrayals of lesbianism required the contrast of Heartland culture and perspective for
definition, implying that queerness and midwesternness are fundamentally irreconcilable cultural, political, and market identifications. The
effectiveness of these episodes—the judgment of whether or not they
are funny and whether they represent significant, "quality" incursions
within the prime time status-quo—thus depends on the degree of success with which anxieties about the "difference" of lesbianism are transferred to the national viewing audience's presumed, consensual understanding of the U.S. Heartland as, necessarily, "straight" and at a remove from cultural and market trends. *Roseanne, Ellen,* and *The Ellen
Show* each emerged during the completion of the transition from the
traditional broadcast era to increasingly niche appeals within which
market conceptions of the region—as a "down-classed," "flyover" zone
compared to "elite," "niche"-markets—were invigorated and powerfully articulated to *political* allegiances. (This association of geography
with market identity *as* taste culture and political point-of-view is later
revisited in the epilogue, which discusses network branding in a "neo-
network" era). While the Midwest and the midwesterner are clearly the
butt of the joke in these programs (based on shared assumptions in
the program narratives and between the programs and their presumed
audience—an audience that is, itself, largely midwestern) the humor is
double-edged. Its effectiveness relies upon a powerful imagination of
the American Heartland as a pre-modern, hermetically sealed land of
squares, hopelessly un-hip and out-of-the loop. Yet, the Midwest is also
a place whose "less complicated," un-faddish, community- versus indi-
vidual-focused nature marks it as a site of *desire* for and placement
within a "knowable" universe.

Longing and affection for the Heartland as "knowable," stable, traditional community are at the center of the revivification of the myth in
periods of national and political trauma, and used as a key rhetorical
appeal to cultivate broadly national audiences in a "neo-network" era.
Together, chapter 6 and the epilogue consider the Heartland myth's renewed prominence, from the mid-1990s to the present, as a region and
people explicitly allied with populist pragmatism, "plain folks" tastes
and desires, and as the home of innocence and spirituality in the contemporary, mass-mediated world. Chapter 6, "Fertility Among the Ruins: Reconstituting the Traumatized Heartland" examines news specials
focused on the anniversaries of the April, 1995 bombing of the Alfred P.

Murrah Federal Building in Oklahoma City.[54] Significant in relation to coverage of the World Trade Center bombings in 1993 and the catastrophic events of September 11, 2001, anniversary coverage in Oklahoma City inscribes the metropolitan capital as the epitome of a timeless, pastoral Heartland. Commemorative accounts contextualize the shock of the event in terms of its rupture of the illusion of an idealized American middle landscape—the Heartland imagined as rural American safe-space, untouched by the contemporary, worldly strife "expected" to be visited upon the country's primary coastal urban centers. Also, however, these programs allow for the memorialization and recovery in Oklahoma City to be imagined through frontier ideology, characterized by a producerist ethic, pioneering spirit, and the values of self-sufficiency embodied in the idealization of the reconstructed family circle.

The epilogue, "Red State, Blue State, Purple Heartland," examines current network branding practices and industrial appeals to an imagined "red state" audience, as seen in TV industry rhetoric and promotion, in network programming, and in popular television criticism—each of which powerfully articulates "realism" and "authenticity" to the Heartland. I focus particularly on network and program branding strategies in the early 2000s from three key sites: the rise and fall of PAX television—which staked its identity on Heartland programs with overtly spiritual content; CBS's public and trade industry embrace of its role as the "last true broadcast" network, appealing to "flyover" America; and reality television's now ritual linking of "real people" to the Heartland as presumptively "innocent," uncalculating, and untainted by coastal "fads." At each of these sites, the Heartland stands in as shorthand for "authenticity" and, increasingly, as the home of an "underrepresented" majoritarian population rhetorically synchronous with political appeals to a red state populace "outside the Beltway" and between the coasts.

Unlike other regions of the country that have been singled out analytically for their perceived exceptionalism, the Heartland is typically represented as an *un*exceptional locus of consensus. While several scholars, for example, have closely studied the myth of the imagination of the American South, those mythologies have, at their core, a traumatic "visibly" "raced" history and history of regional exceptionalism in relation to the nation-at-large. Central to the myth of the Heartland, by contrast, is the overdetermined "invisibility" of racial tensions and the presumption that the region is emblematic of *national* ideals more often than not. That is, while the South—particularly in the earliest years of television through the civil rights era—was not imagined, on television, as nationally representative, the Heartland often was. Indeed, arguably, the tensions regarding the social value and cultural worth of the region have been so provocative because of this "middle-ground" quality. Whereas the South, East, and West have each always held onto distinctive mythologies resistant to being claimed as "all-American," the Midwest, historically, is recuperated and reiterated as "America's hometown."[55]

Heartland TV issues a call to actually *see* such "ordinary," "obvious," "common sense" regional representation as integral to national discourse. What is at stake here is not a privileging or revaluing of dominant cultural practices, but, rather, a call to make visible their *active* construction and function in the re-iteration of "national interest" as it is energized and revised through regional appeals. It is a challenge to consider how, historically, we consistently resist the possibility to think differently with regard to regional mythology and the politics of place. This book asks readers to consider that common TV industry and popular press terms such as "flyover" have *real* social power. This term, for example, encourages a lack of awareness of the diverse, underrepresented populations and real social and economic needs that exist in the Midwest. It also encourages the notion that, within national media discourse, the Midwest can continue to function as a ritually reinvigorated place-holder for ideologically powerful, politically resonant investments that often run contrary to actual regional affiliations and needs. As reports of the Center for Rural Strategies have recently noted, the diverse populations of the Midwest (particularly Native Americans, African Americans, Latin Americans, and Asian/Pacific Islanders) are woefully underrepresented in popular and political discourse. Additionally, though "only 1.78 percent of rural residents earn their primary living from the farm" nonetheless, "a recent national survey by the W.K. Kellogg Foundation showed an overwhelming perception across the country that agriculture is the dominant industry of rural America" with the Midwest being the home to the majority of the nation's rural population.[56] Such misperception is significant particularly in a neo-network and new media era which threatens to reinscribe historically uneven access to technology and corresponding limits to the representational imagination.

From 2000 to the present, "divided nation" rhetoric has been invigorated and expanded in popular discourse. The frequency, ease, and generally unquestioned adoption of this rhetoric largely inspires the work of this book—particularly, as these "simple" assumptions about cultural and political difference have been explicitly significant to network expansion, industry policy, promotion, and program practices, and presumptions about television's audience as a market entity with variable economic, social, and political capital. As James Shortridge has observed, regional mythologies are powerful because "we seem to *need* to believe that places exist with certain characteristics and, so needing, we *will* such places into existence."[57] The text that follows examines the tenacity of this will and the variable cultural needs that the Heartland myth addresses as a mythology "so persistent and so appealing, even among people who 'know' differently."[58] While *Heartland TV* examines historic tensions regarding place-identity and national values specific to the United States, the struggles it points to and the questions it raises enter into dialogue with contemporary discussions of community, nation, and media in a broadly international context. Though the case-studies featured in the following chapters are by no means all-inclusive of the nationally televised programs that imagine the Heartland, it is hoped that the included analyses will encourage further study and might suggest new questions about and approaches to television history and the regional imagination.

1

"Essential, Desirable, and *Possible* Markets"
Broadcasting Midwestern Tastes and Values

As a technological, infrastructural method of content distribution and market organization, networking developed in the United States coincident with and integral to the final solidification of cross-continental settlement, the emergence of the mass consumer market, and the conceptualization of a *national* audience, or conjoined, national community. From its emergence in vaudeville, through the radio age and television's standardization, networking has been prerequisite to the modern, cultural imagination of the nation. Ideally, it allows for the "special kind of contemporaneous community" and "unisonance" theorized by Benedict Anderson as "the technical means for 're-presenting' the kind of imagined community that is the nation."[1] And yet, this idealized notion of "unisonance" effaces the tensions and struggles between region and nation that consistently appear in historical discourse. Such struggles encourage us to consider the significant *unevenness* with which networking was actually realized (both spatially and temporally). This unevenness is structured into networking by the geographic expanse of the United States, but it also has been encouraged in institutional, regulatory, and cultural struggles to balance the system's inherently conflicting imperatives: Organized as a for-profit market, broadcasting is also mandated to serve in the public interest.

While, in the interest of national integration, network promotional rhetoric promised "unisonance" via the broad American public's equal access to broadcasting service, economic imperatives encouraged a much more cautious developmental approach. Behind closed doors, network strategy emphasized universal access as a distant "possibility," focusing, instead, on the practicality of selective market cultivation. Regional "difference" from the national network remained simultaneously powerful, however, as law and regulatory policy's locus of expected service ideals and obligations.

"Public interest" refers both to access to broadcast media outlets and to a judgment of the content or "character" of programming provided therein. While national network programming is idealized as shared public culture, locally affiliated stations are charged with providing programs that meet the particular needs and interests of the specifically regional viewing audience each serves. Historically, lawmakers and regulators relied upon recourse to presumed, distinct regional differences to challenge monopolistic network practices and, periodically, to re-calibrate network profit motives. As broadcasting developed and stabilized, nationally, it relied upon regional difference to manage and balance its founding paradox. In network planning documents, broadcast law, and regulatory policy from the 1920s through the immediate postwar era, the Midwest and midwesternness often became the site through which "service in the public interest" and profit imperatives were assessed and defined.

Struggles over regional definitions are, across this history, struggles to define representative American ideals through comparative market value and social ranking. The formation of national corporate culture required the development of differentiated, "perceived . . . 'taste markets.'"[2] The history of broadcast networking exemplifies how these markets were created and addressed. Specifically, network development rationales, broadcast law, and regulatory policy can be studied in terms of broader assumptions regarding midwesternness as a comparative *capital* relation or "classed" disposition allied with rurality, traditional modes of cultural expression, and relatively homogenous tastes. The networked Midwest is uniquely imagined as distant from cultural trends and as the most "mass," homogeneous, stable market within the continental expanse.

This chapter examines three interrelated phenomena in network broadcast development, chronologically, from the 1920s until 1950: the emergence of the Midwest as cartographic region and symbolic Heartland in relation to "national" ideals in the period; network development and expansion as it was marked by a conflict between public appeals to universal access and an internal focus on economy of scale; and broadcast law's and regulatory policy's struggle to define, balance, and apply local "service" ideals within the framework of national market development. The history of broadcast networking and localism in the United States most typically has been told in one of two ways: either through analysis of broad macro-political institutional struggles (focusing on network development in technical, physical, infrastructural, and economic terms), or through analysis of cultural tensions at the level of everyday engagements with media (focusing on, for example, local resistance to network representation and battles over scheduling and sponsorship control). Here I argue that if the histories of network development and broadcast policy are read in dialogue with contemporary understandings of regionalism, then institutional and cultural struggles over networking, instead, emerge as integral to and inseparable from one another. This chapter interrogates how broadly circulating mythologies of geographic "difference" shaped and became codified within network development plans, broadcast law, and regulatory policy independent of programming and reception. It argues that a particularly selective and limited way of imagining the Midwest as Heartland has been encouraged and reinforced *structurally* as well as symbolically in broadcast history, and considers how this, in turn, has encouraged certain understandings of the region's value for the nation.

Historian Leo Marx once proposed that if geography was "a perpetual reminder of American differences," then technology represented "the possibility of plenty shared by all."[3] Here, Marx points to a key, if often implicit, assumption in media history and theory—that "region" and "network" are conceptually antithetical terms. The basis for this opposition rests in an understanding of networking as a "space-binding" structural and technological phenomenon, while conversely region and region-based markets and culture are "place-bound." The network expands over territory in ways that benefit national and international market goals, exploiting spatial reach for efficiencies of scale. Networking is understood as a technological, economic, social, and cultural framework for the reorganization of space and time *from* the region and local expression to seemingly "placeless," modern, national modes of production and consumption.[4] Networks' "bias" relations toward a "high communications policy, . . . aimed solely at spreading messages further in space and reducing the cost of transmission."[5]

Media scholar David Morley nuances this conventional network/region tension by pointing out that "while, of course, it must be acknowledged that new communications technologies are producing new definitions of time, space, and community, these are not necessarily erasing but rather overlaying old understandings of distance and duration." Analysis of this dynamic in broadcast history thus requires interrogation "of how physical and symbolic networks become entwined around each other."[6] This sense of entanglement is particularly significant as regards the Midwest-as-Heartland, a geographic and perceptual region that, in a real historical sense, can physically and symbolically only be imagined through networked media.

The Physical and Symbolic Entwined: Regional Labels and National Value

James Shortridge argues that "more than seventy years elapsed between the first use of the term Middle West" in the late 1820s, and the second, in the 1880s, concurrent with the active spatial reordering of a U.S. map that now differentiated the "comparatively settled and stable 'middle' states" from the far western frontier and from the newly incorporated southwest.[7] This sense of the Midwest as comparatively settled was encouraged by the region's increased centrality in transportation and commerce. With the expansion of railroads and telegraphy through the end of the nineteenth century, the northern channels of trade, which extended west from New York, and the southern channels of trade, which flowed through the Mississippi and Ohio rivers, converged to complete the transformation of Chicago from "hinterland" outpost to critically central, national hub. The Midwest was the nation's cartographic "middle," balancing between the relatively untamed West and the established East. And, the region was the nation's economic "middle," representative of "the rise of middle class values and institutions of capitalism."[8] By extension, the Midwest was linked in the popular discourse of the period to qualities of "balance" and solidity of character—particularly as evidenced in increased reference to the region as the nation's "heart," as the country's "most sensible" region, as a place more "evenly American in tone" than others, and, explicitly, as the "most American part of America."[9]

British cultural studies scholar Raymond Williams's *The Country and the City* suggests that this late nineteenth-century valorization of the Midwest as the nation's "heart" should be considered in the context of a broader western cultural revaluation of pastoral life in the face of new national communication and transportation systems, which forged unprecedented modern, economic, and extra-regional relations. The Midwest's persistent association with the pastoral as temporally past tense—as evocative of former life and culture, as the storehouse of "traditional" modes of production and consumption—here contrasts with the "nation," imagined as allied with the same sense of simultaneous "empty time" that characterizes space-binding network technology. Rural life and culture are thus counterpoised to modernity and national imperatives of progress. And yet, the Heartland also conjures a nostalgic realm of possibility as the "last" bastion of face-to-face, "knowable" community in modern, market-oriented culture. The apparent need for the Midwest as imagined locus of unchanging values and traditions is striking, considering the market centrality of Chicago and other urban midwestern sites—especially Cleveland, Detroit, and St. Louis—in the development and success of a truly national economy. However, by the late 1920s, once cross-continental markets were achieved and stabilized, popular representations of the region began to excise such urban hubs from their storehouse of images. The myth of the U.S. Midwest as Heartland began to coalesce around a highly selective set of pastoral values and ideals positively associated with rural life and folk-cultural traditions as a national repository for the values of producerism, thrift, and humility. By the 1930s, cities such as Chicago were explicitly considered "extra-regional" exceptions to the Midwest status-quo which was now, thoroughly, allied with pastoralism and considered to be home to "natural peace, innocence, simple virtue," a producer ethic, and "authentic" American idealism.[10] Pastoral/rural life and culture and industrial/urban life and culture were now "segregated mentally: the former was assigned to a regional 'box' called Middle West; the latter to one called East. . . . This left the term Middle West free to be employed . . . as a synonym for rural America."[11]

Network Development and the Social Ranking of Markets

Though this chapter focuses on network development, broadcast law, and policy particularly as each relates to television, any such history necessitates reference to "pre-TV" precedents. Networking emerged out of transportation and communication infrastructures of the late 1800s. Television followed the same service patterns and is legislated and regulated by the same guidelines and bodies as radio before it. This chapter thus uses the term "broadcasting" to refer to *both* radio and television, particularly as the laws, policies, and development plans studied here pertain to the development and operation of the "Big Three" radio and TV networks, NBC, CBS, and ABC. Additionally, I here refer to local stations that are affiliates of these networks (rather than independent stations or those of the Big Three's challengers). While such focus risks "privilege[ing] national consciousness at the expense of local identities," my intent is exactly this—to theorize how the national imagination is itself built up by reference to the "local," particularly in ways that license or limit understandings of place.[12]

In historical focus here is the period from the late 1920s through the immediate post–World War II era. Between the late 1920s and the mid-1950s, the "Big Three" television networks of NBC, CBS, and ABC were formed, expanded nationally, and solidified as the controlling U.S. network powers—a position of dominance they each held until the early 1990s when cable homes began to outnumber over-air broadcast reception homes for the first time in U.S. history. Paradoxically, as the networks became increasingly national in their distribution capabilities they became simultaneously more "local," concentrating all network production and business operations in New York City and Los Angeles by the late 1950s. This period includes the development and institution of broadcast laws that remained fundamentally unchanged until the passage of the Telecommunications Act of 1996. The period of analysis thus begins with the opening of the broadcast era and concludes with the preeminence of the "Big Three" networks, anchored on either coast, as broadcast policy undergirded the growth and stability of network television which realized its promise to be a national presence in U.S. homes.[13]

While network promotional rhetoric promised that television would be an "immediate" postwar service for all Americans, the reality of the medium's gradual availability was much more staggered and uneven. The speed with which networking developed to serve a truly national audience—particularly in midwestern and mountain west regions—was biased heavily by the way the pre-existing "bones" of the system encouraged expansion along certain channels of transportation and communication over others. Network expansion plans were mapped to maximize economy of scale and to prioritize service only as it was economically strategic. Thus, while television's introduction at the New York World's Fair in 1939 showcased the Middleton family's eagerness to adopt TV, regular network service in their hometown of Riverdale,

Indiana was not yet a guarantee. The public promise of universal access and national service was tempered by institutional imperatives.

In 1926 the Radio Corporation of America (RCA) famously took out full-page newspaper advertisements to announce the formation of its programming and distribution arm, the National Broadcasting Company (NBC). The ads promised that, through networking, events of national importance would never again escape a broad American public now guaranteed the best possible programming on an everyday basis. The advertisement promoted networking as an idealized venue for national integration. The resources of a large corporation would allow for "better programs permanently assured . . . in the interest of the listening public."[14] And yet, the advertisement also qualified that

> [t]he National Broadcasting Company will not only broadcast these programs through station WEAF, but it will make them available to other broadcasting stations throughout the country *so far as it may be practicable to do so,* . . . It is hoped that arrangements may be made so that every event of national importance may be broadcast widely throughout the United States.[15]

RCA, here, seems somewhat more circumspect regarding the prospect of rapid and immediate network service to the majority of the country than is recounted in most broadcast histories. Perhaps experiences within NBC's corporate family contributed to this qualified tone. According to historian David Nye, General Electric and Westinghouse were so eager to expand into rural farming markets in the early 1920s that one-fifth of the companies' magazine advertisements were directed to that market, while each also invested in promotions such as an "all electric farm" installation at the Pennsylvania State Farm Products Show.[16] By the close of the decade, however, these corporations and power companies servicing such areas concluded that " 'the purchasing power of 1.9 million [rural Americans] is too low to put them into the potential customer class.' . . . the cost of installation was too high to make it profitable to reach them."[17] Nye quotes *General Electric Digest*'s assessment, here, that whereas

> "[a] mile of distribution line can serve 50 to 200 customers in a city, in the country the average is three customers to a mile." . . . it would be

far more profitable to increase appliance sales to urban dwellers than to extend services to isolated farmers.[18]

In this sense, rural Americans—who in the 1920s were still, predominantly, midwesterners and Southerners—were characterized as a bad market risk, with the double hex of "low and irregular demand spread over a dispersed area."[19]

And yet, broadcast media posed *qualitatively* different benefits to consumers than did other electrical products. This implied the possibility that broadcast media might have wider immediate success across rural markets than other electric appliances. Additionally, broadcast receivers did not necessarily require access to the power grid as other major appliances did. Nye notes that the "one electrical device common to both farm and city was the radio, first marketed not as a plug-in device but as a battery operated crystal set, to be heard using headphones."[20] Broadcast receivers were thus unique in their promise to close the gap between rural listeners' geographic distance from centers of production and the resulting cultural distance created by this gap. According to Pierre Bourdieu:

> In other words, a group's *real social distance* from certain assets must integrate the geographical distance, which itself depends on the group's spatial distribution and, more precisely, its distribution with respect to the "focal point" of economic and cultural values, . . . Thus, the distance of farm workers from legitimate culture would not be so vast if the specifically cultural distance implied by their low cultural capital were not compounded by their spatial dispersion.[21]

Broadcast networking suggested the possibility to shift one's local disposition and reorient one's cultural expertise through space-binding media engagement.

With passage of the Rural Electrification Act in 1936—accompanied by President Roosevelt's declaration that electric power must be regarded as a necessity for all Americans rather than a luxury for a few—the slow but eventual emergence of truly national broadcasting service became possible. Addresses by President Roosevelt and by Postmaster General Farley at the 1937 dedication of NBC's new broadcast studios in Washington, D.C., made this promise explicit. Roosevelt claimed, sooner than any of us realize television will be established in homes throughout this country. . . . it may not be long before . . . it will be possible for us to visualize at the breakfast table the front pages of daily newspapers or news reports, no matter how remote we may be from the place of their publication or distribution . . .

And, according to Farley:

Radio . . . has aided immeasurably in developing musical culture and banishing sectionalism, thereby preventing the disintegration of our people into classes.[22]

It was with this sensibility that the appeals were crafted to introduce television to the public at the 1939 World's Fair.

Fairgoers surveyed by NBC were notably realistic about expectations for the new medium's rapid, universal adoption. Reactions to the television exhibit were gathered from attendees representing twenty-one states, with "26% from states other than New York." Respondents were enthusiastic regarding programming, but clearly perceived TV to be an urban, northeastern phenomenon. Respondents from locations including Pennsylvania, Tennessee, Florida, and Virginia emphasized that they "Would buy [a] set if programs are available at our distance from New York," and "We would be willing to buy one as soon as television networks are established near my town," or "I think television will be one of the most useful inventions when it can be made so as to be in reach of the average citizen."[23]

However, even as the network was promoting TV as "the People's" medium at the Fair, internal plans for corporate growth were much more focused and strategic. The network first planned to target "early adopters" whose word-of-mouth would carry great weight. For example, a memo distributed in 1939 noted that

sets should be placed, at once, in a dozen of the top-flight country clubs in the metropolitan area (Greenwich, Atlantic Beach, Sleepy Hollow . . .) where they would evoke much interest among the membership which . . . enjoy that "social leadership" which others are inclined to follow. We should place sets in the Mayor's office, and in those of the President of the Board of Education, the Police Commissioner and the Fire Commissioner . . .[24]

NBC's plans for growth show a methodical timeline for "realistic" patterns of infrastructural expansion outward from New York City, proposing gradual interconnection from major cities across the United States out to "lesser" markets. In 1939, the original plan was to expand program service in New York City and to then acquire broadcast facilities in "key markets" identified as Philadelphia, Chicago, Boston, Washington, Cleveland, and San Francisco. The next step was to establish "regional service" from Chicago that would interconnect the cities of the Midwest, including St. Louis and Milwaukee. Finally, the network would originate a West coast regional service that would connect Los Angeles and San Francisco. The 1939 plan was to create three parallel North-South networks along the East coast, in the Midwest, and on the West coast. Once established, "with three regional networks operating a transcontinental circuit would make possible a *national* television service."[25]

A key dilemma in television's further geographic distribution was that the network broadcasting system depended upon a centralized point of control from which to deliver its programs. The national system was, thus, inherently localized or skewed toward the markets and culture of the urban East (later, in the 1950s and 1960s Los Angeles became an equal partner in broadcasting and soon overcame New York's dominance in programming and distribution). In an internal report, NBC Vice President of Affiliate Relations, William Hedges, emphasized that the northeastern part of the United States was the economic center of the country and, as such, provided the "economic base on which a profitable network business may ultimately be built." In order to maintain an edge over CBS, its principal competitor, NBC, embarked on a plan for network development that emphasized the retention of "its superiority in facilities and coverage in the northeastern United States," while adding stations only "judiciously where the addition is economically justified."[26] NBC's strategy was to maximize its existing strengths in its most populous markets with high-quality, easy interconnection to New York, in order to build a base of profitability and marketability from which TV *might* expand.

NBC's policy for television network growth was first codified in 1945 as the "Four Phases of Development Plan." The plan identified three categories of affiliate markets that would guide the network's development through the mid-1950s. "Essential markets" included seventy-three principal cities that ranked highest in population and had 150,000 or more families in their service area. These were each cities within easy interconnection reach of New York and its relays in the East, Chicago and its relays in the Midwest, and Los Angeles or San Francisco and each city's relays in the West. "Desirable markets" included fifty-three regions that had at least a population of 100,000 families in their broadcast area. "Possible markets" "might be affiliated depending on the economics of wire line costs, service charges, etc." These markets each had populations of 25,000 and above in their broadcast area.[27] Areas that were not slated for development through the mid-1950s included markets in the South, the Plains Midwest, and the mountain states of the West. According to NBC projections, "costs of electrical interconnections, it is calculated, would preclude electrical connection . . . to this group until well after 1953." Statistical data from the period confirm that NBC's plan was shared by the broader industry: In 1955, television households averaged seventy-eight percent in cities with a population of 50,000 or more, while in rural areas only fifty percent of households had television. Rural farm families reported the lowest percentage of television households, at forty-two percent. And, as a region, the Northeast outpaced all other sections of the country by almost ten percent—eighty percent of households had television.[28]

In 1948 an NBC internal report entitled the "Master Plan" noted that NBC had a *"moral* obligation to add" such rural markets as "Wilmington, Lancaster, Johnston, Altoona"—communities that were perceived to be of "nominal importance" for advertisers at this stage, but would be "necessary to any plan for the development of television as a national advertising medium." A moral commitment to "lesser markets" would only be made, however, when such cities were "on routes between major markets or close enough to permit economic justification" for their network addition. Off the public record, NBC's definition of a "national" system of television was clearly limited to affiliation with cities that were already viable in their own right within the national market—those towns between such sites that could serve as valuable relays between major markets, or those communities within a corridor already slated for expansion.

All planning documents of this period emphasize the importance of slow growth based on market density and ease of interconnection. Thus, the NBC Television Master Plan acknowledges that, while "the National Broadcasting Company plans to operate a television network on a truly national scale, with the *ultimate end* in view of bringing television service to a *great majority* of the population of the United States," that majority could almost be met by 1948 with the fifty-three percent combined U.S. population coverage of NBC affiliates and owned and operated stations provided by New York and Los Angeles alone. NBC's Vice President for Network Operations, William Hedges notes, specifically:

> Although the objective of network expansion is truly national, the only fixed point in the contemplation of this plan is that while it *may* be possible to extend network facilities to a total of 148 stations in as many markets . . . it is impossible that such a number will be attained within the five year period. . . . The long range plan of NBC is to establish a network of interconnected stations covering the most important markets, *providing* such markets are on routes between major markets.[29]

Though coast-to-coast network connection was realized by 1953, television remained a primarily urban phenomenon through the 1960s (as the nation itself underwent the final transition to a predominantly urbanized country). In the market logic of networking, the Heartland became important only as its residents' consuming power could strengthen its economy and enhance its strategic position.[30]

"In the Public Interest": Codifying Regional Difference in Broadcasting

In the period between the establishment of networking and the introduction of television into American homes, several laws and policy statements struggled, specifically, to define broadcasters' local service obligations. Particularly important here are key passages of the Radio Act of 1927, as well as the Davis Amendment (1928) and its later repeal, the Great Lakes Statement (1929), the Communications Act of 1934, the Network Case of 1943, *The Blue Book* (1946), and the Programming Policy Statement of 1960.[31] While these documents represent a diverse collection of guiding laws and regulatory principles, each is connected by specific attention to the public interest standard and its explicit articulation to geography. Specifically, the public interest standard is, in each case, understood to be a geographically comparative standard. Indeed, reading the history of broadcast law and regulatory statements in dialogue with prevailing regional mythology unveils a process of selective tradition engaging and encouraging a certain characteristic way of thinking about the Midwest as Heartland that shaped conceptions of what would meet the standard of "service in the public interest" in different, geographically defined markets. To quote policy historian Thomas Streeter,

> law is not just an occasional constraint on the behavior of broadcasting, it *creates* broadcasting. . . . Law, then, is a key to understanding the media as a product of meaningful habits of thought and action, as socially constructed. . . . any discussion of it . . . involves us in debates and struggles over values and the distribution of power in society. . . . law happens when bargains are struck, hierarchies are enforced, and conflicts are initiated and resolved.[32]

Specifically, midwesterners were understood to be a *market* characterized by "mass," relatively "homogeneous" tastes and proclivities for rural, folk, regionally based entertainment; but, as a *public,* the Midwest was perceived to be distinguished by local commitment to community values and active oversight and engagement as pitted against "crassly commercial" "outside" media influences and interests, and representing a "solution" to network "excesses."

Several scholars have interpreted the language and specifics of the Radio Act of 1927 in terms of the influence of Progressive-era ideology and the progressive orientation of its writers.[33] Progressive ideology presumed that "America's strength lay in its successful assimilation of the diverse cultural elements swirling throughout the country"—elements that could really only conceivably be united through shared communications media.[34] Radio waves seemed particularly important to think about in terms of integrative ideals, if only to begin to grasp, define, and codify their ethereal character, thus creating a framework and rationale for their federal oversight and control. Were radio waves "national" in character? Were they analogous to a natural resource? Did the "air" belong to the people? Or, if radio waves were essentially "interstate in scope and character," were they comparable to transportation and commerce routes between states and the province of corporations?

Defining radio waves as "interstate in scope and character" implied the need for a certain amount of centralized, federal oversight and control that fit the precedent established by the Interstate Commerce Commission. Invoking the commerce clause of the Constitution (Article I, Section 8), the Radio Act of 1927 allowed that "Congress shall have Power . . . to regulate Commerce . . . among the several states." This power was formalized with the Act's creation of the Federal Radio Commission (FRC) as radio's overseeing regulatory body. The FRC was charged to license stations in order to prevent "chaos" in the air. Stations were licensed according to the standard of "public interest, convenience, or necessity." Operating licenses would be granted to stations, "but not the ownership" of the airwaves. These are the core elements of the Act that are most familiar to students of broadcast history. They establish a tenuous balance between private operation and federal oversight in order to shed the possibly distasteful associations in the period with either monopolistic business practices *or* fascistic military/state-control. They define radio waves as commerce and transportation *and* as ethereal, "owned" by the People, and operated in the "public interest."

Another set of clauses here are less often mentioned and—while short-lived in their legal standing—each is important to theorizing the lasting significance of the Act as a grounding precedent for succeeding broadcast law and policy. Sections 2, 3, and 9 of the Radio Act "regionalize" the broader document's focus on national integration by emphasizing broadcasting's promised appeals to representative democracy and equality of service as geographically defined. While the preamble and first section of the Act acknowledge the relatively borderless, potentially unruly nature of radio communication, Sections 2 and 3 propose that the United States should be divided into five distinct "zones" of broadcast service, each to be represented by a FRC member. The zones were designed to be roughly equal in geographic size and population. Each commissioner was conceptualized much as a Congressional Representative, responsive to regional concerns as "an actual resident citizen of a State within the zone from which appointed at the time of said appointment." Additionally, to maintain representative balance between geographic zones, "not more than one commissioner shall be appointed from any one zone." Alongside the FRC's requirement of balance regarding commissioners' political party affiliation, then, stood a requirement for regional representation.

In Section 9 of the Act, the FRC was charged to equalize service by geographic region as nearly as possible:

In considering applications for licenses and renewals of licenses, when and in so far as there is a demand for the same, the licensing authority shall make such a distribution of licenses, bands of frequency of wave lengths, periods of time for operation, and of power among the different States and communities as to give fair, efficient, and equitable radio service to each of the same.[35]

Of the five zones, zone IV was predominantly composed of midwestern states, including Indiana, Illinois, Wisconsin, Minnesota, North Dakota, South Dakota, Iowa, Nebraska, Kansas, and Missouri.[36]

In 1928, as the reauthorization bill for the FRC came under discussion, an amendment was proposed that would make the language of Section 9 more specific. The Davis Amendment (named for its author, Representative Edwin L. Davis, Republican of Tennessee) modified the second paragraph of Section 9 of the Radio Act of 1927 to read:

It is hereby declared that the people of all of the zones established by section two of this Act are entitled to equality of radio broadcasting service, both of transmission and reception, and in order to provide said equality the licensing authority shall *as nearly as possible* . . . to each of said zones. . . . *Provided,* that if and when there is a lack of applications from any zone, . . . the licensing authority may issue licenses for the balance of the proportion not applied for from any zone, to applicants from other zones for a temporary period of ninety days each, . . .[37]

Here the public interest standard is equated with equal provision of broadcast facilities across the country and with the listener's equality of access to broadcast content, regardless of locale. The Amendment provides language that could allow the representative government analogy, as regards broadcasting and geographic equality, to have regulatory teeth.

As the phrases "as nearly as possible" and "provided, that . . ." indicate, however, the Davis Amendment and "geographic zones" of service were short-lived. Characterized by broadcast historian Frank Kahn as "an administrative nightmare for a new commission plagued with the problems of an overcrowded broadcast spectrum," the Amendment was viewed as an unwieldy and unwelcome limitation upon the Commission's regulatory power.[38] Regulatory clauses requiring equality of access and service, regardless of geographic location, also ran counter to the *market* logic of broadcasting, as exemplified by NBC's "Four Phases" approach. The Rural Electrification Administration would struggle with this same dilemma, encouraging and developing rural cooperatives to relay power where "profit power" refused to go.[39] Equal access and viable market development were irreconcilable goals.

In the summer following the Davis Amendment's passage, the Commission issued a statement on "The Interpretation of the Public Interest" in which it made its support of market preferences explicit. The FRC now took the position that the most equitable regional service would likely be achieved through extra-regional means, by broadcasting that crossed "zone" jurisdiction. By emphasizing the logic of interstate commerce rather than the analogy of representative democracy the Commission defined appropriate regional service as greater free-market choice. Equality of service could be met by the provision of a variety of types of service—envisioned as extra-regional, regional, and specifically local.

The Commission proposed that "clear-channel" service, whose signal power was strong enough to cross zone borders, would "permit . . . a *high order of service* over as large a territory as possible." In fact, only the largest broadcasters with extra-regional, clear-channel capabilities *could* allow for "the distant listener in the rural and sparsely settled portions of the country [to] be reached." As broadcast historian Susan Douglas explains,

> the rationale for such 'clear-channel' stations was that listeners in rural areas with inexpensive or even homemade sets who were not within range of a radio station, or a station with adequate power (most rural stations in the 1920s were 50- to 100-watt stations; some even as low as 25), could now be served, especially at night. By the 1950s it was these clear-channel, or Class I stations, like WDIA out of Memphis, that listeners at night delighted in reeling in.[40]

However, this rationale later became the foundation of and precedent for subsequent policy statements that presumed networks to provide inherently higher-quality service than independent, local stations.

In market terms, the Commission aligned quality broadcasting service with economy of scale. Equality of service, the Commission argued, would only be created by thinking *beyond* representative zones and conceiving of a hierarchy of channels based on transmission capabilities and contrasting content expectations. While clear-channel stations could transmit cross-zones, "regional stations" would serve specific zones, and "low-power channels" would serve communities within each zone. While clear-channel providers could program for broadly diversified audiences with a mix of content, "channels . . . which desire to reach a more limited region" would, accordingly, serve increasingly specific publics, "distinctly local in character. . . . without any attempt to reach listeners beyond the immediate vicinity of such towns."[41]

This last statement becomes more interesting when tracing how its principles are embedded in later documents such as *The Blue Book*. Understood, from this document forward, is the premise that urban stations are, inherently, "extra-local," as exemplified by programming exhibiting high production values, genre diversity, and audience breadth. For example, in this same statement on the Interpretation of the Public Interest, the FRC proposes that urban areas are, inherently, diverse markets, while rural communities are removed from the cultural flow:

> The public in large cities can easily purchase and use phonograph records of the ordinary commercial type. . . . The commission realizes that the situation is not the same in some of the smaller towns and farming communities, where such program resources are not available. Without placing the stamp of approval on the use of phonograph records under such circumstances, the commission will not go so far . . . as to state that the practice is at all times under all conditions a violation of the test as provided by the statute.[42]

The more diversified urban market and its consumers navigate and sustain a plethora of program types, while rural remove is compounded by homogeneity; hence, the potential advantage to rural listeners of clear-channel urbanity. Significantly, then, the 1928 Interpretation of the Public Interest concludes "that the test—'public interest, convenience, or necessity'—becomes a matter of a comparative and not an absolute standard when applied to broadcasting stations."[43] Comparative standards applied not just to access, but to qualitative concerns as well—one market's "ordinary commercial" consumer purchase was another's cultural programming.

The Davis Amendment was formally repealed by President Roosevelt in 1936, restoring the language of Section 9 (now applied to the Communications Act of 1934) to its 1927 form and adding that

the legislation is recommended for practical reasons of administration
. . . [as] the drawing of artificial zone lines for guides in allocating radio
facilities cannot satisfactorily be applied because of the physical laws
governing radio transmission. As a consequence, the policy of Congress,
to so distribute radio facilities that every section of the country will be
adequately supplied, has been very difficult of effectuating.[44]

Unable to be confined to specific geographic regions, radio waves are,
here, naturally allied with national service. Rather than "equitable" service by geographic zone, the language was changed to conform to the
original text of 1927, proposing "fair" and "efficient" service instead.
While the establishment of geographic zones of service was short-lived,
the assumption that different geographic markets required different
types of service and that "small town" content and "big city" content
were necessarily counterpoised emerged from these documents as precedent and de facto principle of subsequent regulatory statements and
strategy.

In the Great Lakes Statement of 1929, the FRC turned its focus to
broadcast content as a key standard in licensing considerations. It argued that broadcasting was in a unique class of market goods. Because
it was both "intangible" (as "naturally" occurring airwaves) and "vital" to everyday life (as shared public discourse), broadcasting was to
be considered in the same class as public utilities. Broadcasters are licensed "not for the purpose of furthering the private or selfish interests
of individuals or groups of individuals," but in order to serve a broad
listening public. Broadcast content serves "the listening public" and not
"the sender of the message." In this respect, the communal "tastes,
needs, and desires of all substantial groups" among a station's listening public "should be met, in some fair proportion, by a well-rounded
program, in which entertainment, consisting of music of both classical
and lighter grades, religion, education and instruction, important public
events, discussions of public questions, weather, market reports, and
news, and matters of interest to all members of the family find a place."
The Great Lakes Statement seems to tip the balance back toward broadcasting's promised democratic service mission, away from its more expressly market-oriented functions. And yet, the statement also prioritizes national networks' capabilities as networks alone have the economic strength to provide widely diversified programming with broad

appeal. Critically, however, the statement underscores that public interest, as a comparative standard, can really only be assessed through *content.*[45]

With the Communications Act of 1934, the FRC was reconceived as the Federal Communications Commission and its commissioner ranks were increased from five to seven. In keeping with the now-established national, corporate conceptualization of broadcasting, no reference is made requiring that Commissioners represent particular geographic regions or that the Commission itself reflect equal representation from across the country. The language of the 1934 Act now firmly "nationalizes" broadcasting and its service obligations. The clause establishing the FCC reads:

> For the purpose of regulating interstate and foreign commerce in communication by wire and radio so as to make available, so far as possible, to all the people of the United States, without discrimination on the basis of race, color, religion, national origin, or sex, a rapid, efficient, nationwide, and world-wide wire and radio communication service . . . and for the purpose of . . . centralizing authority heretofore granted by law to several agencies.[46]

Through the 1930s, communications law and regulatory statements actively encouraged and prioritized national network development and its success in commercial terms. However, by the early 1940s, concern grew regarding the sheer dominance of network interests in broadcasting, increasingly evidenced in battles between the networks and their locally affiliated stations. In 1943, *National Broadcasting Co., Inc., et al. v. United States et al.* (or "The Network Case") exposed these concerns. Justice Frankfurter's decision in this case upheld that national, commercial networks were the foundation of the U.S. broadcasting system, and yet, the networks' overwhelming market control and increasingly restrictive business practices begged for judicial intervention. Frankfurter argued that, "without networks, broadcasting in a vast country like the United States would not be a national communications medium," but *within* the national communication system, "local program service is a vital part of community life." So, the "national" character of networking was upheld, while reiterating that different regions had different service needs.

The Network Case led to both an industrial and a regulatory shift. NBC was found to have significantly restrained its affiliates when it required exclusive affiliations and oversight of station scheduling decisions and local advertising rates. The network was ordered to divest itself of one of its two radio networks. This enabled the formation of the American Broadcasting Company (ABC) from the divested "chain." Additionally, the court's decision argued for increased awareness of the FCC's role in oversight per the public interest standard. According to Frankfurter, the FCC "must not confine itself to technical considerations," but must also consider *content*. Beyond the "supervision" of broadcasting "traffic," the Commission was charged with "the burden of determining the composition of that traffic."[47]

The FCC's expectations for broadcast licensees' service in the public interest were most clearly enunciated with the 1946 publication of the *Public Service Responsibility of Broadcast Licensees* (hereafter *The Blue Book*, by which it is most commonly referred due to its distinctive blue cover). *The Blue Book* also codified ambiguity, however, as it was not an official publication of the FCC, but an independent report solicited by Chair Paul Porter from the primary author, Professor Charles Siepmann of New York University. Thus, while the guidelines for license renewal, program service expectations, and public interest found in *The Blue Book* implied reinvigorated FCC concern over postwar broadcasting's responsibilities, it had no binding power. Still, *The Blue Book* presents perhaps the most sustained account of regulatory logic regarding public interest as a comparative standard based on *geographic* differentiation.

The Blue Book restates the 1928 Interpretation of Public Interest to emphasize market and, apparent *civic* distinctions between urban and rural locales. While "metropolitan" markets are presumed to be diverse in both program choices and program content, "rural" markets are imagined to have much narrower "tastes" and cultural proclivities. Significantly, in this respect, its comparative case-studies primarily reference urban northeastern and rural midwestern markets. *The Blue Book* codifies that the "appropriate" programming service standard by which these markets would be judged interpreted taste and cultural fluency to be region-specific. Expectations for the different requirements necessary to meet the particular social welfare of a locale, further, imply comparative standards as regards the region's broader *social* value. Specifically, the report supports the idea that the Midwest is synonymous with rural America while New York City represents the contrasting "metropolitan" market standard. In its examples *The Blue Book* argues that the rural Midwest is best served by familiar, local talent presenting popular genres of expression and appealing to popular tastes, whereas "legitimate" tastes and cultural production may be a common program feature in the metropolitan market. In this critical document, then, a *policy* principle—service in the public interest—links the Midwest and midwesterners to a *necessarily* rural disposition explicitly associated with folk-expression and with traditional cultural production, as opposed to the "legitimate" and progressive possibilities of metropolitan programming.

For example, *The Blue Book* notes that the "rural people" of Missouri would definitely like and be appropriately served by the type of entertainment offered by the "Happy Millers," a singing group of "hillbilly and western" music:

> Public acceptance has been phenomenal, partly because of the interest of rural people in the type of entertainment afforded but also because the entertainers are all local people and well known in the community.[48]

The rural, midwestern locale—as presumptively "knowable," face-to-face community—is assumed to respond favorably to vernacular performance styles, program genres, and "familiar" faces, whereas the report's reference to the New York City market argues for a range of entertainments from "high" cultural productions to "ordinary commercial arts." The report states:

> In metropolitan areas where the listener has his choice of several stations, balanced service to listeners can be achieved *either* by means of a balanced program structure for each station or by means of a number of *comparatively specialized* stations which, considered together, offer a balanced service to the community.[49]

New York City is characterized by "a considerable degree of specialization on the part of particular stations . . . [with] one station featuring a preponderance of classical music, another a preponderance of dance music, etc."[50] For metropolitan areas, then, a different public service standard is in effect:

> The Commission proposes in its application forms hereafter to afford applicants an opportunity to state whether they propose a balanced program structure or a special emphasis on program service of a particular type or types.[51]

The metropolitan station can either address a broad, shared audience, or can target focused markets within that audience, whereas the rural station must necessarily address a broad, "mass" listening public.

Thus, *The Blue Book* introduces a paradox into the consideration of the public interest standard: The larger the "local" audience and greater the local broadcasting competition within a market, the less diversified each station's programming within that market need be. Those stations serving the most dispersed audiences with relatively little competition have a greater onus for diversity of service. And yet, simultaneously, the expectations for "rural" broadcasters also remain, arguably, "low" in the expressed limited understanding of what type of program service will satisfy such audiences. Specifically, "hillbilly music," amateur hours, and commercially available phonograph records are each referenced as appropriate and strategic program types for midwestern markets, while other types of programming—particularly those with "high" cultural appeals—are considered to be much more at home in urban, northeastern locales.[52]

The value given to comparative program balance-by-market in *The Blue Book* explains the striking tone of betrayal evidenced in the report's accounts of local affiliates' misrepresentations of their service to the public in their applications for license renewal. In featured cases, the local station is admonished for betraying its community when it caters to commercial interests—in essence, when it acts like its network parent (or, for non-network affiliates, when it acts like a network). After applying for an increase in broadcast time, for instance, station WTOL in Toledo "became affiliated with a national network. By 1944 the 'local' programs . . . were conspicuous by their absence. 91.8 percent of the broadcast time was commercial."[53]

Embracing a consumer market ethos is seen to deny local public interest. To outline counter-examples of positive conceptions of local service and civic expression, however, *The Blue Book* refers to several sites of public activism from the Midwest, each of which represents the protection of local interests and tastes from corrupting outside influences, and stands for "character" against the sway of commercialism. Imagined, placid, pastoral Heartland community cohesiveness is evoked, here, to underscore the dangers of imbalance in broadcasting. *The Blue Book* quotes a radio report, for example, that illustrates the dismay of

> a Midwest jeweler who operated a first-class . . . store [and] reported that he had cancelled his use of radio because he felt that radio management in his city had allowed the air to become too crowded with spot announcements . . . purchased by firms selling cheap and shoddy merchandise.[54]

Here, the midwestern businessman is exemplary of local taste-standards and a civic ideal, as he stands up against crass commercialism in the name of his fellow citizens' best interests. Similarly, *The Blue Book* heralds the *St. Louis Post-Dispatch*'s campaign against advertising within newscasts which argued that informational broadcasts serving civic interests should be free of "plug-ugly" commercialization.[55] Thus, while advertising serves a *national* interest and is common to networks' appeals, in local programming time, the sanctity of the community's "own" airspace "must be protected" through vigilant civic oversight.

This association of midwestern markets and stations with traditional appeals extends to the report's valorization of the perceived authenticity and upstanding character of broadcasters who epitomize service in the public interest in these terms. In the example of a "250-watt station located in the Middle West," for instance:

> All attempts at copying outside stations were eliminated. . . . Station facilities were made available on a free basis to civic institutions such as the Chamber of Commerce, women's clubs, parent-teacher association, public schools . . . making the station a real local institution and a true voice of the community.[56]

Additionally, *The Blue Book* heralds the public engagement and activism of Midwest-based "listener's councils," singling out groups in Cleveland, Ohio and in Madison, Wisconsin.[57]

Although there is certainly truth to many of these presumptions regarding public service requirements in the Heartland during this period (for instance, the need for daily agricultural market reports, etc.), the values held up as particularly midwestern and the accompanying absences here suggest that popular discourses about the Heartland had made a significant incursion into the conceptualization of broadcast law and the resulting expectations for public service requirements.

Considering the FCC's apparent valuation of local place and taste specificity here, it is not surprising that the affiliates taken to task in *The Blue Book* are those who filed local interest-friendly broadcasting plans with their license applications but subsequently ignored these schedules in an apparent quest for greater commercial success and market dominance. The potential disparity between proposed service plans of local licensees and their subsequent broadcast performance establishes a tone of wariness and vague mistrust of local stations throughout *The Blue Book*. The authors systematically question the sincerity of local affiliates with regard to ideals of character, citizenship, and community. While admitting that "the evidence is overwhelming that the popularity of American broadcasting as we know it is based in no small part upon its commercial programs"—those programs associated with network-provided prime time programming—the local broadcaster is required to strive for balance between commercialism and service in the public interest and will forfeit its license should it unbalance this equation.[58]

At the same time that it berates stations for giving in to commercial interests, *The Blue Book* upholds the profit-making, commercial network system as U.S. broadcasting's necessary, structural status-quo. Throughout *The Blue Book,* the networks are presumed to be crassly commercial, in contrast to their local affiliates. However, the networks' national programming voice is nonetheless assumed to have a distinctly valuable pedagogical and nationally unifying function, particularly for the rural, local community. Drawing a parallel between local newspaper layout and affiliate scheduling, for example, the report's authors state that network prime time programming, "the hours from 6 to 11 p.m. are the 'front page' of the broadcast station."[59] National programming and commercial sponsorship thus represent a common language that is held out as a consensual ideal while "local material" engages only the "particular interests" of a given community.

Finally, the status and value of networking as a national market is made explicit: Networks provide "consumer knowledge of the new and improved products which contribute to a higher standard of living" and, therefore, network viewership "is one of the steps toward achieving that higher standard of living." The "indispensable . . . essential role [of advertising] in the distribution of goods and services within our economy" is only provided by network programs as they are sponsored by major advertisers.[60] While acknowledging that advertising is largely contrary to emplaced local (and, specifically, midwestern) sensibilities, *The Blue Book* also still upholds the basic principle of national connection and the networks' definitive role in a nationwide system that, ultimately, overrides local concerns. According to this logic, intervention in the development and national spread of the commercial network system would mean tampering with national progress.

On July 29, 1960, the FCC released its "Report and Statement of Policy re: Commission en Banc Programming Inquiry," also known as "The 1960 Programming Policy Statement." This document reinforced *The Blue Book*'s stance regarding licensee obligation for service in the public interest. The statement added an "ascertainment" obligation, requiring each licensee to "discover the 'tastes, needs, and desires' of people in the local service area through surveys of community leaders and the general public; to evaluate the findings of such surveys; and to propose programs responsive to the evaluated 'tastes, needs, and desires.'"[61] Ascertainment was, however, arguably qualified by the Commission's simultaneous assertion that "there is no public interest basis for distinguishing between sustaining" programs—those underwritten by stations or networks themselves—and commercially sponsored programs in evaluating station performance."[62] Local citizens and licensees remained responsible to ensure service in the public interest. However, if "hinterland" stations were portrayed as correctives or the counterbalance to the "commercial excess" emanating from the coastal network hub, these markets were simultaneously encouraged to take advantage of and become fluent in national consumer ideals. "Rural" and, specifically, midwestern stations, historically, were urged to guarantee a breadth of program types within one station's schedule, while the FCC held "northeastern" urban broadcasters to a significantly different standard—allowed, as those stations were, to "narrowcast" based on the broad field of competition in which they were operating and the diversity of voices that composed their audiences.[63]

Out Where the Tall Antennas Grow

Reading the history of broadcast networking through the interpretive screens of cultural geography encourages a new critical awareness of regional mythology's legacy and activity in contemporary media rhetoric and policy. Reference to broader cultural "common sense" regarding the Heartland—as, alternately, idealized civic center, or perceived island of "difference" within the nation—remains central to many appeals regarding media technology, access, and purpose. Such attention allows us to query, for example, why, strategically, the Clinton administration's initiative for universal internet access in public schools was promoted as an "electronic barn raising," or, conversely, why network programmers consider "Middle American sensibilities" to be *necessarily* divergent from those of the people who live in New York and Los Angeles.[64] Writing regional mythology back into historic analysis thus opens up new avenues for examining the prevailing cultural "common sense" with regard to technology and society, cultural capital, and political voice.

Early network promotional rhetoric and structural development, broadcast law, and regulatory policy each critically re-conceptualized region and nation in ways that encouraged a broader modern revaluation of U.S. culture from regionalism toward national markets and culture. This was achieved by establishing and reinforcing the idea that rural "place" was resistant to urban market values and national, space-binding ideals. Broadcasting's founding principles of division were not neutral but, rather, "by categorizing . . . legitimate[d] social inequalities," presented "social differences between people as if they were differences of nature."[65] Yet, to the extent that national networking made possible the literal and figurative connection "between regions and forces otherwise kept conceptually distinct" it "seemed to create a permeable space" not just between different geographic regions but also between their presumed dispositions and cultural worth in contrast to other regions and values.[66] With the solidification of TV's place in postwar homes and the growing success of 1950s television programming perceived to appeal to imagined midwestern sensibilities, public discourse about television and U.S. culture increasingly evinced an undercurrent of perceived *threat* at the heart of national networking—a threat linked to these relational understandings of geography as capital. Even as the FCC had apparently suggested (in its *Blue Book* case-studies) that the Midwest was innately home to upstanding citizens able to resist the sway of crass commercialism, still, on the *national* stage (the "front page" of nightly prime time broadcasting), it seems the following dilemma now rose to the fore of public debate: If the midwestern disposition could be "upclassed" through "enlightened" programming, might

Heartland programming have the potential to "down-class" the broader nation?

In a particularly stark, if not unique, example of this broader postwar revaluation and distantiation in national media discourse, a *Harper's Magazine* satire from 1956 details a New Yorker's trip to visit his in-laws in Iowa. The urbanite discovers that the Hawkeye state has been turned on to symphonic music, operas, and the Broadway stage, thanks to television. "Out where the tall antennas grow," TV is newly accessible, forging a shared national culture wherein New York—as cultural center—is all the rage. William Zinsser writes that

> the weekend in Iowa left us demoralized and we wondered if we should buy a television set so we could keep up with the Iowans. But they have too much of a head start. I'm working on another plan. I have subscribed to *Agricultural Digest* and the *Pig Breeders' Weekly*. I went to a revival of 'State Fair' and took notes. . . . I'm hoping that my in-laws will watch television so much that they'll forget all they ever knew about Iowa. That's when I'll go out and tell them a thing or two about corn.[67]

While clearly humorous in intent, this article suggests that there is a deeper felt threat at the heart of the joke—the threat that television, as a site of shared, national audience attention, might have the power to blow open local domains of cultural provenance, to disarticulate disposition from place, or to close the gap between geographic distance from cultural centers and the social capital required for cultural conversance and political voice. If television achieved its early rhetorical "promise" to bind far-flung spaces, it might, indeed, challenge *The Blue Book*'s codification of the "appropriate" alignment of the metropole with diverse and "high" cultural offerings and the hinterland with "shared" folk programming. If Iowans could become like New Yorkers, what would prevent New Yorkers' sudden appreciation of state fairs, pig breeding, and corn—in both stalk and cultural form? Chapter 2 is devoted to interrogating the ways in which this broadly public struggle over regionalism, taste, and national purpose was energized by popular TV programming and network "branding" practices in the 1950s, whereby ABC-TV launched itself as a new national network and viable "mass" market entity specifically through appeals to Heartland audiences and by staging regional expression in prime time.

2

Square Dancing and Champagne Music
Regional Aesthetics and Middle America

We told them, with the advent of television, Broadway as they knew it, and Main Street, U.S.A., as we knew it, were almost becoming one and the same because the population was exposed to the same entertainment . . . Instead of being tremendously apart, New York and the Ozarks were like super highways running parallel to one another—and getting closer all the time.[1]

The big and real difference seems to lie not in what [TV viewers] do but how they feel about it. What the majority accepts as a legitimate use of television, the minority may think of as abuse of it (or *its* abuse of *them*).[2]

At the same time that network development and regulatory policy was defining broadcasting through national market ideals, the promise of national *cultural* integration through television programming was engendering broad, public conflict. Alongside regional markets' revaluation toward national corporate culture, regional *aesthetics* and audiences were also critically contemplated and reassessed. Particularly, in the period from television's rapid postwar entry into American homes through the early 1960s, network programs that were identifiably "midwestern" in their content, aesthetics, and appeal to a Heartland audience (wherever that audience may physically live), were hailed by producers and fans as emblematic of TV's democratic cultural promise, while bemoaned by critics, politicians, and regulators as a sign of TV's "low" cultural pull upon the broader polity. In a postwar, Cold War, and emergent New Frontier era that now positioned U.S. culture at the front guard of the free world, debates catalyzed over cultural images that appeared as surprisingly stubborn, counterintuitive icons, resistant to national incorporation in their regional distinctiveness. Whereas through the 1930s "official" histories, national political culture, and arts and media had valorized historian Frederick Jackson Turner's frontier myth, the internally directed strategies of the New Deal, and the regionalist expression of artists such as Thomas Hart Benton, in the postwar era, the residual "localism" of each of these seemed no longer adequate in the emergent international-looking, New Liberal, modern (and modernist) context. Regionalism was now reassigned from its pre-war status as "official" explanatory discourse of national identity and value. Regional appeals remained exceptionally popular and active in everyday discourses, however.

As Erika Doss has argued, regionalism was the dominant American art practice during the 1930s, associated with "images of what seemed to be ordinary, everyday Americana," a "uniquely American art aimed at widespread popularity, an art intelligible and meaningful to all" through "a language that was plain, direct and devoid of any of the fancy specialisms of Art."[3] Regionalism—especially as characterized in the work of Thomas Hart Benton—was explicitly associated with the Midwest as emblematic of "the indigenous or the primal basic America."[4] However, by the mid-1930s and, in full flower by the conclusion of World War II, regionalism was increasingly critiqued as a threateningly provincial, stereotypical, and anti-modern style that suggested an inward-looking, conservative isolationism which stood in stark contrast to the perceived need for global engagement and an expansive postwar political and cultural vision. The aesthetic address and favored content of regionalist art was thus reevaluated as an art of the past, focused on the American interior, naïve in its appeals to "the people," and out-of-touch with cultural trends and progressive movements centered in New York and in Europe. Similarly, historian Frederick Jackson Turner's "frontier thesis"—which had, from its introduction in 1893 been the reigning paradigm for defining what was unique or particular to American history and development—was now also actively reassessed. Placing the Midwest at the center of American identity, the thesis was a rationale for the "advance of independence on American lines" and, therefore, for "a steady movement away from the influence of Europe."[5]

Turner's thesis had allowed its proponents to explain "almost all that was desirable in American life and character" as emanating from the pioneer experience and westward expansion.[6]

Others, however, challenged the appeal of this mythology, pointing to the pioneer's "social conformity" and "naïve" politics.[7] Criticism of Turner's thesis was crucially tied to *place*. As historian Warren Susman has argued, by the 1920s:

> The frontier thesis in effect had made the contemporary Middle West 'the apotheosis of American civilization,' and that was exactly the problem . . . the significant point here is that the kind of character produced by the pioneering experience was no longer valued in any way by an important body of American intellectuals. . . . The revolt against this particular 'useless past' was part of a larger revolt against what was considered to be the Midwestern domination of American life and values. . . . It admitted that American development had been the creation of the frontier process. Yet it insisted that the consequences of that process had been detrimental to the creation of a valuable political and cultural life.[8]

The valorization and disparagement of regional representation and explanatory narratives use strikingly similar language to that which described both television's promise for postwar audiences and its failure in the eyes of its critics. Debates over television were riddled with discussions questioning "program taste, often opposing . . . New York programming to the standards of the rest of the country" and the "complaints of television critics" versus "the popular success of the disparaged new program forms."[9] Arguably then, just after regionalist expression was revalued from its earlier status as the nation's *representative* art to "escapist" "kitsch," television programming adopted and re-presented some of regionalist art's aesthetic characteristics and popular appeals, transposing and reinvigorating them for the postwar era.

Thus, while *popular,* commercial venues continued, in this period, to promote and circulate idealized myths of the Midwest, "official" discourses of cultural critics, politicians, and regulators critiqued these mythologies with a renewed vigor and, often, vitriol. Arguably, in much "official" discourse from the 1950s through the 1960s, the Midwest became the reigning cultural symbol for past life and peripheral culture—

"a museum of sorts"[10]—while in other everyday uses it often remained conversely revered as central to or centrally representative of U.S. life and culture—as a site associated with tradition *within* progress and as the American Way. In this regard, public discourse regarding the region and its relation to broader national identity and purpose was thoroughly bound up with a broader revaluation of U.S. artistic, cultural, and political identity *from* regionalism and narratives that emphasized the centrality of the Midwest to national identity *to* modernism, internationalism, and *New* Frontier narratives focused on expansive leadership of the free world. In this revaluation, the Midwest most typically remained associated with pre-war understandings of national identity and representational culture that were increasingly considered archaic or threateningly provincial.

Serge Guilbaut argues that this reassignment of values was particularly energized at this historical conjuncture because, in the Cold War context, these debates took on a moral, nationalistic, value-laden burden reflecting the "degree to which culture had become politicized and important in a world sharply divided between the forces of good and the forces of evil."[11] In the radical shift that occurred in aesthetic values, "within the context of a major cultural and political transition," "*politics*" came to be understood "as a set of cultural beliefs."[12] In this politicized climate, since regionalism emerged from the Midwest and was inextricably connected to its myths and "ideals," the postwar revaluation of regionalist expression—as aesthetically impoverished and politically passé at best, and "low," degraded culture evoking retrogressive ideology at worst—was now fully part of the mythology of midwestern *political* identity. Guilbaut additionally proposes that, ironically in this period, the avant-garde

> rebellion of the artists, . . . gradually changed its significance until ultimately it came to represent the values of the majority, but in a way (continuing in the modernist tradition) that only a minority was capable of understanding. The ideology of the avant-garde was ironically made to coincide with what was becoming the dominant ideology, . . . [the Vital Center, New Liberalism proposed by Arthur Schlesinger, Jr. and embraced, particularly, by the Kennedy Administration] Avant-garde art succeeded because the work and the ideology that supported it . . . coincided fairly closely with the ideology that came to dominate American political life after the 1948 presidential elections.[13]

In its newfound role as the central medium of information and entertainment in everyday U.S. life, television moved to the center of these debates linking aesthetics, market success, and political ideology. As several scholars have carefully detailed, critics, regulators, and politicians increasingly expressed alarm at the "TV problem," arguing that the medium was not living up to its potential to enlighten rather than pander to the public.[14] While Heartland series through the 1960s share this critical attention with other popular genres of the period (particularly westerns and quiz programs), debates regarding series such as *Jubilee, U.S.A.* and *The Lawrence Welk Show* are distinguished by the comparative venom they direct toward the programs' perceived aesthetic impoverishment, "mass," "simple," popular appeal, and audiences whose cultural tastes are presumed to reflect misplaced priorities for the times. While ratings for these series bear out that they were tremendously popular from coast to coast (for example, Welk's highest ratings came from the Philadelphia market, particularly in the 1966–1967 and 1967–1968 seasons), critics of these programs and their fans considered them to be explicitly representative of "the fundamental regionalism that pervades the Midwest," positing these programs' success and tenacity as "rare regional phenoms" that, counter to national trends and values, "always . . . cling to the known and comforting, maybe half an emotional century behind the times."[15]

As Raymond Williams argues, at every stage of cultural development there remain "residual" tendencies, or, in other words, cultural elements that have been "effectively formed in the past, but (are) still active in the cultural process, not only . . . as an element of the past, but as an effective element of the present."[16] Residual elements are thus potentially symbols of a useless past, and yet, especially in times of social upheaval, "there is a reaching back to those meanings and values which were created . . . in the past and which still seem to have significance because they represent areas of human experience, aspiration, and achievement which the dominant culture neglects, undervalues."[17] Indeed, the perceived time-bound qualities of these series *within* the flow of the premier national space-binding medium offered a touchstone of stability and loyalty for viewers and their nurturance of imagined midwestern values at a time when national transformations fundamentally challenged the future of roots and fealty to one place or region.

In this chapter, I argue that key prime time ABC-TV programming of the 1950s points to such a "reaching back" and, in so doing, explicitly overdetermined and located residual American ideals in the rural American Heartland. This chapter thus examines the popularity and "problem" of 1950s and 1960s Heartland TV, to consider how "low" cultural expression and "mass" market desires were, increasingly, allied with regressive and potentially dangerous politics to the extent that, by the close of the 1960s "the relationship between television and the national economy had achieved the status of common sense for many Americans who reasoned . . . that popular cultural forms had no necessary connection to particular places."[18] "Local" expression was revalued to the extent that, on the national stage, the U.S. entered "an age which attached little or no value to vernacular culture in any form."[19]

ABC's Rural Strategy as "Democratic" Appeal

Compared to NBC's and CBS's successful legacies as radio networks, their capital-intensive roster of stars and vaunted high-production value programming, and also their commercial primacy within major television markets, ABC was at a competitive disadvantage upon its entry into television. To "brand" ABC as a viable competitor to its rivals, its executives rhetorically allied the network with "rural" values and with those viewers on the postwar cultural periphery, perceived to be underserved by the "Tiffany" network (a nickname both promoted by CBS and embraced by critics as early as 1950 to describe the network's quality—particularly as regarded its star talent and the rigor of its news division), or by NBC's "spectaculars." President Oliver Treyz argued that the network's goal was to forge an entirely new audience of television viewers—an audience as yet "left out" of the postwar TV boom. Said Treyz: "We aren't as concerned with taking audiences away from other networks as we are getting the people who aren't looking to tune us in."[20]

While expressive of a democratic ethos, this populist, rural strategy was also reflective of structural conditions particular to ABC. A relative late-comer to network television broadcasting, ABC was geographically disadvantaged in relation to NBC's and CBS's populous, urban market share. ABC's audience was thus initially fairly restricted to those who received low-power VHF transmissions and many less-desirable, rural UHF affiliates. Because of VHF's stronghold in large markets, UHF allocations were generally located in smaller urban areas, broadcast with weaker signals, and often intermixed and interfered with by directly competing VHF stations. UHF stations usually reached a small audience due to area population and lack of UHF receivers, and so they were not particularly attractive as network affiliates—their small-market appeal could not attract mass-market advertisers. Into the 1960s, "ABC had twice as many UHF affiliates as either CBS or NBC," serving "smaller cities [such] as Madison, Wisconsin; . . . and Rockford, Illinois."[21] ABC needed to build upon its existing market strengths to develop a base from which it might expand.

Technically (for ease of reliable "national" distribution), ABC relied largely upon filmed rather than live broadcast programming. Such programming—thanks in large part to ABC's partnerships with Disney and Warner Bros. studios—led to a concentration on genres such as action-adventure, westerns, and detective programs. Though typically unexamined, ABC also featured music-variety programming for the same reasons. As Christopher Anderson's *Hollywood TV: The Studio System in the Fifties* points out, "in contrast with programming forms that traded on uniqueness"—such as the live anthology dramas featured on CBS or the variety spectaculars on NBC—ABC's weekly series "encouraged an experience of television viewing as something *ordinary,* one component of the family's household routine."[22]

ABC President Oliver Treyz rationalized ABC's emphasis on filmed programs as both an economic survival strategy *and* in the best service interest of the network's new family audience, focused on "those households formed since World War II." Treyz testified to the FCC that the more focused ABC's programming was on popular genres of filmed entertainment, the more "mass" its audience would be

> with more than five times as many markets unable to receive an outstanding ABC-TV program on a live basis, it is obvious that our program planning must be restricted to a narrower range than that which is required to accomplish fully our purpose of reaching the maximum number of different people. . . . Therefore, our planning, in contrast to the other networks, necessarily concentrates on the development, production, clearance and sale of quality film programs, such as *Ben Casey, Naked City* and *The Roosevelt Years.*[23]

Considering that *critically* successful shows of the period were, largely, live anthology dramas originating on CBS or "spectaculars" with major stars on NBC, ABC's programming strategy explicitly positioned it as an alternative network through "accessible," popular, time-worn entertainment programming. The network proposed to offer the "all-American" democratic *choice* of the "low" in evening entertainment in contrast to its "high"-cultural competitors. The competition embraced this rhetoric. NBC's Pat Weaver, for example, "expected to make the common man the uncommon man," promoting TV's enlightening possibilities over what he called the "broad stuff" making up "ABC success."[24] Calculatedly, as Laurie Ouellette has argued, "By aligning itself with a 'voting' majority of its own constitution, the industry justified in populist terms its enormous cultural power, as well as its marketing strategies."[25] ABC-TV executives, in particular, argued that, "through counter-programming we seek to present offerings, different in type and different in fundamental appeal than the programs scheduled in the same time periods on other networks," promoting such programming as what "ordinary" people want, in spite of criticisms lobbed by "haughty elites who looked down on 'plain folks.' "[26] ABC would compete by featuring family programming in accessible, "complete, self-contained" shows featuring familiar genres populated by "ordinary" non-stars.[27]

ABC's audience's tastes were presumed to run toward active, group entertainment. Aesthetically, the most popular programs on ABC could be considered both stylistically impoverished or "pre-televisual" and *interactive,* engaging an unusually participatory audience, rather than one characterized by distanced contemplation. John Caldwell has defined "televisuality" as "aesthetic facility," a "self-conscious performance of style" whereby "style itself" becomes the subject. [28] This is a phenomenon, it should be noted, that Caldwell historically locates from the 1980s onward. However, discourses of aesthetic "quality" in TV—often used to distinguish the "class" programming preferred by critics and a selective, well-educated audience from the "mass" programming popular with wider television audiences—are often staked on such contrasts. Aesthetic "impoverishment" is typically linked, therefore, with "low" taste and, by extension, the audience of such programming is often written about as a relatively indiscriminate "mass." Notably, while publicly embracing the broad, popular audience as savvy "voters" who democratically choose cultural winners from free-market offerings, internally, network executives shared much of their critics' disdain (though the networks profited handsomely in spite of their skepticism). An example of correspondence pertaining to program audiences at NBC indi-

cates the ambivalence, here, as it explicitly connects geographic affiliation to taste and behavior:

> The loud and phony audience reaction is not only encouraged, but
> sought after by the package producer, who incidentally, is highly critical
> of us if we do not deliver the "right" kind of audience. (Out-of-towners
> are more cooperative in the matter of "proper" reaction and New York-
> ers or metropolitanites are not welcome because they are much too
> blasé and independent).[29]

Caldwell uses the example of *Ted Mack's Original Amateur Hour* to
theorize the links between a "zero-degree studio style"—emphasizing
the amateurish, staged, "visually uninteresting" qualities of such programs—and such programs' connection to pre-televisual arts and media. Caldwell argues that 1950s TV genres emphasized the uneasy tension between "art and the East"—as envisioned in "quality" dramas
and specials noted for "auteur" contributions—and programs that "celebrate . . . self-deprecation . . . form[ing] a populist alliance with viewers."[30] These latter series forge what Charlotte Brunsdon and David
Morley have described as

> a close and 'homey' relationship with [their] audiences . . . massively
> linked with the rural aspects of regional life and hence with the past
> and with a kind of cultural nostalgia for old folkways, values, and
> customs.[31]

Their "project is to be accepted by . . . audience [members] as their representative, speaking for them, and speaking to them, from a perspective, and in a language which they share."[32] Each of these programs,
for example, explicitly address their audience as "neighbors" or as
"friends"—implicitly understood to be, in the main, white, rural, Protestant midwesterners.

Originating from Springfield, Missouri . . .

Jubilee, U.S.A. and *The Lawrence Welk Show* epitomize many of the
ways in which national network TV was still in a period of considerable
transition through the 1950s. Both programs originated in pre-televisual

networks—from vaudeville and traveling shows to radio programs—
before making the transition to TV. Both programs' telecasts originated
outside of New York City, with *Jubilee, U.S.A.* telecasting from Springfield, Missouri and Welk's broadcasts originating from Santa Monica,
California. During the series network run (1955–1960), *Jubilee* was
broadcast from Springfield, which prompted its co-producer, Si Siman,
to boast, based on audience draw, that

> Springfield, Missouri was the third highest origination point for na-
> tional television—third only to New York and Hollywood. More than
> Chicago. More than Washington, D.C. . . . We were able to convince
> ABC that "country" was a lot more popular than people realized.[33]

This quote points to another shared claim the programs could make:
Each drew a very broad geographic and multi-generational audience to
each week's telecast. As *TV Guide* noted,

> ever wonder which show attracts the widest family circle to the TV set
> each week? Wal, now, it's that li'l ole *Ozark Jubilee* that you don't hear
> so much about but that sure does pack in the country-music fans on
> Saturday night. . . . According to the American Research Bureau, *Ju-
> bilee* has 28 percent more people per set watching than the average of
> all evening shows. In other words, it appeals to Grampaw and all the
> tads, too.[34]

Jubilee boasted a per-set audience estimate of 3.32, higher than that for
either *Disneyland* or for *Lassie*.[35] And yet, the *genre* of the program, allied as it was with regional expression, consistently raised puzzlement
regarding its popularity. *Time* magazine posed the question, considering
the "hillbillies . . . moaning and wailing, . . . Why is it so successful?"
To which co-producer Ralph D. Foster replied, "there are more country
people in America than any other kind of people. Most city people were
from the country and are still sentimentally attached to it."[36] The program producers and network promoters thus concurred with the critical
discourse's presumption that these programs were "mass" and "majoritarian" in their appeal, rather than catering to an "elite," objectively de-
tached audience.

Featuring a cast populated by amateur performers or country and
western performers familiar from *The Grand Ol' Opry* radio show and

stage-tour circuit, the program's reviews indicate befuddlement over its "supreme lack of show-business knowledge," its relatively impoverished "two-camera, no-ulcer" look, and its "far from subtle, but . . . forth-right . . . sincere" charms.[37] Each week's closing credits explicitly positioned the "heart of the Ozarks" at the geographic center of America and, conceptually, as the bed-rock of postwar society from which all good things radiate outward—as a residually place-bound corrective to the anxiety, materialism, self-involvement, and distance from "real folk" perceived to be ever-more prevalent in modern life.

Typically following a two-camera approach to shooting action on-stage, the snazziest uses of TV technology in the series come during square dance routines, wherein a third, overhead camera is often used. Even here, however, it would seem that the additional view on the action only serves to further familiarize audiences with particular dance routines, popular for community gatherings. Thus, rather than distin-guish between expert and amateur cultures or exhibit the revelry in technological expertise common to programs such as CBS's *See It Now,* ABC's pre-televisual, populist programs treat the television camera as a necessary but not particularly remarkable extension of the family that enables the cast's weekly meeting with its friends and neighbors at home. The camera helps to reinscribe local place within the program's address, as it allows studio audience members to acknowledge their own hometowns via banners and signs from the Midwest, Southwest, and Great Northern Plains. For example, in *Jubilee, U.S.A.,* audience members hold up placards sending out greetings from the studio to "Cedar Rapids, IA" and "Waco, TX," among others.

Bound to rural place and proud of it—these shows imagine an insu-lar, homogeneous, shared community by staging folk traditions that ref-erence the cultural past and exhibit a knowing, even defiant difference from urban life. Reinforcing local insularity, in particular, are comedi-ans whose stock characters include the country rube (like Uncle Cyp and Dr. Lew Childres). On *Jubilee, U.S.A.* each repeats routines already familiar to the audience from pre-televisual venues such as the stage, ra-dio, and traveling versions of *The Grand Ol' Opry,* reviving and recir-culating shared rural narratives within the "new," "modern" TV forum —often at the expense of urbanites. For example, in one Uncle Cyp sketch, when questioned over a malapropism by host Red Foley, Cyp re-sponds, "I don't know what it means—a 'hillbilly' writer from Boston wrote it!" Similarly inscribing residual Heartland insularity, each of these programs encourages audience participation in forms of entertainment that—considered to be nostalgic or evocative of "old folkways"—might not be seen elsewhere on TV. Thus, here, the loyal viewer is made partially responsible for the preservation of Midwest-regional, rural, and past cultural practice, as the program features guests from barbershop quartets and square dancers to 4-H award-winners.

Finally, these programs profess to be made for and by the people, as their representative, through their homiletic address to a presumed Protestant audience. Each program features one or two country and western renditions of popular hymns—often in front of the façade of a rural church. Red Foley, host of *Jubilee, U.S.A.*, ended every episode with a sermonette. These gospel segments explicitly reinforce the Heartland community's imagined, steadfast adherence to pre-modern values of family, church, and hometown in the face of rapid postwar change.

An Unlavish Square Takes on the TV Experts

While *Jubilee, U.S.A.* was distinctive for its "local" origination, its mass audience, and its key role in ABC's network development and solidification through regional appeals, no Heartland program could match the popularity and longevity, or the equally passionate and ongoing critical disdain, of *The Lawrence Welk Show*'s "clodhopper charm." The Lawrence Welk Orchestra began hosting weekly "dance parties" on television after twenty-six years of entertaining on the road, on radio, and in the ballrooms of Pittsburgh and Chicago. In August, 1951, after Welk had spent about a month at Santa Monica's Aragon Ballroom in Pacific Ocean Park, KTLA Los Angeles agreed to telecast one of his appearances. According to Welk biographer William Schweinher, "viewers began to call before the show was over," requesting more appearances of the orchestra. KTLA aired Welk's program for the next four years.[38]

The key to this incarnation of Welk's television success would seem to have been a combination of the orchestra's rapid-fire musical transitions (from waltzes to swing tunes to polka, etc.), and the bandleader's rather awkward but sincere persona. Welk's producer Don Fedderson has characterized this appeal as "genuineness . . . credibility and actuality . . . which enables people to relate."[39] Mark Williams's detailed study of KTLA quotes station manager Klaus Landsberg as determined to promote such sentiments through programming that needn't be elaborate. The people look at those lavish furnishings and they feel betrayed. They don't belong to them . . . they'd much rather find a warm, friendly personality on the air that's considered one of them—one they would welcome in their homes . . . there's far greater appeal in that than in all the lavishness.[40]

According to his sponsors, the Dodge Dealers of Southern California, Welk's unlavish appeal instilled

confidence in his viewers by projecting an image of sincerity and honesty [so] that they buy the product he recommends. We know of actual instances of people buying Dodge automobiles who couldn't even drive, just because Lawrence Welk recommended them.[41]

Locally, then, KTLA presented Welk as an ordinary personality and familiar presence—qualities enhanced by the fact that his orchestra played arrangements of folk music and dances that were common to many viewers' family or community heritage. Welk's phenomenal sales success for Dodge brought his program to national network attention in 1955. While Welk's success in the Los Angeles area recommended him for a national prime time trial, network executives initially saw his unglamorous persona and thick accent as risks to widespread audience attraction. However, Welk ultimately fit with the network's overall strategy of counter-programming that, comparatively, encouraged Welk's plan to expose a *national* audience to geographically characteristic folksy attributes. While broader industry rhetoric implied that a unified market/community of viewer/consumers would raise the cultural literacy and commercial fluency of the nation, Welk assumed that television could promote communal gatherings and activities evocative of shared ideals that had historically informed American traditional behavior (including celebrations or ritual festivals, courtship and marriage, family). If television's nationalizing trends promoted America's technological future to be one nation under shared consumer ideals, Welk embraced television's ability to celebrate his audience's shared connections to the *past*, underscoring the benefits of citizenship and free enterprise.

Indeed, Welk not only achieved his first television popularity by appealing to imagined midwestern ideals, but he did so in the context of immediate postwar Los Angeles, whose boom of this era was largely attributable to its affordable housing, new industries, and sunny climate, which attracted a mass of G.I. family migrants from Midwestern states. Thus, rather than change his program content and strategy, Welk interpreted his position in the network schedule as an affirmation that his "local" approach and production style were right on target with the desires of the American television audience. Echoing Landsberg's comments above, early Welk interviews and essays point to his strategy of attributing his orchestra's popularity to his knowledge of "the people." Here, Welk combines his awkward, amateurish, immigrant farm-boy persona with an expert awareness of the public's musical zeitgeist. According to Welk, the national community of viewers was not an "ultra-sophisticated," intellectual elite but "essentially an audience of simple people." Therefore he and his orchestra "are more content than ever to remain exactly what we always were, and always will be—a group of musicians dedicated to entertaining the great millions with the danceable, bouncing beat of Champagne Music which they tell us they understand, and like."[42]

In these terms, *The Lawrence Welk Show* is suggestive of residual cultural ideals in the post–World War II American consumer landscape via its chosen content, aesthetic composition, and audience address. The program most often features a single set and uses only two studio cameras, while its content features familiar folk tunes, historic dance steps, and promotes a family atmosphere with rural, midwestern, and church-going ties. It addresses its audience as participants who interact with the weekly "dance party" rather than merely observe with a contemplative gaze. As an ABC voice-over promotion from 1958 exhorts:

Dance around in your stocking feet or high-fashion formal shoes! Dress as you like because the dance party is in your home . . . with music and entertainment provided by all the Champagne Music Makers led by Lawrence Welk! . . . Fun and music for the whole family—that's Lawrence Welk's Dancing Party—and everyone's invited![43]

And, in a *TV Guide* feature from 1956, interactivity is portrayed as "The Philosophy Behind Lawrence Welk's Tremendous Success."

Welk himself says the secret of his popularity is that he appeals to the "most important" member of the family. "Mother likes our music," he says, "Mother isn't as dull as you think. Oh, she does the laundry and the housework, but she hasn't forgotten she likes to dance. . . . And she is so happy, it makes us popular with the whole family."[44]

At the crux of much of the debate about *The Lawrence Welk Show*'s cultural worth is the association of this audience's pleasures as regionally territorialized and resistant to an erasure of local identity. Welk's audience is consistently particularized as "midwesterners." The imagined, shared vernacular attributes and communal bond of this group are those of the culturally ill-equipped provincial viewer of the Midwest and of the rural plains states (especially the senior citizen, and particularly older women)—a portrayal that remains surprisingly consistent in both academic and popular press criticism. David Marc's book-length analysis of television comedy, for example, includes a passage regarding the popular cultural fluency of the rural viewer:

> Though it baffles the imagination, the ratings coolly substantiate an image of a lone TV antenna standing against the stark Nebraska prairie pulling down a snowy black-and-white image of Sid Caesar performing in a spoof of Japanese art films, written by Carl Reiner and Mel Brooks.[45]

Marc purposefully locates a hypothesized rural spectator in order to illustrate television's educational value for even the most presumptively marginal of American viewers. Should it equally "baffle the imagination" that Lawrence Welk's 1950s ratings as a national program on ABC were strongest in Boston and Philadelphia? Significantly, here, Cincinnati, on the cusp of the Midwest, handed Welk his lowest ratings during the 1950s. Notably, Welk attracted his largest nationwide audience after ten years on the air, from 1965–1968,[46] at a time when the networks were increasingly attentive to counterculture interests and demographic appeals.

During Welk's network run, his approach to musical selection, production numbers, and "family" assignments all demonstrated the program's apparent concerns with specificity of place and its audiences' imagined midwestern sympathies—those residual elements of the pioneering experience that regionalist art and the frontier thesis found to be positive, "square" ideals. Considering this approach and the above critical conventions, it appears logical that much of the popular criticism and network apprehension about *The Lawrence Welk Show* stemmed from concerns that the program, its star, and its audience were not in tune with national ideals of progress. The program was considered to be irrevocably associated with the past, and not indicative of the latest available techniques in television production.[47] These concerns are manifest in responses to Welk's persona, the series' production values, and his orchestra's musical style. Welk and his music are alternately criticized and praised according to the different weight given to his North Dakota homestead pioneer past or his Horatio-Algeresque rise to fulfillment of the American dream, his image as an amateur-performer or expert-entrepreneur with regard to the television and music industries, and finally, his role as a "moral" celebrity who prioritizes ideals of "citizenship" and character over those of consumerism and personality.

In the network premiere, which was broadcast July 2, 1955, to serve as a summer replacement for *The Danny Thomas Show,* it is clear that the "amateur" television performer is uncomfortable with the camera, as Welk fastidiously fidgets with his hands and baton when he is not conducting the orchestra. At this early stage in the series' tenure, remarks from the bandleader such as "Well, now we have the opening out of the way," and "Thank you kindly. Now, on with the show," underscore Welk's intent to just get on with the music and dancing. There are two primary camera set-ups in this episode: one focuses on the bandstand and moves in for medium close-ups of Welk, while another hovers over the field of dancers on the floor. As the dancers are all dressed in similar formal attire and are primarily shot in high-angle, they are not particularly distinguishable. Apart from the unique trademark bubble machine, which makes for a lively backdrop, there is no visual standout in the program's organization and presentation. As a *Newsweek* review stated: "For all there is to be seen, as Welk himself admits, 'you can turn your TV set upside down while we're on the air.' "[48]

For the industry experts who were poised to redeem America's broadcast future from past midwestern "domination" of the nation's life and values, Welk's persona clearly emphasized his North Dakota farmer upbringing, complete with the unmistakable German accent that led to malapropisms and verbal tics ("babbling" for bubbling and "wunnerful, wunnerful"). This grated upon critics who read this "unsophisticated" presentation as unsuited to a new technology with so many more progressive possibilities. As Hal Humphrey remarked in 1955 in the *Detroit Free Press,* "I doubt that even his most fervent fans would credit him with being the Heifetz of the Accordion . . . his personality holds a sort of shy, clodhopper charm."[49] In 1963, *The Charlotte News* agreed, and attached place to these qualities, stating: "Welk is good in his own way. Whatever it is about him that is unique is one-hundred percent Midwest American, red, white, and blue, though lacking in musical taste."[50]

Although these assessments envision Welk's audience as tasteless, graceless klutzes, Welk's production staff, whose perception was that they were already on "the fringe area of show business," encouraged portrayals of the orchestra leader as a "farm boy" man of the People in contrast to the elite, coastal "television experts."[51] For his proponents, Welk embodied a Horatio Alger novel come to life. As Susman observes, Alger's novels were directed to an ostensibly rural population, and they provided "an easy and terror-free way of making possible rural adaptation to urban life."[52] While *The Lawrence Welk Show* did not serve this same function, it did position Welk as a rural "common man"—navigator of modern technological airwaves and surrounded by a schedule of programming that contrasted with his show's "environment" and appeal (notably, *Jubilee, U.S.A.* preceded *The Lawrence Welk Show* on ABC each Saturday night from 1955–1959, then followed Welk's show in its final full season, 1959–1960. Neither CBS nor NBC ever programmed musical series opposite Welk during his network run, instead competing with quiz shows, westerns, comedy-variety, sitcoms, legal dramas, or movies).

The notion of Welk as an amateur in an expert's business appealed to positive conceptions of the American frontier past that were foundational to both Turner's and Alger's myths of the country's successful entrepreneurial future. A wistful 1980 interview in *The Saturday Evening Post,* for example, recalls that Lawrence Welk was "one of us—the farm boy who made good . . . he seems to personify all that is best in the American character, a man who made good by being good" and who "reflects almost exactly the musical tastes of the average American."[53] There is an exuberance here, in the idea of Welk and his audience's uniquely shared cultural fluency through a homesteading, rural past. Welk's "making good" is closely tied to value-laden ideals of honesty, faith, and bootstrap entrepreneurism—what Welk has called the "underlying toughness about Americans that comes from our farming experience."[54]

Welk's amateur, ordinary, farmer persona also inflects his field of expertise. When asked about his accordion playing in interviews, Welk repeatedly stated his inadequacy. In a *Life* photo essay from 1957, he emphasized orchestra member (and lead accordionist) Myron Floren's proficiency by downplaying his own, stating, "I make no claim to being a great musician . . . Even as an accordion player I just don't rate."[55] Critical responses to this amateurishness frequently zeroed in on both the aforementioned lack of musical "taste" and the "non-televisual" aspects of Welk's program. While network officials in New York and Chrysler executives in Detroit had wanted Welk's transition to prime time to include "some improvements in his traditional musical variety format including the suggestion of a chorus line, a recurring comedian, and featured guest stars,"[56] Welk resisted any changes in favor of a series of musical numbers of different genres presented in rapid succession. Significantly, while network executives' rhetoric of the time suggested that the ideal television program would have no sense of place apart from an amorphous national character, Welk's program stubbornly called attention to the importance of regional and local places in the history of particular musical numbers, especially with regard to the origination of his orchestra members, known as his "musical family."

During the 1955 premiere, for example, Welk clearly introduces each of the members of his orchestra and feature singers between musical numbers, such as "our little Champagne Lady, Alice from Dallas," and tenor Jim Roberts, "a typical young American from Madisonville, Kentucky." Even though the cast's hometowns range from New York City to Escondido, California, Welk and his orchestra highlight the importance of the Midwest as centrally defining the Welk community. Myron Floren—"a very talented young man from South Dakota"—speaks for the entire orchestra as a preface to his accordion solo, stating, "It's really wonderful to go coast to coast and to see all of our friends way back in the Midwest and the Mideast . . . We hope to do it for a long, long time." Welk's efficiency in moving from number to number, though very prompt—often breathtakingly so for the musicians—never precludes the performers' introductions according to heritage and place. This was attached, throughout the years, to Welk's theory that each of his musical family should be perceived as familiar and next door neighbor-like. Rather than viewed as untouchable celebrities, the "family" was to be seen as hometown friends or nonprofessionals who happened to have some musical talent. This amateur appeal, which was overtly localized in an unstylized way, ostensibly underscored Welk's fluency with the desires of "the people."

Welk's impression of folksy amateurishness is in no small part attributable to his musical style, featuring instrumental arrangements known as "champagne music." While only a few of the musical numbers in each show feature champagne arrangements, this is the characteristic Welk sound. The champagne style emphasizes woodwinds over brasses, which is further accentuated as the brass instruments are muted. Clipped sixteenth notes establish these arrangements' dominant beat, moving the music along and giving it what Welk calls a "bubbly" character. In terms of tone quality, the reedy and quickly paced champagne music evokes Welk's favorite instrument, the accordion, and its home genre of the polka, but these arrangements are conceived as a mélange of big band, folk music, and upbeat popular dance tunes.

For Welk's detractors, "champagne music" most clearly epitomized the presumed "uncultivated taste" of his audience.[57] For example, in 1975 reviewer John Bull of the *Philadelphia Inquirer* proclaimed:

> If sugar could kill, I'd be dead by now for listening to Lawrence and his Musical Family. Saturday night was a saccharine venture into a world that no longer exists. . . . Music seems fizzingly artificial. . . . Welk insinuates that life really is free and easy and we can merely dance our troubles away. . . . There are sure a lot of people who like to pretend that's the way things still are.[58]

Mentioned in these discussions of a "world that no longer exists" and "resistance to innovation," is the "nostalgia that is Welk's stock in trade."[59] If there is nostalgia at play in the loyalty of Welk's audiences, it is focused around his persona's fusion of the "amateur" and the successful entrepreneur in the name of "vernacular" history—a shared language of place, tradition, and "pioneering" bootstrap values. Welk's celebrity evokes legacies of the past (like the community festivals and celebrations at which the polka would be danced) in order to manipulate the technology of the present in a meaningful way for his audience.

In this context, while network "experts" may appear crassly material in their designs for retooling Welk's program to have more zip and flair, Welk appears to be a staunch man of the people, playing for "the public" rather than himself. *Life* magazine's interview with Welk in 1957 supports this assessment, arguing that his farm-boy values have influenced every phase of his life in Hollywood, including the fact that he has no swimming pool, and therefore no worries. If Welk rejected the swimming pool, the ultimate 1950s object of Hollywood's conspicuous consumption, how could he with good conscience not only sell Dodge automobiles, but become the most successful pitchman in Dodge automobile history?

The Citizen Consumer and the Car You've Been Dreaming Of

Lawrence Welk's residual emphasis on the importance and inscription of place, as well as his program and persona's valuation of the qualities of character, suggest his position as a mediator between vernacular ideals—the older community-based culture assumed to be common to his viewing audience—and the consumer realities of a postwar America in which he had risen as a show-business personality and individual entrepreneur. Sponsored by the Dodge division of Chrysler throughout his network run, Welk was positioned as a citizen spokesperson who "evoked the experiences of the past to lend legitimacy to the dominant ideology of the present."[60]

George Lipsitz has meticulously outlined this task with regard to the 1950s subgenre of working class ethnic sitcoms, which disappeared by the 1960s in favor of suburban family sitcoms. As Lipsitz states,

> television's most important economic function came from its role as an instrument of legitimation for transformations in values initiated by the new economic imperatives of postwar America. For Americans to accept the new world of . . . consumerism they had to make a break with the past.[61]

One route to ease this break "consisted of identifying new products and styles of consumption with traditional, historically sanctioned practices and behavior,"[62] thus merging traditional ideals of adherence to the values of character and community while also anchoring them to the contemporary reality of consumerism. By this strategy, Lipsitz argues, "morally sanctioned traditions of hearth and home could be put to the service of products that revolutionized those very traditions."[63]

Welk's "citizen" stature as a man of tradition, community, and character was essentially defined by his denial of conspicuous personal gain in favor of a rigorous code of moral and behavioral standards. If Welk refused to play Las Vegas because it might offend some of his staunchly religious fans, must it not be the moral thing to do to drive a Dodge? Characterized as "one of the shrewdest citizens on Main Street and in Middeltown,"[64] Welk's moral reliability was illustrated by a constancy to that imagined Midwest community which was characterized by political fixity and ideological stasis: "In practicing his art, Mr. Welk shoots away from the hippie—and other current distractions—straight to the heartland."[65] He is also seen, in the 1960s and 1970s, as the only musical series star to counter the medium's "current kick of exalting teenage beat music and the weirdos who play it."[66] It is important to note that Welk's supposedly moral, family-focused, citizen ideals—rooted as they were in a residual stability—were contrasted with images of urban-affiliated youth and Left political activist movements that suggested a "rejection of American values" and of "straight American society."[67]

Significantly, as with many other TV variety hosts, Welk's spokespersonship for his sponsor is an implicit one. He did not appear in print ads for Dodge, nor did he do any voice-overs or testimonials on the automobile's behalf—these were done solely by orchestra family members and on-air Dodge announcer Lou Crosby. Advertising copy, however, was closely affiliated with the same values promoted by Welk and his musical family. Each weekly installment of the program was nationally sponsored in the name of local Dodge dealers, and Crosby's introduction offered "best wishes from the friendly Dodge dealer in *your* community." The automobiles were portrayed as offering "traditional reliability" and "champagne glamour." Themes and values emphasized in each advertisement included corporate trust, product accountability, and consumer safety. Above all however, Dodge was associated with a solid return on one's hard-earned money. Offering a series of models to fit different budgets, Dodge promised that small amount of glamour acceptable to the good citizen, but at a traditionally cost-effective price.

In the premiere episode of *The Lawrence Welk Show*, driving is associated with healthy social activities or community gatherings. Here a Dodge Lancer floats playfully to the front of the credits in a Welkian bubble, which bursts as announcer Lou Crosby says "Dodge: the car that says 'Let's go!' brings you the music that says 'Let's dance!'" A 1964 episode clinches the idea that Dodge can be a communal joy, no matter how large or limited the budget. Crosby shows the television audience the Lawrence Welk Orchestra parking lot lined with every model of new Dodge available on the market. Trusting that a loyal viewing audience is in some sense sympathetic to Welk's claims that his musical family is an extension of the viewing family, this is a powerful testimonial.

The family reliability of Dodge is underscored in one of the program's special broadcasts from the Aragon and Pacific Ocean Park. Here, the Lennon Sisters demonstrate the torsion-air feature of the new Dodge Dart. The advertisement is neatly tucked in at the end of the Sisters' performance of "Round, Round, Round." As they approach the automobile, surrounded by an eager and curious tourist crowd, the song lyrics change to a serenade of the car and its ability to provide effortless freedom. Featuring the Lennon Sisters here might appeal to the new teen drivers in viewing households, but equally, having the group—the oldest of whom was 18 at the time—demonstrate the ease of "push-button" driving technology suggests that the car is safe for all members of the family and, in accord with conventional gender stereotyping, does not require "expert" mechanical knowledge. In fact, in his 1960 introduction to the Dart line, Crosby sets up an opposition between the "experts" and "you, the motoring public," implying that the citizen-consumer is wise to the value of Dodge long before the consumer-experts who insist upon first test-driving "cars costing a thousand dollars more."

Blue-Haired Ladies and the Rural Welk Masses

The Welk program's homespun, community, and family-oriented advertising was successful on cross-class and cross-geographical lines, as is evidenced by its sixteen-year successful national network run. What seems to consistently mark the program and its popularity according to an imagined place and shared community is its focus on tradition *within* "progress" (e.g., Dodge value over a new sports car for the sake of keeping up with the Joneses), and family over "theatrical types" (that is, "ordinary people" populate the musical family). In Welk's world, these valued attributes give the word "square" a positive meaning. Embracing one of the most consistent terms in Welk criticism, the bandleader notes, when I was growing up, "square" was a compliment. You gave a man a square deal, looked him square in the eye, stood four square on your principles. . . . I grew up in a community of squares . . . squares as a group . . . enjoy clean fun, understandable music, pretty and wholesome girls.[68]

During the 1950s and through the mid-to-late 1960s, Welk's program may have intended its message for a shared community of "squares," but it was very concerned with attracting squares of all ages. The bulk of Welk's audience in the first ten years or so of his success formed an inverted curve, attracting children and pre-teens, and then viewers who were twenty-five years and older. In 1956, the most loyal members of Welk's audience were between the ages of twenty-five and sixty-eight.

Even in the last episodes of Welk's national network run, dancers Bobby and Cissy continued to attempt to attract an audience of younger viewers interested in a variety of steps. Aided by "upbeat" music, vividly bright lighting, and Welk's jarring combinations of costume colors, the pair took advantage of extant color and sound stage technology. One example is their tribute to the history of rock dances in which they demonstrate such steps as the pony, mashed potato, and alligator, in rapid succession. Aesthetically, this segment is very different from the show's black-and-white period and remains distinct from the syndicated series. Not only are the colors splashy, with clashing contrasts, but the television technology is revved up with floor camera transitions that simulate rapidly animated movement—a departure for Welk, but characteristic of shows marked by counterculture appeal such as *The Smothers Brothers Comedy Hour* or *Laugh-In*.

Despite Welk's cross-place, cross-generational ratings appeal, the popular representations of his fans continued to recall the imaginary uncultivated middle of America, a middle that was further marginalized and ridiculed according to generational and gender stereotypes. In 1964, Thomas Murphy of the *Hartford Courant* perfectly encapsulated the most popular strategy for the quick, critical dismissal of Welk's program and its significant ratings:

In both Welk and Liberace the design is to make little old ladies like them. And both succeed beyond the fondest dreams of man. . . . There must be some solution to the enigma, for . . . [Welk], like Liberace, is not what anyone would say conforms to the standards of masculine beauty. Both share . . . cornball music and fantastic success.[69]

After the critic distances himself from the object of adoration, he evokes the image of old women enamored with a television celebrity. At Welk's live local performances the appearance of dancing mothers and grand-mothers—women "out of control" with pleasure and desire—is apparently so threatening that the object of adoration must be desexualized in some way.

In a 1964 *Jack Benny* episode, the guest Welk is portrayed as a much bigger star than Benny himself.[70] Two featured Welk fans are portrayed as stereotypical "little old ladies" who have changed their passionate allegiance and club booster support from Benny to the orchestra leader. The fan club officers are dressed in predictably frumpy hats and dresses and joke about their weight gain, respective attractiveness, and their desire to stand in for the accordion Welk is squeezing. From these women, heralding from that midwestern enclave in southern California—Glendale—to the "wig flippers" in Milwaukee,[71] Welk fans are not only marked by gender and generation, but, again, by specificities of place.

On the surface, the joke here seems to be a jab at any amount of loyal devotion to Welk, an unlikely celebrity with "clodhopper charm." Fundamentally, however, the notion of a midwestern housewife or farm woman as desirous or sexually active outside of the sphere of motherhood "down on the farm," evokes a cultural threat based on notions of "proper" place and what is nationally seemly or tasteful regarding older women, midwesternness, sexuality, and desire. Finally, such discomfort would also seem to signal a fear of the threat of regional difference and what is assumed to be concomitant cultural regression from urbanity and progressive ideals; the threat that televised exposure to "unenlightened," residual cultural artifacts might literally hold the nation back from its future promise.

Such perceptions of Welk's audience were, in part, perpetuated by Welk's own attitude toward each program as a potential musical journey to and education in different types of instrumentation, tempo, timbre, and orchestration. The "ethnic other" in these journeys was defined as non-Anglo and generally non-Agrarian. The most frequently performed and implicitly natural or shared ethnicity on *The Lawrence Welk Show* was the German polka-culture showcased by Myron Flo-

Dancing to champagne music on *The Lawrence Welk Show.*

ren's accordion solos. Welk emphasized that each member of his cast came from a place with specific characteristics and that each element of his family was part of a "mini democracy." Along these lines, Welk wrote of his program:

> Whenever I feel truly downcast, I look at our orchestra . . . a little "America" . . . democracy all its own. And if a German bandleader and a Jewish musical director can become such pals, that's a very positive sign! We are Gentile and Jew in our band, and Catholic and Protestant, and black and white and old and young, Republican and Democrat . . . but we're alike in our devotion to what's best for all of us. . . .[72]

In practice, however, ethnically or racially "distinctive" family members were asked to literally perform their ethnicity in stereotypical ways under the scrutiny of Welk—the symbolic white patriarch.

During the show's early years such ethnic and folk numbers are the domain of Irish tenor Joe Feeney and "Aladdin" (no last name is given) the violinist. "Aladdin's" unidentified ethnicity allows him to assume various identities in these set pieces, from a "Gypsy Violinist" to a German beer cellar proprietor. By the early 1970s, Anacani (again, no last name is given), a Mexican American woman, assumes this multi-purpose ethnic character role. According to Anacani, "Mr. Welk always liked [for her] to sing Spanish songs on the show," (referring to the language), and so she generally sang either songs that were already familiar to a predominantly non-Mexican audience or novelty songs that were translated into Spanish, such as "Feliz Navidad" and "Happy Farm," respectively.

However, Welk's program generally featured the cheerful Anglo couple, Bobby and Cissy, doing a "dance like Carmen Miranda," rather than Anacani. In production numbers which featured whites "doing" ethnicity—as in Bobby and Cissy's case, or when a white country singer performs "Jambalaya," or the orchestra joins in unison for that "favorite folk song" "Jimmy Crack Corn"—the dance or song was thus "demonstrated" for the audience's education. Severed from any autobiographical connection with the Welk Family cast, such performances were able to remain generalizable community property.

Calling All Revolutionaries: The Welk Community Comes to PBS

Once Welk was cancelled by ABC in 1971, he jumped into syndication under a new sponsor banner, Geritol. The changes in television markets and sponsors mirrors a conscious shift on Welk's part to retool his program to a very particular demographic. After years of reading *Billboard* and planning programs around teenage dance parties, Welk wholeheartedly embraced an older audience, stating, "some people ridicule us for playing what they call 'mom and dad music.' We think it would be wrong to pace the show for the teenage audience that isn't home on a Saturday night."[73] Welk was taking an ideological and political stance which he had previously, if very thinly, disguised in the name of a national network audience. Now, his "squares" were rhetorically positioned as the Silent Majority who "pay their bills . . . keep their children clothed and fed, send them to Sunday school, raise them to believe in God and this country."[74] Now his tunes were played as the alternative to musical "extremes" in the contemporary environment.

According to Welk's son, Lawrence Welk, Jr., his father's career was marked by an attempt to mediate "the tensions between an old-world culture from rules and tradition and a new-world culture of curiosity, independence, and diverse values . . . Few men and women of his generation integrated these two worlds so successfully into their lives and work."[75] Historian Alan Nevins has written that "unity in American life and political thought certainly does not stem from general agreement on any body of doctrines . . . It is not the look backward but the look forward that gives us cohesion. The great sentiment of America is hope for the future."[76] The look backward, however, was where Welk saw his mediation skills, his hope was for the young members of his cast family to learn rules from this old-world culture that they might apply to the present day.

In the first years of syndication, Welk began doing theme shows that examined "Americana" for the holidays (Christmas and New Year's Eve only), including a tribute to the Rose Parade at New Year's. In 1972, fresh off the sting of network cancellation, Welk did a country and western show in which the family performed the Roy Clark song, "Music Revolution." Welk himself does not seem to know what to make of Clark's intent in penning the lyrics, but states, "even if you're only kidding, I'm flattered." With wholehearted family gusto, the cast sings:

> We're goin' through a music revolution
> The hippies say they'll overcome us all.
> But while they're blowin' smoke in air pollution,
> we're hangin' on with the help of Geritol.
> They're roundin' up the squares in California
> They're pickin' off our heroes in New York
> But they'll never take away our champagne music
> As long as Lawrence Welk can pop his cork.
> They still do the polka in Milwaukee
> Still do the waltz in Tennessee
> Still singing' bluegrass in Kentucky
> With old-fashioned country harmony.

So give me some good ol' champagne music
And play that double-eagle march for me
For they still do the polka in Milwaukee
So let me hear that one-a-two-ah-three.

This production number seems hyperbolically poised to reterritorialize the Welk audience's geographical and ideological space within the nation, to reinstate the vernacular within the market, to insist that folk traditions are part of a useable past that is rapidly threatened, here, by a diffuse hippie-led deterritorialization or the assertion of a common national culture. While claiming "square" bastions in New York and California, the revolutionaries are firmly ensconced in the frontier community behavioral traditions of the Welkian Middle West.

Indeed, if ABC's "populist" programming and Heartlander appeals generated criticisms throughout the 1960s that placed the network on the "low" end of debates regarding television and national purpose, by the decade's conclusion, the imagined *audience* of such programming was, additionally, increasingly linked to regressive *political* allegiances. The "typical" fan of *Jubilee, U.S.A.* or *The Lawrence Welk Show*—imagined in the mid-1950s as a square midwesterner—was, by the 1970s, also routinely associated with Middle Americanness as a *political* identification. This transition is exemplified best by a *New York Times* feature story by *The Vital Center* author, Arthur Schlesinger, Jr. "The Amazing Success Story of 'Spiro *Who?*'" prefigures the current, imagined "red state, blue state" divide—a breach that is critically conceptualized as much through cultural disposition as it is on political ideology:

[With] his Lawrence Welk records and his Sunday afternoons with the Baltimore Colts, Mr. Agnew was the archetype of the forgotten American who had made it. He took pride, he used to say, in his "belief in dull things—dull things like patriotism. Dull things like incentive. Dull things like respect for the law." "The disease of our times," he said in June, 1968, "is an artificial and masochistic sophistication—a vague uneasiness that our values are corny"[77]

The latter years of the Welk program attempt to affix "traditional community" to the Midwest by imagining it as a stable center against which the nation is defined as following any new whim that comes its way. By 1975, Welk began taking these political implications seriously in an eerily Ross Perot-like fashion. One of his fans began a drive to nominate him for President of the United States, and Welk wrote three books outlining his "system" and his "plan" for the restoration of the strength of the country through family, morality, and free enterprise. In *My America, Your America,* Welk suggested that successful television production could serve as a model, stating that "what we had been able to do in our Musical Family on a limited scale could be done for our great American family."

While *The Lawrence Welk Show* lives on in syndication, exhibiting a popularity and cultural stamina that continues to this day, ongoing "common sense" use of Lawrence Welk as shorthand for cultural waste is most provocative—especially as it is used similarly by figures occupying opposite poles of the political spectrum. [78] In an installment of the mid-1990s summer series *TV Nation,* Michael Moore sent twenty-something and former MTV icon Karen Duffy to investigate "North Dakota: The Least Visited State." The segment ironically defended the state's tourist industry by uncovering its significance for fellow Americans. At the state capitol, Duffy is told that the first person inducted into the North Dakota Hall of Fame was Lawrence Welk, although the tour guide cannot think of a single reason why he was chosen. In rural Strasburg, Duffy sees the Welk Homestead, where its director cannot recall the name of any tune made famous by the bandleader's orchestra. If Welk's "archaic" status in the 1950s would make him seem, by the 1990s, an obvious comedic target for the liberal Moore, it should be recalled that Republican President George H.W. Bush *also* attacked Lawrence Welk's legacy in his 1992 State of the Union Address. In light of an uproar over Congressional funding for a German-Russian Pioneer and Homesteading museum—planned to celebrate North Dakota's centennial and to boost tourism in Welk's hometown—Bush pilloried "the annual ritual of filling the budget with pork-barrel appropriations" such as "a Lawrence Welk Museum."[79] Bush's reference was most effective, in part because speechwriter Peggy Noonan and her staff omitted the not so subtle distinction made by the museum's planners between a "German-Russian Pioneer and Homesteading Interpretive History Center" and a Lawrence Welk Museum. As Bush would have it, the nation's funds were not to be whittled away for a "Graceland on the prairie," in honor of the "Liberace of the accordion."[80] In leveling criticisms at the farm boy as a wasteful cultural icon the President was also implicating Welk's following—ostensibly the President's own peer constituency—as part of a useless past.

In *both* examples, Welk's "low" worth appears to follow from his native connection to a Midwest whose presumed geographic remoteness (the "least visited" "prairie") irrevocably defines the region as culturally void. In both, the speaker skewering Welk—and by extension his fans, if not midwesterners at-large—attempts to establish a conversely tasteful and knowing relation to the cultural products and places that *matter* as politically engaged and relevant within the United States and for its broader public. Inherent to both references is the awareness that a majority of the audience will *get* this joke, will know who Welk was, what his program was like, and, therefore, why his image conjures up such loaded presumptions about American identity, place, and cultural worth. These associations of the Midwest with "a remoteness . . . that is not wholly geographical"[81] are the focus of my examination in chapter 3 of the 1960s "quality" documentary genre through *CBS Reports'* 1960s visits to a Heartland Midwest imagined as home to an emerging Silent Majority invested in the "belief in dull things."

3

"Strictly Conventional and Moral"

CBS Reports *in Webster Groves*

On February 25, 1966, an installment of CBS's critically acclaimed documentary series, *CBS Reports,* focused on the daily lives and dreams of teenagers growing up in Webster Groves, an affluent suburb south of St. Louis, Missouri. *CBS Reports: Sixteen in Webster Groves* was followed, seven weeks later, by *Webster Groves Revisited,* an unprecedented though carefully planned defense of the contents and conclusions presented in the original telecast that incorporated the responses of Webster Groves' residents to their earlier portrayal and their rebuttal to the image of their community presented to the nation-at-large. From a control room booth, narrator and reporter Charles Kuralt began the *Webster Groves Revisited* broadcast, stating:

> Where that [first] broadcast ended, this one begins. Television usually only works one way—we talk to you, and you can't talk back. Or, if you do laugh or applaud or mutter or curse, we can't hear you. Our voice is loud, because it is amplified. But we know that amplification should not necessarily be confused with wisdom. And we've always thought it would be interesting to hear what you say back to the picture tube.[1]

This chapter closely examines two examples in which a public self-identified as midwestern talked back to the television set during the 1960s peak reform years of 1961 to 1966: FCC Chairman Newton Minow's "Vast Wasteland" address of May 9, 1961, which initiated this period and the Webster Groves documentaries, which aired at the close of this era. Minow's speech ushered in a period of interventionist activity at the FCC and encouraged a brief but prolific boom in network documentary programming. Examined here are viewers' responses to Minow's address and to documentary production personnel during this period. Letters are relatively unreliable historical documents in the sense that letter writers are not "typical" viewers, tending to be more invested in particular issues than those who do not write. Additionally, these documents are somewhat unreliable in that it is often unclear which letters were kept and which were discarded from archival collections, perhaps skewing the sample of letters available. However, correspondence, press, and televised public responses to television's regulators, producers, and journalists do, nonetheless, help to excavate traces of an often overlooked voice in the debate over television and "national purpose" —a debate that typically has only been represented by the "official" discourses of regulators and producers.[2] The Webster Groves documentaries expose participants' deep ambivalence regarding competing popular and official discourses. This ambivalence particularly is revealed in conflicts regarding who should speak for the local community within national programming and over the Midwest's portrayal to the nation-at-large as an object of critique, rather than exemplar of national ideals.

As Michael Curtin has argued, the early to mid-1960s represented

> a distinctive and complicated moment when political and corporate leaders as well as network officials embraced the television documentary in an explicit attempt to mobilize public opinion behind a more activist foreign policy . . . an ambitious effort to reawaken the public.[3]

This moment of regulatory, critical, and industrial unity has been characterized as an "elite consensus" whereby "a small body of opinion leaders . . . had common concerns uncommon to the great majority of Americans."[4] As Laurie Ouellette has further noted,

> the definition of good television promoted by reformers like [FCC Chair Newton] Minow was socially and historically bound to urban, upper-middle-class, white Eurocentric, university-bound, and, very often, masculine experiences. Officially available to anyone, it favored those with the required "cultural capital" to belong.[5]

Indeed, as proves the analysis in chapter 2 of the overwhelming popularity of "populist" program genres of the 1960s, the majority of TV viewers were *not* captivated by documentaries. Popular support *did* exist for regulatory reforms and for a pedagogical vision of television's purpose, however. While comparatively small in number, such support is nonetheless significant for its marked investment in television's role as the nation's "voice," and in the value of "good TV" to the broader public. Here, correspondence often reveals letter writers' awareness of the apparent "gap" between "elite" culture makers and "ordinary" viewers; writers frequently propose that television is the solution to this division. Responses to regulators and producers posit documentary, in particular, as a site of social investment and concern regarding claims to citizenship, cultural capital, and the right to speak or to author the American "ideals" of the period. Responses to FCC Chairman Newton Minow's "Vast Wasteland" speech also broadly indicate alliance with critical and regulatory discourses that questioned "mass" taste in television viewing and supported documentary as "one of the most important vehicles of public education in an age of crisis and uncertainty."[6] Such respondents point to the success with which (given the histories outlined in chapters 1 and 2), regulatory, industrial, and market investments in television had encouraged a broader, modern, revaluation of U.S. culture from regionalism toward national and international goals.

Given the association of midwesterners and the Midwest with populist, mass, "low" entertainments and cultural capital established in previous chapters, expressed Heartlander support for Minow's reforms and embrace of documentary's pedagogical possibilities suggests that this period offered a unique opportunity for viewers to actively, explicitly disassociate from and disavow pre-modern and place-bound associations with programs and fans such as Welk's and to assert allegiance with national imperatives and "elite" consensus. Minow, himself a native midwesterner with Milwaukee and Chicago roots, was arguably a model for this type of disavowal and travel between presumed categories of place and taste (as was consistently charged by his critics, who implied that his ambitions had outgrown his provenance, as seen below). These were viewers who identified with or who actively sought to ally themselves, publicly, with the elite educational and cultural capital and social leadership presumed to inhere in such reformist projects and program genres. TV, in this sense, offered a potentially aspirational site of identification and institutional recognition, distinguishing those viewers who make savvy viewing or culturally tasteful choices from those who do not—preferring *Omnibus* to *Jubilee, U.S.A.* or *CBS Reports* to *The Lawrence Welk Show*. Viewers making such choices and identifying, explicitly, with such distinctions also identified as in step with the New Frontier's reform ethos and its broadly international orientation.[7]

Respondents conform, in these senses, to the viewer category defined as "Academicus" in Gary A. Steiner's *The People Look at Television: A Study of Audience Attitudes,* a report funded by CBS and published in 1963. According to Steiner's survey,

> Academicus obviously watches little if any television himself. . . . His chief concern is with the social and cultural implications of so much television "escape" among the masses. To him, the country needs a more informative educational schedule, as it needs speed limits, better public schools, and racial integration—*not necessarily* for his personal benefit or use, but for the common good when adopted by others. As a middle-class, striving American, he more acutely feels the need to spend time usefully than his less ambitious counterparts; and his formal schooling has placed a high value on reading and serious study. . . . "Waste," which probably tends to be an issue for him in many areas, seems especially evident here in the case of time, his most valuable resource.[8]

Such identification and support was fraught with ambivalence, however, when documentaries "came home" to portray, for the broader nation, locales that were part of viewers' everyday familiarity. In such cases, viewers' belief in the network documentary's "national" voice—staked on the "genre's claim to objectivity" which "achieved peculiar force through its association with the political project of the New Frontier"—suddenly had to confront the fact that "the ways in which documentary programs explored and explained the world" might contradict local sensibility regarding community identity and social value.[9] Documentary's truth value and educational potential met skepticism and resistance when journalists focused their pedagogical address and urge to reform upon program participants themselves, rather than upon mass "others." Thus, the "two way flow" between the *CBS Reports* staff and local residents in the Webster Groves documentaries illustrates a profoundly ambivalent relationship between participants' and audiences' *popular* knowledge and "good" television's "official," cultural expertise. Exposed here, particularly, is the apparent disjuncture between local belief that Webster Groves' identity is fully synchronous with national ideals—indeed, representative of the apotheosis of the American dream—and "outside" expert cultural findings that the community is out-of-step with New Frontier imperatives, judging its cultural worth to be closer to Welk's than to Camelot's.

Newton Minow's Frontier and the Public Interest

As detailed in previous chapters, by the late 1950s, television was at the center of political, popular, and industry debates regarding cultural value and "national purpose." This debate was expressly aligned with the political imperatives of the New Frontier during the 1960 presidential campaign. In speeches and writings throughout the campaign, John F. Kennedy envisioned television as a venue to educate Americans regarding pressing international issues and to mobilize public activism and support regarding a variety of the administration's initiatives. This vision was generally accompanied by a critique of the alternative—the threat that Americans might, instead, choose to occupy a postwar "valley of complacency." With suburban and Middlewestern voters particularly in mind, Kennedy argued that

> too many Americans in the 1950s, I believe, have been living too much of the time in such a valley . . . contented and complacent and comfortable. Now it is time once again to climb to the hilltop, to be reinvigorated and reinspired.[10]

As Kennedy's choice for Federal Communications Commission Chair, Newton Minow assumed office fully inspired to initiate regulatory reform and to encourage the general public's participation in broadcast oversight.

On May 9, 1961, Minow delivered his famed address to the thirty-ninth Annual Convention of the National Association of Broadcasters in Washington, D.C. Minow's central theme was that broadcasters should consider whether their program schedules included a variety of genres, intended audiences, and programming oriented toward public service rather than ratings numbers alone. States Minow:

> Let me make clear that what I am talking about is balance. I believe that the public interest is made up of many interests. There are many people in this great country, and you must serve all of us. . . . We all know that people would more often prefer to be entertained than

stimulated or informed. But your obligations are not satisfied if you look only to popularity as a test of what to broadcast.[11]

Minow was himself a fan of television of all kinds—though he claimed to particularly favor *Omnibus,* the Sunday afternoon series sponsored by the Ford Foundation featuring multiple segments dedicated to the arts. During the speech (drafted, in large part, by John Bartlow Martin) he demonstrated his awareness of the broader program schedule, singling out series including *The Fred Astaire Show, Twilight Zone,* and *CBS Reports,* as well as specials such as *The Fabulous Fifties* and *The Nation's Future.* Minow thus emphasized that the question facing broadcasters was whether to choose a path characterized by diverse programming, balance, and flexibility, or to continue a quest for the highest ratings, at any cost.

> A rating, at best, is an indication of how many people saw what you gave them. . . . it never reveals what the acceptance would have been if what you gave them had been better—if all the forces of art and creativity and daring and imagination had been unleashed. I believe in the people's good sense and good taste, and I am not convinced that the people's taste is as low as some of you assume.[12]

Here Minow also attempted to shame broadcasters and raise their competitive ire, pointing out that while "newspaper publishers take popularity ratings too"—contests in which comics and advice columns always win out—"the news is still on the front page of all newspapers, the editorials are not replaced by more comics."[13] In television, by contrast, Minow implies, comics are always the lead, with news and editorial content buried.

Thus echoing Kennedy's call, above, Minow posits that broadcasters have settled into their own "valley" of contentment and complacency by offering schedules dominated by popular program genres while, increasingly, neglecting less majoritarian interests and service. Though networks were not required to program in the public interest in the same way that local stations were, Minow appealed to such standards as a shared, national programming obligation as well as a local licensing standard. Throughout the address, Minow also emphasized public ownership of the airwaves, noting that broadcasters were "trustees for 180 million Americans" who profit "by using public property." Minow signaled the newly activist stance of "the New Frontiersmen's" FCC, warning that each broadcaster volunteers "for public service, public pressure and public regulation."[14]

Finally, Minow appealed to the public to embrace this newly activist position. At the close of his speech, the Chair states that license review will no longer be a pro-forma exercise for the Commission. In order to institute serious review and to uphold the public interest standard, Minow proposes to

> find out whether the people care. I intend to find out whether the community in which each broadcaster serves believes he has been serving the public interest. . . . I want the people who own the air and the homes that television enters to tell you and the FCC what's been going on. . . . The FCC has a fine reserve of monitors—almost 180 million Americans gathered around 56 million sets.[15]

Following the speech, Minow received 2,745 letters from the public which he took as a mandate that people did, indeed, care, and that the general public was supportive of a more activist FCC and would embrace its own role as industry watchdog. Geographically, the majority of the letters came from the Northeast (fifty-one percent), followed by the Midwest (twenty percent) and then by the South (fifteen percent) and by the West (fourteen percent). Though the responses were fairly evenly split according to gender lines, the majority of responses were sent by "housewives." These were followed by sizeable responses from "teachers," "lawyers," "doctors," "ministers," and "professors," after which correspondents were each lone representatives from a variety of fields. Most correspondents had high school diplomas, followed closely by those with college degrees and then those with post-graduate degrees. According to Minow's aides, an overwhelming majority (all but fifty-five letter writers) "expressed support of Chairman's position."[16]

Indeed, though Minow's calls for reform *were* harshly critiqued, such criticisms were primarily lobbed by broadcasters themselves, and in newspaper editorials committed to a political point-of-view expressly opposed to the Kennedy administration's. These critiques coalesced around the idea that the administration intended to institute a "socialist" national culture, imposed by an elite cadre of minority interests, upon "the people." *Sponsor* magazine and an editorial in *The Peoria Journal Star,* respectively state, for example:

> Is that genuinely "private enterprise," Mr. Minow? Or is it a kind of creeping state socialism, implemented by a potent government bureaucracy and by minority pressure groups?

and

> It appears more and more that this administration has recruited a corps of bigots . . . All businesses are sinful, and these bureaucrats are nice, cleanhearted, pure chaps to make ours a gloriously pure land of cultured people. . . . whenever people with such monumental conceit try to force their own superior opinions and tastes on everybody by government action, this kind of ridiculous situation develops.[17]

Letters from the general public, however, indicate both agreement with Minow and a sense of genuine relief at having one's own cultural preferences or viewing frustrations publicly ratified within official discourse. Indeed, most letter writers take their responses as an opportunity to explicitly ally themselves with the cultural "elite" against "mass" tastes. This sense of intellectual and cultural recognition and ratification seems particularly important when considering the seventy letters from self-identified "housewives," for whom television functioned both as a relaxing reward at the end of a long day of labor *and* as a significant accompaniment to labor in the home. By responding to Minow's address, these correspondents found a uniquely public, institutionally legitimated outlet for their heretofore "invisible" opinions about the *quotidian* failings of television and its adverse impact on domestic labor. A viewer in East Lansing, Michigan, for example, supports Minow's call for balance by offering an intimate example of local broadcasting's lack of diversity:

> The claims made by the television industry about serving the interest of the public are just so much unadulterated eye-wash! . . . My sons were watching the Detroit-Chicago baseball game, and after they went to bed, I had planned to do some ironing, and at the same time watch some of my favorite Monday night programs. I got the shock of my life when I discovered that the ball game was on all three channels that we receive here in the Lansing area—channels 6, 10, and 12. . . . It is just completely unrealistic to expect all your viewers to have the same

tastes. Obviously there are exceptions—such as a Presidential message or some special event, but a ball game is not on a level with these. . . . Is it asking too much to expect a mature attitude on the part of the TV people?[18]

Significantly, however, the letters also demonstrate an unquestioned expectation that network television should continue as is. That is, there is no call for a fundamental change in the structure of the industry—letter writers instead appeal for "better programming" within the existing system. Thus, broadcast networking, national broadcast service, and market inclusion are ratified while viewers critique the quality of programming and advertising appeals therein. A letter from Mrs. J.M. Stillwell, Jr. of Upper Marlboro, Maryland demonstrates clear affiliation with the New Frontier in these terms, as she draws a direct line between popular TV programming and political and technological complacency:

> The question is, are we a Nation of Escapists, or are we ready to face the challenges of the future? . . . Being a Housewife, I have very little time to waste my precious evening hours watching a sadistic murder or a corny adventure yarn. . . . Maybe the Russians have a point, MONEY is God over here . . . we have here a wonderful instrument, more marvelous than most of us can imagine . . . It reaches and touches everyone in our Country and we are taking it for Granted. The Russians are riding off into Space and the Future and we're sitting comfortably in our easy chairs One Hundred and Fifty years in the Past watching Matt Dillon shoot someone in the belly.[19]

Similarly, a viewer sent the Chair a copy of a letter she had originally sent to the general manager of WGN in Chicago, with the complaint that there was no programming that spoke to her "influential" interests:

> My dear gentlemen, I'm the consumer—you're trying to reach ME—or are you? . . . Have you ever considered that there is a market besides the one you're using? Have you ever wondered how it is that WFMT and *The New Yorker* are economic successes? Have you ever tried to scout out and toady to advertisers who can be trained into worrying about "the influentials" as those of us with some brains and some taste are so ironically called?[20]

Significantly, as in two of the three letters, above, many correspondents reported locally "responsive" service to be a key source of their frustration (WGN's programming for Chicago and East Lansing's Detroit-originating telecasts of the home-market's baseball team), rather than network-originating programming. Indeed, beyond the frustrations expressed by letter writers who identified as under-served by "majority" programming, Minow discovered that relatively few people cared about *local* service obligations in broadcasting. In hearings held in Chicago and in Omaha in 1962 members of the "general" public were not only largely absent from the hearings but, often, overtly hostile to the idea of the FCC riding into town to exert paternalistic oversight. As television historian James Baughman points out, for example, a resident of Omaha wrote to the Commission that "if any of your members watched one of these local, live television programs, you would readily acknowledge that such programs are so poorly planned and ineptly done that we certainly need no more of them cluttering up the T.V. channels."[21] Thus, while relatively few people cared about local service obligations, these same citizens remained generally committed to and broadly accepting of *network* television programming and the ethic of "national" service and market inclusion those programs represented. Such hearings revealed a tension that inflected responses to TV programming as well: Each exposed the fine line between public eagerness to ally with "official" recognition *and* skepticism regarding the "outsider's" view of local investments and goals.

Documentary as Elite Discourse?

Network documentary series of the 1960s capitalized both upon the New Frontier's call for quality programming that would address issues of national and international importance in the context of the Cold War, and upon the public's acceptance of network programming as the "gold standard" of television address and uniquely shared national forum. As Curtin's *Redeeming the Wasteland* notes, many of the documentaries of this period were "specifically about foreign policy issues," "superpower struggle," or "the space race," synchronous with the New Frontier's international outlook and concurrent with television networks' own growing investments abroad.[22] However, those programs that featured "local," domestic concerns—which Curtin has called

"documentaries of the [Cold War] home front"—were significant engagements with New Frontier calls for reform, ranging from examina-
tions of civil rights, poverty, and the housing crisis to broader interrogations of "the meaning of life in a 'free' society."[23] The Webster Groves
documentaries represent entries calculated to educate and "awaken the
public" to a critique of the "average" American's middle-class consumerism for its "contented, complacent, and comfortable" disposition in a
time of broader social and political upheaval.

CBS Reports was a regularly scheduled, weekly documentary series
during the 1961–1962 and 1970–1971 television seasons. Prior to and
after those dates, episodes were broadcast periodically, as CBS News division specials with the title *CBS Reports*. Though each network offered
flagship documentary series and periodic news specials (including, for
example, *NBC White Paper* or *Bell & Howell Close-Up!* on ABC), *CBS
Reports,* as noted by Minow above, was considered qualitatively distinctive. The series was recognized particularly for its strong narrative
sense and compellingly intimate engagement with each episode's featured "characters." As a review by Jack Gould of a 1960 installment
noted, "as is typical of the Murrow-Friendly team at its best, the fasci-
nation of the program lay not only in the sharply conflicting opinions
voiced . . . but also in the close ups, which reflected the personalities
involved."[24]

As Curtin's study notes:

Network producers now spoke of narrative forms as important tools
for organizing information and attracting the attention of audiences.
. . . proposing that many of the conventions of fiction be applied to documentary television. . . . As Fred Friendly, executive producer of *CBS
Reports,* put it, "We hope each show will be just like reading through
to the last page of a detective story to discover whether the butler did it.
You won't know the outcome of any of our shows until you see it."[25]

For Friendly and his staff, "narrativizing" *CBS Reports* was part of a
strategy to create "a high-quality film image that could compete with
the entertainment programming produced by Hollywood studios."[26] To
achieve this end, *CBS Reports'* crews shot on 35mm film, incorporated
dense and multi-layered sound, and adhered to the classical Hollywood
cinema style of "invisible" filmmaking (keeping the story and central
"characters" at the center of attention and concealing the technology

and construction involved in the production and editing of the pro-gram). States Curtin, "the details Friendly most avidly pursued were those of character. He looked for people with strong convictions," and then produced intimate engagements with those characters by filming them in familiar settings and entering their personal space through close-ups and medium close-ups. And yet, *CBS Reports* was simultane-ously hailed for its investigative journalism and its "aura of dispassion-ate, professional expertise."[27] Each program was thus energized by a tension between the commitment to "Hollywood" style narrative and formal elements and appeals to objectivity and "a cold war elite under-standing of the uses of visual culture" as "a tool for teaching responsi-ble citizenship on multiple scales, from the interpersonal to the institu-tional to the national."[28]

As detailed below, the Webster Groves documentaries point to the potential crisis that can emerge from this attempt to balance "Holly-wood" and classroom appeals. More broadly, however, documentaries that focused on locales known to viewers exposed disjunctures between local identification—forged through emotional bonds of community and native knowledge—and the dispassionate, "expert" point of view of documentary production staff. As those historically absented from national media representation know all too well, such fissures often provoke viewer concerns regarding who gets to speak to the nation on behalf of the community. Whose knowledge represents the community to the nation-at-large? What real social power do such images have? Be-cause "many viewers identified network documentary with the reform agenda of a political and cultural elite,"[29] positive responses to home-front documentaries were reminiscent of the supportive letters Minow received. They allied the viewer with the news expert's tastes, especially as measured against "unsophisticated" audiences. Conversely, however, critical viewers struggled with the presumption of journalistic expertise and the inherent credibility of the national network voice. Such corre-spondents disputed the objectivity of the documentary point of view and argued that their own local, quotidian, intimate expertise had higher truth value because it was based on native, everyday knowledge that an "outsider" could not quickly adopt.

Viewer letters written to David Brinkley following an installment of his *David Brinkley's Journal: Our Man on the Mississippi* (NBC, Febru-ary 5, 1964) offer examples of both such critiques. According to a Dela-ware junior high teacher:

It is only programs such as this that make owning a television set worthwhile. . . . I cannot bring myself to believe that the taste of the American public is so unsophisticated as to prefer a show like "The Beverly Hillbillies" over a show like "David Brinkley's Journal." If this is so, it is a sad commentary on our educational system in this country, for we, somehow, must be failing in our task to educate those placed in our charge to appreciate those things which have true worth.[30]

Conversely, another viewer snaps, "we 'hinterlanders' (as New York Egomaniacs term us) have an image deserving of more than a riverboat barge orgie at a beatnick bar or the scene of immersion near a mispronounced town called Alton."[31] Interestingly, the *Variety* review of this program also noted that, "to viewers with a knowledge of any piece of the spread, the NBC treatment thereof may have seemed sketchy." [32]

Again, however, viewers' passion to respond—and to *correct* the experts with native knowledge—is largely provoked by an assumption that national network television is and *should* be the national "voice" for issues significant within the public forum. In this respect, viewers' dismay reflects a newfound feeling of betrayal provoked when their expectation for institutional performance and "elite" objectivity does not conform to their personal sense of place. Apparent viewer investment in the rhetorical promise of documentary—as objective locus of truth and national significance—allows that for these correspondents the felt betrayal of that promise provokes more mistrust and confusion than the quiz scandals that had earlier helped encourage the documentary boom. While "low," frivolous programs such as *The $64,000 Question* could be dismissed as "only entertainment" and always crassly commercial in orientation, documentary's "elite" promise of objectivity and import, when otherwise "exposed," provoked an interpretive crisis.

Further, this sense of betrayal generated fears of the potential damage that might ensue from a locale's misrepresentation to the nation-at-large. As an Iowa viewer wrote to Brinkley:

I feel the whole feature brought about a feeling of degradation to the beauty of the mid-west and to the intelligence of the people who make their living on and near this great waterway. In this great country in which we live there is no part which is completely void of the ugliness which humans can bring about, but it seems to me that there is too much dwelling on that which is bad. . . . Mr. Brinkley, you represent a powerful and influential medium. I hope you can justify what you have done to the image of a great portion of our country. . . . to millions of people only the visual impressions will remain.[33]

Thus, when viewers "talk back" to the television set, they do so to debate the medium and its purpose, but also to engage and struggle over tensions regarding local identity and national citizenship. These tensions are expressed as both ideological and textual conflicts.

The Webster Groves documentaries, for example, exhibit an apparent ideological disjuncture between the reporting staff's narrative conceptualization of the "American Dream" (as the youthful pursuit of individual self-expression and idealism) and that of the Webster Groves residents selected to be featured in the program (as insular, "knowable" community characterized by material comfort and security, suburban homogeneity, and corresponding social and political consensus). Textually, the aesthetics and address of *Sixteen in Webster Groves* and *Webster Groves Revisited* are marked by an internal clash between reporting that emphasizes journalistic and social scientific appeals to "scientific rationality" and photography and editing reminiscent of classical Hollywood cinema (characterized by an intimate, personalized, affective investment in the community and its "characters"). Journalistic and social scientific appeals to quantitative evidence imply that Webster Groves was part of the *problem* of the 1960s. This evidence, as it shaped the documentaries' select iconography, characterizations, and "story," allies the suburb with associations of the Midwest outlined in chapter 2—as a community characterized by "a remoteness . . . that is not wholly geographical"—rather than with a broadly national, mobile orientation at the leading edge of the New Frontier's future.

"The Whole Truth Is a Difficult Thing to Squeeze into an Hour"

As the above quote from reporter Charles Kuralt acknowledges, clearly, choices about content and focus must be made when creating a documentary. The choices for *Sixteen in Webster Groves'* focus emerged from a sociological study of its high school students.[34] Both Webster Groves documentaries were produced by Dr. Arthur Barron, who collaborated with the University of Chicago's National Opinion Research Center and sociologist John Johnstone to interpret the results of a thirty-two page questionnaire administered to students at Webster Groves High. Following the written survey, one hundred students were selected for follow-up interviews. Based on the survey and interview responses, the CBS staff concluded that the community's teens "have lost their youth because of tremendous pressure to make good grades, get into college, and be a 'success.' . . . love of learning and intellectuality are being lost in the shuffle in Webster Groves."[35]

According to Barron, Webster Groves youth demonstrated that " 'the American dream of affluence and security' has been achieved," but " 'The survey also discovered that the students were strictly conventional and moral in most of their attitudes.' . . . 'We should worry about their . . . over-conformity and lack of questioning.' "[36] Thus, the "story" arc of *Sixteen in Webster Groves* follows a questioning of misplaced postwar priorities in the context of suburban affluence. Specifically, the program asks what is "missing" from the lives of white, upper-class suburban youth, and what ramifications will this hollowness have for the future leadership and progress of the nation?

While Webster Groves was the locus of the program's critique, the producers proposed that the documentary should serve as a cautionary tale regarding the suburban "good life," nationally. Says Kuralt in the program's conclusion, "their town is the America we are becoming—affluent, suburban, and secure." However, critically (and locally) the program was interpreted to be a highly particularized case-study. According to Rick DuBrow's UPI-syndicated column (which ran in the *St. Louis Post-Dispatch* locally),

> there can be little doubt that CBS-TV justified showing its Friday night hour if the intent was to make people in suburbs all around the country think about themselves and the relationship of the younger and older generations—and this, of course, was a stated objective. . . . CBS-TV mentioned this, but I don't think it mentioned the point enough by way of broader suggestion of the national view. . . . Frankly, although Friday night's hour was effective, I still find it difficult to fairly judge a town on the basis of a one- or two-hour television look.[37]

And, according to *Variety*'s reviewer:

> Not to be believed, those future stalwarts of the power elite via plush Webster Groves, MO. . . . the CBS crew under producer Art Barron

(one of the more sensitive in the biz) turned in a neat job of giving those split level folk all the rope needed, and all the fine country clubbers took it from there. . . . nightmarish Webster Groves.[38]

And, in Kuralt's prologue to the program itself, Webster Groves youths were identified as particularly insular and localized:

> Theirs, it turns out, is not the world of rebellion, dissatisfaction, and adventure. Theirs is the world in which silverware makes you *feel* good.
> . . . [they are] two-thirds Protestant, ninety-six percent white, more than one-half the people were born right here in Missouri . . . [there is] virtually no room for anyone new and no desire to move out.

The "community" of Webster Groves is thus imagined to be a homogeneous group of white, upper-middle-class, consensus "strivers" and club members with whom the audience is presumed to identify (as in the presumptively white, middle-class, affluent "America we are becoming") but also to be a bit frightened by, warned against, and educated to refute (for the community's staid satisfaction and consumer comforts that have apparently immobilized its citizens and undermined their will to critique, or even engage, the broader world).

The program reinforces its vision of Webster Groves by focusing on a small, interrelated group of "characters" whose adult members belong to the same country club and whose youth are the "Socies," or, social successes and student leaders at Webster Groves High School. "It is an article of faith," intones Kuralt, "that the Socies will inherit the earth." The insularity of these groups' interactions with one another and the prematurely "aged" behavior of the youth is reinforced by the program's portrayal of the groups' separate but analogous behaviors (as when the parents dance at the country club while their children attend Mrs. Condon's Dancing School).

While other students, individually, represent other "types" of characters as oppositions to the "norm" of the primary group, they each appear only once, as stated opposites, and thus function to throw the status-quo reign of the Socies into relief as the majority way of being in Webster Groves. These voices include that of a male and female "intellectual" student, a student from metal shop class, and two African American students, one of whom is a football player and the other a cheerleader. Each of these "non-Socie" students is represented as orbiting around the fringes of the featured group by virtue of having a "distinct" identity that "stands out" from the Webster Groves' "norm."

Notably, while the producers propose that the program's core, featured students are "in no way average, they are the *best* of America," these "outsider" students provide a completely different vision of the community to viewers—one that, in fact, embodies the "expert" culture's expressed ideals for America's youth. Each of the non-Socies is self-possessed, has a pragmatic point of view on social issues, is unaffected, and demonstrates a clear and even joyful awareness that there is a broader world beyond Webster Groves (including the nearby St. Louis city center). On the de facto segregation of Webster Groves' schools and culture, for example, the students state, "they have always gone their way, and we've always gone our way," and, acknowledge that the college-bound competition is "dog eat dog—you have to excel more so than the white students."

By contrast, the Socie students seem particularly vacant and out-of-touch through their involvement in traditional activities in which their parents might just as likely take part (and, the program implies, most surely *did,* in their own time in high school). Footage features the youths singing "It's A Great Country" in chorus, making a turkey in home economics class, golfing, talking about marriage plans, and exiting church. The Socie group occupies a pre-modern vision of a small town, "safe, secure, happy in their own little group." And yet, there are clearly cracks in the façade—most of which appear when the students' parents are encouraged to speak. Following the *CBS Reports* style of characterization, Molly McGreavey's father (identified as Dr. McGreavey), in particular, embodies the atmosphere of rigidity, control, pressure to succeed, and social and political conservatism that the students are themselves beginning to adopt. Indeed, the answer to Kuralt's opening question, "But is there something missing from their lives? Is something missing?," is that what is missing is the students' urge to stand up to their parents or to have an opinion other than their parents.' What is missing is "the rebellion of youth."

Sixteen in Webster Groves' production staff returned to town to film the participants' reactions to its screening. Based on those reactions and the ensuing local community outcry, *CBS Reports* produced and aired *Webster Groves Revisited,* a strategy that critic DuBrow praised as "adapting the letters-to-the-editor idea into effective television form."[39] Local responses were gathered by filming screenings with the featured "characters" on the program (with Kuralt attending the "youth" screening) and interviewing them about their reactions. Responses were also gathered from phone calls to KMOX, St. Louis's CBS affiliate, immediately following the program's airing. Additional responses were gathered from community members throughout Webster Groves in person-on-the-street interviews the morning after the screening. While a few of the local respondents were thrilled that "CBS has let everyone know what goes on in Webster Groves," the majority of participants and viewers were concerned about the community's new image in the national consciousness and with the selective combination and editing of materials by CBS's reporters to create a particular "point of view" regarding Webster Groves.

Specifically, many respondents charged that CBS had selected images that produced an "inauthentic" or "not true" vision of Webster Groves that "failed to cover the real average youngster for the country-club set." Callers and interviewees seemed particularly dismayed at the lack of diversity by which Webster Groves was represented, leading to "fears about what the rest of the country now thinks of us." The blame for this was placed with the reporting staff. Interviewees of the *St. Louis Post-Dispatch*, for example, worried about what had been left out of the program. "I think that it reveals that when you do a special program in television you have to have a point of view. . . . You just can't come out and record the fact. I thought it was unfair." And, " 'I thought it was an interesting program, but I didn't particularly recognize it as the place I live.' . . . the values exhibited by some of the parents in the program certainly exist, but are not the only ones to be found in the community."[40]

CBS Reports: Webster Groves Revisited allowed the staff to incorporate these complaints and to refute them through recourse to journalistic expertise and documentary objectivity as buttressed by quantitative, statistical evidence. In an opening voice-over, Kuralt explains the broadly representative importance of Webster Groves, referencing statistical support for the network's claims. "We chose it for a study of teenagers because it is suburban Middle-Western and upper-middle-class—a town of 30,000 people which happens to be statistically fairly representative of such communities in America today." Combined with the sociological data from the questionnaire and interviews, this "gave us *exact* knowledge about our subject and a *scientific* basis on which to plan the filming." Kuralt then quantifies the filming process (nine crew members shot twenty-eight hours of film over thirty-two days' time) in order to deflect criticism that the crew came to Webster Groves with "preconceived notions" to which they conformed interviews, photography, and editing. In response to this criticism, Kuralt counters, "Well, if we expected to find anything, it was youthful rebellion and dissatisfaction." Instead, he continues, the crew found that "we should really call the film *Forty in Webster Groves.*"

Kuralt next softens this somewhat defensive tone and appeal to scientific documentation, by emphasizing the productivity of the criticisms brought out by the program as they underscore television's key function as a site of public debate—as key national, cultural forum. *Webster Groves Revisited* thus proposes that "the raising of discussion alone is worthy of telecast." In the time since *Sixteen in Webster Groves* aired, Kuralt argues, the "Socies" began "to wonder if people have been honest with you your entire life," and a local bond issue that granted better support to Webster Groves High School vocational programs passed. *Webster Groves Revisited* posits that the documentary raised civic awareness and created dialogue that has already had a powerful, proactive, social effect.

However, in response to the charge that the program used "trickery" and deceit in the way in which it edited and compiled images, Kuralt acknowledges that an opening sequence—a stark black and white medium close-up pan of the "Socies" standing outside with severe, dour expressions on each of their faces—had been shot just after a memorial service for a peer. Kuralt also acknowledges that, perhaps the parents were not "so bad" as the first program indicated. In *Revisited*, Dr. McGreavey is able to respond to his earlier portrayal, arguing that he appeared to be "the special guest villain on CBS's answer to *Batman*" but also acknowledging the success of *CBS Reports* pedagogical vision, stating that he was now aware of "how little I truly know." Here, Kuralt acknowledges the affective relations developed in his time in Webster Groves, detailing the ways in which that created difficulties as regards journalistic objectivity. In his concluding monologue he states:

> It was the first time we've ever seen our audience except as numbers on a Nielsen rating. They're much more appealing as people—even people who are angry with us. Digits on a chart don't advance the debate

about where we are in America and where we're going. Only people do that. . . . We wouldn't take back anything we said before, but we probably *would* add something—that, obviously, Webster Groves has its mountain-climbers, too.[41]

Webster Groves as Emerging "Silent Majority"?

Together, the Webster Groves documentaries propose that, while the suburb's citizens possessed the economic and educational capital that had traditionally signaled achievement of the American Dream, such affiliations did not carry the same value as they had in the past *unless* they were marshaled for expansive or socially progressive ends in line with New Frontier and Great Society commitments. Indeed, each program exposes a disjuncture between featured citizens' sense of themselves as in accord with the cultural affiliations and investments that mark the production crew's "elite" journalistic expertise and worldly awareness. However, the programs construct the featured citizens as part of the postwar population that, instead, requires pedagogical intervention or, an "awakening" to the "true" American spirit of the 1960s—particularly in the interest of returning youth, independence, political awareness, and freedom of expression to the community's young. Suburbia did not have to be a "valley of complacency," the programs suggest, but, if Webster Groves is representative of the new suburban norm, the broader U.S. viewing public is encouraged to see the community as a cautionary example. One wonders whether a demonstratively different social and political landscape of the community might have emerged had *CBS Reports* visited Webster Groves to focus on the "different" students who were singled out as "exceptions" to the Socie world. This would have, arguably, created a much less "readable" image of the community as a site of consensus and conformity and would have forced a somewhat confounding complex vision, for the period, of diversity in suburban St. Louis that would significantly challenge geographic myth and deflate Webster Groves' value as a contrast to the national ideals of the era.

Although this image of the suburb as a bubble of conformity was evoked throughout the New Frontier era as a cautionary tale regarding the betrayal of national progress for local comforts, by the late 1960s that same image had been recuperated and was now aggressively marketed by the political right, as iconic of a "Middle American" ideal. If Webster Groves' featured characters were representatives of the "Silent Generation" in their 1966 portrayal, by the end of the decade, the Socies and their parents would be held up as iconic of the "great Silent Majority." As Thomas Sugrue points out, the "Silent Majority" did not emerge strictly out of the 1960s, but, rather, reflected "the culmination of more than two decades of simmering white discontent and extensive antiliberal political organization."[42] The political right's reaction to social and institutional gains from the New Deal through the Great Society, was the creation of an image-based, classed category of labor identified as "populist" in its orientations and conservative in its politics ("Middle America")—characteristics that were geographically articulated to the Midwest as "at home" in the Heartland.

Indeed, in a brief but intense period from the mid-1960s to the early 1970s, the Midwest became explicitly re-mapped and reimagined in popular discourse and political rhetoric as *the* regional and cultural placeholder for patriarchal, white conservatism, in terms that resonate completely with Dr. McGreavey's expressed vision of the American Dream. Thus, while the progressive policies and activism of the 1960s challenged citizens of communities such as Webster Groves to extend themselves into the broader world and become involved in social change, the "new right" simultaneously seized the image of community, family, and insular, face-to-face "knowability" at the core of CBS's Webster Groves—"the language of the small republic . . . the scale of the local fraternal lodge, the church organization, the block club"[43]—to argue that it was the mainstream U.S. identity and "virtuous middle" against which "others"—particularly "blacks, liberals, antiwar protesters," and women's rights activists—were "demonic outsiders."[44] A keystone upon which this image was built, was taste, which now also increasingly referred to *market* segmentations and appeal. Specifically, as seen in chapter 2, the contrast was drawn between "square" entertainments (the Socie club dances, for instance) and urbane, mod engagements and affinities. Lizabeth Cohen has thus recently urged that such rhetoric and articulation of place and politics must be considered in relation to shifting conceptions of the market in the 1970s, in ways that encouraged marketers to emphasize what *differentiated* consumers over what united them. Writes Cohen:

Their embrace of market segmentation thereafter lent marketplace recognition to social and cultural divisions among Americans, making "countercultures" and "identity politics" more complex joint products of grassroots mobilization and marketers' ambitions than is often acknowledged.[45]

It is striking, in this light, to consider that the 1960s opened with Newton Minow's address encouraging greater news and documentary coverage and urging broadcast reform, and the decade closed with Spiro Agnew's attack on the liberal "bias" of television news and its

little group of men who . . . wield a free hand in selecting, presenting, and interpreting the great issues of our nation. . . . these commentators and producers live and work in the geographical and intellectual confines of Washington, D.C. or New York City . . . a tiny and closed fraternity of privileged men, elected by no one.[46]

Both discourses—the urbane, "elite" perception of television as a site of enlightened discourse and rational debate, and the square, "populist" understanding of television as driven by everyday investments and the "vote" of the people—have been re-energized in these terms in various moments throughout broadcasting history. Indeed, in 1992, Dan Quayle's "Murphy Brown" speech to the Commonweal Club of California is a virtual restatement of several different Nixon and Agnew addresses from the 1960s, dividing the nation into "the cultural elite and the rest of us."[47] Significant in each of these moments—from the New Frontier's claim for television's purpose to Agnew's "belief in dull things"—is the powerful articulation of image to place *as* political investment in ways that constrain other types of thinking. Laurie Ouellette argues that from the 1970s to the present such rhetoric has, in fact, increasingly "legitimated the Right and disenfranchised the Left as the *people's* ally" in battles over television (examined here regarding 1960s documentary, but later and regularly staged over funding for PBS, which is Ouellette's focus).[48] I would extend this legitimation to broader political discourse regarding cultural value, place, and presumed political identification—issues centrally at stake in chapters 5 and 6. And yet, there are conjunctures—intersections of political, cultural, televisual, and market discourses—in which "popular" and "official" investments, along with region and nation, momentarily appear to synch up in productive relation. Chapter 4 focuses on one such moment, wherein the Midwest was revalued from "right" to center in the 1970s as a site of "stability" and balance in the face of broader social upheavals and the demise of the Nixon administration. This revaluation took place, in part, through MTM Productions' "quality" sitcoms' seemingly counter-intuitive imaginations of a Midwest far removed from Webster Groves.

4

"You're Gonna Make It After All!"

The Urbane Midwest in MTM Productions' "Quality" Comedies

Although broadcast history lore states that the creators of *The Mary Tyler Moore Show* were greeted with consternation upon proposing that their series would feature a single woman over the age of thirty, less often mentioned is another relatively controversial element of their pitch—that the program would be set in the middle of America, specifically, in Minneapolis. Minneapolis was a location that, in 1970, did not immediately call to mind the image central to the show and to its hoped-for new audience demographic of hip, young, urban professionals—much less the glamour of a celebrity such as Mary Tyler Moore.

This chapter proposes that MTM Productions' "quality" comedies of the 1970s emerged in the context of, and also encouraged and contributed to, a broader revision of the Heartland myth, pointing to newly *urbane* understandings of regional identity and national value in post-1960s U.S. culture. These programs and the industrial, critical, and popular discourses surrounding them intersected with broader institutional, political, and social shifts that explicitly engaged the larger, national cultural imagination of regional and place-identity, emphasizing that this process is always unstable and constantly renegotiated. This chapter thus takes up Pierre Bourdieu's challenge to understand that what counts as regional identity "is deeply historical and subject to change as other kinds of social identities and formations of everyday life shift among populations."[1] *The Mary Tyler Moore Show* in particular, but also *The Bob Newhart Show* and *WKRP in Cincinnati*, imagined a new American Middle—one populated by urbane "squares" who had "somehow . . . fended off the sixties" and offered an idealized equilibrium for the new decade.[2]

The chapter that follows traces this revaluation of the U.S. Heartland as site of all-American equilibrium, good taste, and calm—a place that "works" through rational discourse among "nice" adults in the 1970s. Specifically, I examine how this shift in the general discursive representation and understanding of the region occurred through a matrix of media, industry, and civic discourses that actively assessed the upheavals, gains, and losses of the 1960s, and consciously revisited traditional ideals of national identity in anticipation of the Bicentennial. In the wake of Watergate, Nixon's resignation, and the emergence of Jimmy Carter as "small-town virtued . . . wonderfully American, born of a thousand Norman Rockwell covers,"[3] the Heartland was integral to popular imagination of national restoration in the 1970s.

Analysis of MTM Productions' newly urbane imagination of the Midwest in the 1970s requires analysis of four key socio-cultural, industrial, aesthetic, and civic sites. First, the quest for a post-1960s, Watergate-era "equilibrium" is a recurring trope in popular discourse during the 1970s. Specifically, popular press features about the Midwest and midwestern values undergo a marked shift from the end of the 1960s to the mid-1970s, significantly revaluing "equilibrium" as at home in the Heartland. Second, regulatory and industrial shifts within television networking between 1969 and 1971 encouraged new business practices and the adoption of "quality" TV programming appeals by which CBS promoted MTM series. Critical and popular press interpretations of MTM Productions' series are examined here, in dialogue with textual analysis of the series themselves, to chart the ways in which the programs were increasingly valued throughout their run, as they were explicitly allied with an idealized, newly urbane imagination of the Midwest. The series and the region were analogized as both reliably based in "common sense" representations of an imagined, square, status-quo Midwest. The popularity of each series particularly was read through Mary Tyler Moore's and Bob Newhart's self-conscious embrace of their "midwestern" star personae as "really quite dull" and "square." Significant here also is each series' plot and character conventions, whereby the humor is based in self-deprecation—in knowing one's "place" and being true to one's inner square—and in the deflation of "outsiders'" pomposity. The "gentle" humor characteristic of MTM Productions, in this regard, was based in a quotidian, *a*political "realism" that was explicitly contrasted to Norman Lear's urban, politically charged series.

"Equilibrium" is thus: a geographic concept associated with the Midwest at this time; a political concept associated with the status-quo "calm" perceived to be at "home" in the Heartland; an industrial concept by which networks attempted to retain a "mass" audience and cultivate a new, younger, urban demographic in the 1970s; and, a cultural concept here explicitly allied with MTM Productions' titular stars, "quality" productions, and programs' "good taste." Finally, this chapter briefly interrogates the means by which Minneapolis in particular has strategically inscribed Mary Tyler Moore as a triumphant civic icon and broader national idol thirty years after the series left the air. Energized, particularly, with the 2002 unveiling of her statue in downtown's Nicollet Mall, Mary's movement off the television screen into the everyday public life of the city can be seen as one of three post-primetime moments which have positioned Minneapolis at the forefront of the new cultural and economic phenomenon of "Heartland Tourism" —a broadly regional strategy to imagine "midwesternness" as both a sensibility and a destination, as *every* Americans' idealized home away from home.

Revaluing the Heartland: From Middle America to Intelligent Equilibrium

As indicated in the preceding chapters, from the immediate postwar period to the end of the 1960s, popular representations of the Midwest coalesced to imagine the region as singularly rural, white, middle class, and, increasingly, politically inflexible, conservative, and out-of-touch with the "outside" world. James Shortridge argues that, in the 1960s, the principal "concept of pastoralism" remained prominent and yet became "increasingly awkward after the late 1960s, as racial conflict and industrial collapse occurred in Detroit, Cleveland, Cincinnati," and elsewhere throughout the region.[4] Since the region's pastoralism had been imagined as fundamentally agrarian, rural, and predominantly "white," the reality of such urban, industrial, and "raced" locales *within* the cartographic region, thus, arguably forced Americans to shift their conception of regional borders in ways that would allow the region to remain the nation's symbolic Heartland.

> It seems clear . . . that Americans made a choice about the Midwest around 1950. As Detroit and Chicago got ever more industrial and ever

more diverse culturally we could easily have modified the regional image. . . . Instead, though, we chose the alternative action. Industrial cities were excised . . . the perceptual region began a migration back to the plains.[5]

In other words, the borders and images of midwestern identity historically have been reworked to excise urban life and culture, "non-white" populations, and marked class differences for the "benefit" of retaining a pastoral storehouse for national ideals and "traditional values." Following the uprisings of the 1960s and economic downturn of the 1970s, for example, public response to "visibly" raced, urban, and industrial incursions upon the imagined, placid, rural regional myth was to "rework [the] cognitive map of Middle-western location,"[6] shifting the regional core of the Midwest north, to the upper-Great Lakes and Great Plains states—now including cities such as Fargo and Minneapolis–St. Paul, while excising Cleveland and Detroit. Thus, the Midwest was actively reinscribed as pastoral due to "increasingly negative perceptions of [an] urban America" presumed to violate that same myth.[7] Urban America was now presumptively Black, working class, and politically charged in contrast to a pastoral Midwest that was, therefore, presumptively white, middle class, and "Silent."

The period's linking of place, politics, and value in these ways climaxed with the January 5, 1970 publication of *Time* magazine's Man and Woman of the Year issue, featuring "The Middle Americans." *Time*'s editors explicitly regionalized the honorees, arguing that they "tend to be grouped in the nation's heartland more than on its coasts."[8] The cover portrait underscores this connection. Evocative of regional folk art, Vin Guiliani's work features wooden cut-outs of a Caucasian man and woman in profile against a field of blue with stars that recall the U.S. flag. The man's face and woman's hair incorporate the flag's red and white stripes. At the base of the couple's necks, in profile, is an ashtray with one cigarette lit and one stamped out, adjacent to a dollar bill upon which lies a wrench that clenches another dollar in its vise. Along the base of the artwork, on the couple's shoulders, in profile are diecast, plastic, and wooden models of a farmer on a tractor, Main Street with a school and church, a plate of processed meat, and three family sedans in a row. The cover image thus places the Middle Americans in the Heartland as it also associates the region with pastoral culture, quotidian investments, and fealty to the flag.

According to Henry Luce's Publisher's Letter, Heartlanders "are the ones who sent President Nixon to the White House and the astronauts to the moon, who feel most threatened by the attacks on traditional values."[9] Significantly, in the featured cover story, *Time*'s portrayal of the Middle Americans' political affinities is not supported by voting statistics or economic data, but is drawn instead through select examples of the region's presumed shared cultural investments as they contrast with the "rest of the nation"—specifically, a taste for middlebrow entertainment and expressions of guileless patriotism:

> The gaps between Middle America and the vanguard of fashion are deep. The daughters of Middle America learn baton twirling, not Herman Hesse. . . . the Rockettes, not *Oh! Calcutta!* are their entertainment. While the rest of the nation's youth has been watching Dustin Hoffman in *Midnight Cowboy*, Middle America's teenagers have been taking in John Wayne for the second or third time in *The Green Berets*. . . . They sing the national anthem at football games—and mean it.[10]

While the editorial staff seemed bewildered at the ways in which Middle America remained resistant to emerging cultural trends through the tumultuous sixties—according to the magazine's own selective examples—these same qualities would conversely soon be revisited to recuperate and revalue the region, imagining it as a beacon of hope that the political and social upheavals of the 1960s might, in the end, be survived without the country having to endure fundamental, structural, institutional change.

Particularly between 1970 and the Bicentennial, but throughout the 1970s more broadly, *Time* joined other popular press and entertainment media in an active reworking of the Heartland myth away from the residual, conservative, and divisive connotations that had broadly marked its national image for the prior forty years, toward a myth that idealized the Heartland as home to "the nation's more agreeable qualities" and the lone national site of "equilibrium," "peace," and "sobriety," post-1960s. Reacting, specifically, to the aftermath of the urban uprisings of the 1960s, the emergence of new nationalist African American revolutionary movements, youth activism on college campuses, and, in the early 1970s, the ongoing war in Vietnam and escalating concerns regarding Watergate and Richard M. Nixon's subsequent resignation, portrayals of the Midwest Heartland now regularly imagined the region as a place "that works" without revolution or confrontations motivated by systemic racism or poverty. The Midwest Heartland was recuperated, popularly, as the place where the traditional American Dream still lived *untouched* by political turmoil. The region was idealized, in this sense, as that which survived the sixties unfazed, unaltered, and in balance. Popular media representations of the Midwest as Heartland are, thus, marked in the 1970s by a shift in discourse wherein the perceived "unaltered," "status-quo" stolidity of the Midwest was, increasingly, embraced as a positive, national value.

This transition in value took place by drawing a contrast between the Heartland and *urban* life and culture "elsewhere" in the "rest" of the country through references that were explicitly raced and classed. Although in the 1950s and 1960s the presumptively rural, "white," and middle-class makeup of the Midwest (a myth that had already excised from its imagination those that did not fit that description and the region's urban areas) was contrasted with the emergent New York– and Washington, D.C.–centered, urban, and international-looking New Liberal Critique and New Frontier, by the early 1970s, mainstream fears—stoked by urban uprisings, backlash toward Great Society programs, Vietnam, and mistrust provoked through Agnew's resignation, Watergate, and Nixon's eventual resignation—arguably encouraged a broader public revaluing of the Heartland. The region gradually shifted, in representations, from its presumptively traditional, conservative, isolationist tendencies, back toward its pre-1930s valorization as home of "authentic" American "common sense" which skewed to the center and mainstream of the political spectrum. For example, according to a "Report from the Heartland" in *Newsweek*:

> In this Rodgers and Hammerstein country, where cerulean skies stretch endlessly over golden plains, . . . All but untouched by the turmoil facing most Americans . . . leading what in the '70s has to be called an idyllic life. Homes are left unlocked . . . There has never been any racial conflict in St. Francis, simply because there is not a single black family living in the county. Women's liberation is incomprehensible to farm wives who drive tractors, operate milk routes and manage the accounts.[11]

This rather remarkable, overtly raced transition in regional portrayal is perhaps best exemplified, once again, by *Time* magazine, whose August 13, 1973, cover story featured Minnesota's Governor Wendell

Anderson, photographed on a dock, clad in a flannel shirt, turtle neck, and khakis, holding a large fish aloft with glee. Behind Anderson is an expanse of lake and a friend in a fishing boat. The cover title, in bright yellow text, announces "The Good Life in Minnesota." Inside, the cover story, titled "Minnesota: A State That Works," proposes that, "if the American good life has anywhere survived [the sixties] in some intelligent equilibrium, it may be in Minnesota."[12] The editorial staff considers the state and its people to be defined by "courtesy and fairness, honesty, a capacity for innovation, hard work, intellectual adventure and responsibility."[13] Unlike traditional "machines" elsewhere, the politics are "clean" in Minnesota. The people are "remarkably civil" and their daily lives are peaceful. Says advertising agency owner Chuck Ruhr of Minneapolis, "California is the flashy blonde you like to take out once or twice. Minnesota is the girl you want to marry."[14] And, while the editors point out that the weather extremes in the state might be drawbacks to some, the seasons also "build character" and weed out "weak-kneed beachboys."[15] Alongside these stereotypically gendered analogies, the crux of Minnesota's good life is, here, explicitly raced and classed:

> Some argue that Minnesota works a bit too well and too blandly, that its comparatively open and serene population is a decade or two behind the rest of the U.S. The place lacks fire, urgency and self-accusation of states with massive urban centers and problems. Minnesota's people are overwhelmingly white (98%), most of them solidly rooted in the middle class. Blacks rioted in Minneapolis in 1966 and 1967, but with only 1% of the state's population, they have not yet forced Minnesotans into any serious racial confrontation. . . . Minnesotans are proud of that.[16]

Though the reality of urban uprising might indeed imply "serious" racial confrontation and problems, the overt articulation of "whiteness" with serenity and the bourgeois status-quo is made even more explicit several pages later:

> In many respects, the Scandinavians, long the largest single group in the state, have shaped Minnesota's character. They, together with its large Anglo-Saxon and German strain, account for a deep grain of sobriety and hard work, a near-worship of education and a high civic tradition in

Minnesota life. Such qualities help to produce the intelligent calm—and the stolidity—that characterize the efficient Minnesota atmosphere.[17]

Time's editors mention Minneapolis's cultural advantages (with references to the Dayton family's patronage of the arts and celebration of the Guthrie Theater), and its social "homogeneity" and "stolidity." However, because the story defines "politics" to be overtly associated with racial confrontation and class inequity, Minneapolis, Minnesota, and the broader region are, by extension, portrayed as *evacuated* of political concerns. Additionally, having rhetorically positioned "massive urban centers" and their corresponding "problems" with extra-regional locales, the Heartland is allowed to be *urbane* (polite, cultured, and refined) but remains, resolutely, not *urban*. "Whiteness," in this equation, is allied with urbane cultural and economic subjectivity, as an apolitical, "universal," normative, status-quo ideal. The "raced" urban, "problem"-filled community is, by extension, home to *political* subjectivity (e.g., expressed through "rioting" rather than rational discourse and assimilation into the market), not cultural or economic subjectivity "logically" characterized by "sobriety," "hard work," or "intelligent calm."

Time's feature on Minnesota was one of many such mainstream, popular press articles in this period that portrayed the region as a salve against tumult and as the core of the United States where things were in balance—"the essential America, where grass, grain, and animals are almost as important as people, and where the old values still dominate, largely unaffected by the waves of fashion and fad that constantly surge over the east and west coasts."[18] The Midwest is "the very crucible of the American experience, our heartland," whereas "New York and Washington, D.C. are of another world. Here is only a vibrant, productive sprawl."[19]

Significantly, such feature stories also revisit the conception that "conservative" and "Midwest" are necessarily conjoined terms, now addressing flaws in this oversimplification. *Better Homes and Gardens,* for example, argued that the Heartland was, historically, home to idealistic movements and the political *mainstream*.[20] According to Thomas Anderson in *The Nation,* for example, "indeed, if one uses the measure of innovative leadership by elected officials, the North Central states may hold first rank in the nation as a center of liberalism." Considering this, Anderson concludes, "perhaps," in thinking otherwise, "people who dwell along each coast find it comfortable and satisfying to their egos."[21] In these examples, the Midwest is hailed as a locus of rational discourse against the "fads" and extremes (both cultural and political) on either coast. The Heartland is allied with ordinary, hard-working folk, in contrast to the outsized "egos" on either coast.

The 1970s Heartland was, thus, revalued by selectively adding new elements to its imagination (allowing urbane, politically mainstream values to enter into the myth) while simultaneously remaking the pastoral, square associations central to past iterations. The region's new image was one that implied that, perhaps there was no real need for structural, institutional change within the United States, considering that Minnesota—and other sites within the Midwest—"work" well through adherence to the assimilative ideology of the American Dream and smooth market functioning. Following the turmoil of the 1960s and the lingering doubts and political scandals of the 1970s, popular imaginings of the Midwest implied that its historically *mundane* identity was, by contrast to the "rest" of the nation, now *exceptional*—the average, ordinary, everyday "square" was also stable, functional, and representative of core, national ideals. By excising cities such as Detroit and Cleveland from this fantasy, while hailing Minneapolis as iconic, the Midwest was also recuperated as an available, "safe" space for travel, exploration, and white, middle-class liberation. Minneapolis suggested a fantasy of urbane community *without* the "city," "reclaiming" the community as familial space for white professional travel and tourism centered on consumption. This imagination prefigured the 1980s reconstruction of downtowns as tourist spaces, which is addressed at the close of this chapter.

"CBS! We're Putting It All Together!"

The CBS television network's promotional theme for the 1970 season was "We're Putting it All Together!" Mary Tyler Moore's image was centrally featured in this campaign, as both an advertisement for *The Mary Tyler Moore Show*—to premiere on September 19—and as iconographic of CBS's new programming strategy and intended audience appeal. Television critic Jack Gould summarized CBS president Robert D. Wood's approach to putting new programming together with new audiences as follows:

[He] feels that TV's major mission in the coming years is to give a better reflection of the contemporary scene in urban centers, rather than dote on such foolishness as "Petticoat Junction," which he has mercifully canceled. . . . Now, without disenfranchising the older segment of the audience, the network hopes to attract younger viewers, many of whom, one suspects, have withdrawn from watching TV entirely.[22]

CBS's throwing over of the mass-audience appeal "foolishness" of such rural-skewing series as *Petticoat Junction* for "contemporary," urban-skewing series such as *The Mary Tyler Moore Show* was encouraged by shifts in the regulatory and business climate of networking as well as by cultural transformations that promoted the pursuit of new markets for television sponsors and viewers.

Several important regulatory moves helped to reconfigure network power in the early 1970s, encouraging changes in the ways networks acquired, promoted, and scheduled prime time programming. First, key rulings and actions in the late 1960s and early 1970s helped to open up prime time television advertising to greater competition. In 1968 the U.S. District Court of Appeals upheld the FCC's earlier ruling that the Fairness Doctrine, which required that opposing views be granted fair opportunity to respond where controversial issues were at stake in a broadcast, applied to cigarette commercials. A station presenting cigarette ads had the duty to inform the public of the hazards of smoking, because its promotion was proved to not be in the public interest. By the 1971 television season, cigarette ads were pulled off the air, opening up a gap in advertising revenue and expanding the market for competitive bidding in advertising.[23]

The FCC, additionally, instituted two sets of regulations that were intended to undercut perceived monopolistic power on the part of networks. The Prime Time Access Rule (PTAR) was issued in 1970. This ruling took the 7:30–8:00 pm eastern and pacific time slot (6:30–7:00 pm central time) away from the networks and returned it to local stations for their programming discretion. With this move, the FCC hoped to encourage an increase in the production of local news and public affairs programs (those programs that *The Blue Book* guidelines would consider to best serve the public interest, as outlined in chapter 1). Even though PTAR did not have this intended effect—with most local stations simply acquiring inexpensive and profitable syndicated game shows or reruns of older TV series to fill these slots—the rule did cut into network profit dominance and scheduling flexibility in evening program hours. Also in 1970 the FCC created the Financial Interest and Syndication Rules, known as the "Fin-Syn" rules. These rules banned networks from owning or profiting from the syndication of shows that had previously run on the network. The FCC argued that networks could not profit from a show once it was no longer running on the network itself.

Broadcast networking had thus made a fairly complete transition from prior sponsorship models, as advertisers not only no longer dominated program decisions, but also had to bid for increasingly smaller and more competitive advertising slots within a given program. Arguably, because of this increased competition, the content of programs could now be more topical and responsive to larger social concerns, as single sponsors would not be solely identified with controversies, should they arise, as they had been in the past. So, by the late 1960s, the network had put advertisers in their place, so to speak, but also faced new regulatory restrictions on their own power over profit-making, due to the Fin-Syn and Prime Time Access Rules. To help protect from greater financial risk in this period, the networks turned to independent producers for more and more program content for their schedules.

This strategy was both beneficial for networks—in that they earned their profit up front with relatively little risk—and very rewarding for the independent producer whose series was successful enough to go into syndication, at which point the profits reverted to the production company. Plus, according to MTM co-founder, Grant Tinker, since "until 1979, networks had over ninety percent of the audience," once one had a secure place on the network schedule with a solid program, "it was very hard to fail."[24] In the 1970s there were two independent production companies, in particular, that dominated the airwaves: MTM Productions, helmed by Grant Tinker, Arthur Price, and Mary Tyler Moore, and Norman Lear and Bud Yorkin's company, Tandem Productions.

In addition to regulatory and industrial shifts in the early 1970s, networks also began to respond to broader social transitions that had made "new" audience markets "visible" to broadcasters. First, advances in the civil rights movement through the 1960s led to an increased market awareness of the economic viability of a thriving African American consumer class. And, according to census data, between 1950 and 1970, the number of married women who worked had doubled, and the percentage of women who made up the workforce had grown to almost forty-five percent. Women's liberation was now aggressively incorporated by advertisers as an appeal to brand products as contemporary and hip. In addition, the structure of the family had shifted—between 1970 and 1980 over forty percent of all households contained a single, divorced, or widowed individual, encouraging commercial appeals to single professionals. Finally, youth culture had come into its own in the 1960s—as a political entity (in protests against the Vietnam War and in support of the causes of civil rights and women's liberation), and as a consumer and professional class (due, largely, to the postwar shift to nearly universal access to higher education for young Americans).

The 1970 television season is thus considered to be the turning point from which networks began to balance the merits of programming that would attract a "mass," multi-generational, and multi-regional audience against the potential benefits of targeting smaller, demographically segmented urban, professional audiences with "niche"-appeal programming. Because the "Big Three" network broadcasters did still hold sway over U.S. television viewers, their approach in the 1970s was hybrid: Each sought to obtain audience equilibrium, balancing appeals to the "old" aggregate audience while also building a new generation of demographically segmented TV viewers whose more contemporary tastes were now enticed to enter and bolster the networks' profit stream. Todd Gitlin quotes Robert Wood explaining his network's new attention to younger, more urban viewers and market areas as largely motivated by CBS's owned and operated stations' loss of viewers and profits due to its pre-1970s rural and older-skewing program appeals: "My interests were obviously insular, or reduced to the welfare of our stations. I recognized that *Gunsmoke* and all these rural shows were doing terrifically nationally. It just wasn't doing much for the company-owned stations division."[25] While not wanting to lose this terrific national audience, networks began to strategize to also attract a more lucrative kind of viewer.

Though CBS is often singled out in this respect, each network made similar moves. As discussed in chapter 2, ABC, for example, cancelled *The Lawrence Welk Show* after the 1970–1971 season, even though it was still a ratings success. Significantly, Welk's primary sponsor in syndication was the senior vitamin-maker, Geritol. CBS's changes were, however, both the most radical and the most successful. In the 1969–1970 season, the top twenty programs from CBS included "rural appeal" programming such as *Gunsmoke, Bonanza, The Beverly Hillbillies, Hee*

Haw and *Mayberry, RFD*. By 1971–1972 most of these programs had disappeared and CBS's new contributions to the top twenty included programs such as *All in the Family, Sanford and Son, The Mary Tyler Moore Show,* and *The Flip Wilson Show*. By the 1974–1975 season, MTM Productions and Tandem Productions, between them, produced nine of television's top ten rated programs.[26] And yet, as Aniko Bodroghkozy has pointed out in her case-study of the demise of *The Smothers Brothers Comedy Hour,* "using the Nielsen-inspired designation that 'eighteen-to-forty-nine' meant youth, the networks found themselves hampered by a demographic that included two generations whose interests, tastes, and ways of interpreting social reality were radically different."[27] Indeed, CBS's fears about the youth and liberal-oriented political content in *The Smothers Brothers'* last two seasons, accompanied by the affiliate and viewer protests that led to the program's 1969 cancellation, would seem to have discouraged the network from being *too* new or contemporary for the 1970 transition.

Focusing on the acquisition of independently produced comedy series helped to establish CBS's sought-after "equilibrium" between contemporary, urban, youth appeal and mass-audience palatability. The serial nature of the sitcom format allowed for the exploration of pertinent social issues within a context that, arguably, "domesticated opposition," released tensions, and allowed for a spectrum of character identifications, encouraging what Jeffrey Miller has called "an ideal of contained comedy" exhibiting "the realism and depth of characterization central to quality television" presumed to appeal to a new niche demographic, while simultaneously "addressing audiences and markets not necessarily liberal, sophisticated, or upwardly mobile."[28] Todd Gitlin argues similarly that, for CBS, "the point was that, at the very least, gung-ho enlistees could watch *M*A*S*H* without being offended; as could authoritarian fathers and youthful liberals delight in *All in the Family,* and career women and sexist men in *The Mary Tyler Moore Show*."[29]

MTM Productions' series fit this mandate exceptionally well: Each offered a distinctly new, modern vision of the Midwest fulfilling Wood's mandate to contemporize the network's appeal—particularly through title sequences that each imagined Minneapolis and Chicago as joyously urbane, mod, upbeat, stylish, and consumer savvy. And yet, each program also offered the comfort of "gentle" equilibrium in a contentious time—particularly by aligning their stars with midwestern ideals and values, and by using the setting of each series as a "character" that created an aesthetic interiority and intimate, quotidian address to the audience. Indeed, the humor in each series' weekly installments coalesced around two alternating, conventional ideas: In the first comic conceit, the star's "square" midwesternness is made overtly comic but triumphs in the end because of the character's awareness (and that of work and friend "family" of supporting characters) of her/his "limits" as a square, along with a happy embrace of that identity, reflective of self-knowledge and stability in relation to the "outside" world. In the second comic conceit, "outsiders"—characters who do not "fit" in the habitus of the Midwest and cannot be incorporated into the cast "family"—are expelled. This plotline particularly occurs through the deflation of pompous characters' egos and the resulting restoration of a "square" equilibrium against the "outside" world. Both series suggest that Mary's Minneapolis and Bob's Chicago are, in the end, relatively sane outposts in an otherwise insane world.

While much scholarship has devoted considerable attention to *The Mary Tyler Moore Show* as "quality" TV programming—particularly as contrasted with the concurrent popularity of Norman Lear's more overtly political, "relevant" comedy series—I propose to elaborate upon and significantly extend such analyses by unpacking the ways in which MTM Productions' "quality" comedies were promoted and perceived as such, in large part, by reference to *geographic* affiliation. Particularly in the cases of *The Mary Tyler Moore Show* and *The Bob Newhart Show,* but also evidenced in *WKRP in Cincinnati,* MTM Productions' stars, settings, and program aesthetics and address were explicitly analogized with the Midwest and midwesternness as the 1970s locus of a liberal humanist equilibrium (that which "survived" the sixties unscathed) and consensus "good taste." The series' thus presented a regional imagination counterintuitive to past understandings, positing a hip and urbane Midwest while simultaneously promoting the prevailing "common sense" understanding of the region as, essentially, *apolitical,* white, and middle class.

Particularly, I would like to extend Kirsten Lentz's exemplary study of the critically raced and gendered distinctions made by scholars and TV critics who have proposed that the MTM series represented "quality" programming while the Lear series represented "relevant" programming in this era. As Lentz notes:

"Quality" does not strive to shock, . . . "Quality" . . . means genteel and civilized. It appeals to the intellect. As such, it relies upon its association with whiteness, class location, and sexual modesty. "Relevance" on the other hand, is a discourse about the "real," not the moral or polite. And reality is allowed to be shocking. It is only through this discourse that race can be spoken on entertainment television in the 1970s.[30]

Lentz argues that whereas

in *All in the Family,* whiteness is a racial category; in *The Mary Tyler Moore Show,* whiteness is made to disappear into a humanist universalism where it serves as the invisible norm. The different approaches to racial representation created a mutually determining circumstance in which *All in the Family* was consistently understood as "about race" whereas *The Mary Tyler Moore Show* could be understood as "about gender" in the absence of race.[31]

I would add that MTM Productions' programs and the comparative understanding of them as apolitical rather than political, "tasteful" rather than confrontational, and "urbane" rather than urban was *also* powerfully raced and gendered implicitly *and* explicitly by the programs' midwestern settings.

As established in prior chapters and above, by the early 1970s, the region was imagined as *presumptively* white, middle class, and a site of "equilibrium" comparatively unscathed by the sixties. This field of associations "ruled in" certain understandings of the region and made others quite literally unimaginable within the programs' setting (e.g., awareness of the region's actual racial, ethnic, and class diversity; awareness of the region as also politicized and a site of potential revolution and "impolite" discourse). The inability to imagine politics and race as *of* the Midwest (or, of whiteness *as* raced rather than "universal" identity "at home" in the Midwest) was strengthened, at this time, by the broad public inability to perceive of Minneapolis as a "city" (as reflected in the popular press examples above) and by the stars' analogous associations with the region as mundane squares with quotidian dilemmas. Occupying a politicized subjectivity is "ruled out" of the Midwest in the apparent need to invest in a Heartland myth for the 1970s of a lone region of explicitly "white," middle-class American "common sense" equilibrium and rationality. Thus, while Maude wrestled over abortion within a subway's ride from New York City, Mary more typically asked: "Why do all of my big problems seem like little ones?"[32]

The Mundane as Exceptional: Mary's "Minnesota Nice"

Though *The Mary Tyler Moore Show* premiered on September 19, 1970 to lukewarm ratings and relatively poor critical reviews, by the end of the series' second season, it was considered representative of the upper echelon of "quality" programming on TV and earned the highest ratings of the series' run (at seventh, overall, for the season). It was in the third season (1972–1973) that MTM's flagship series was joined by *The Bob Newhart Show* on CBS's Saturday night schedule. Newhart's series aired immediately following *Mary Tyler Moore* from its premiere until 1977, when *The Mary Tyler Moore Show* left the air. *The Bob Newhart Show*'s final episode aired on April 1, 1978. From 1972 through 1976, both series remained in the top twenty rated programs each year. Though Norman Lear's *All in the Family, Maude,* and *Good Times* always (and, often, resoundingly) beat MTM's series in the ratings, CBS executives, MTM production staff, TV critics, and popular press features throughout the 1970s consistently portrayed MTM series as more palatable than the Lear series. As Lance Morrow wrote for *Time* at *The Mary Tyler Moore Show*'s conclusion:

> During Watergate and the long ending of the Vietnam War, when the nation was feeling especially baleful, these characters in an out-of-the-way local TV station, with their family feeling, may have suggested that it was possible to deal with the world without being either Patty Hearst or R.D. Laing. They became part of the viewer's family, comfortable to have around.[33]

Whereas the Lear series were often criticized for being shrill and "mean" and for featuring polemic caricatures, *The Mary Tyler Moore Show* and *The Bob Newhart Show* were embraced as "comfortable," "sophisticated," and exceptions to the rule that "anything on television that appeals to everyone should be regarded with suspicion."

Both lowbrows and highbrows have continued to be captivated by a program that verges on the adult, shows sparks of genuine wit, and contains . . . a gallery of certifiably human faces.[34]

The "certifiably human" qualities of these programs and their titular stars were consistently, explicitly associated with the series' midwestern settings and "values" as representative of a comfortable post-1960s equilibrium. This was an association that was, simultaneously, powerfully counterintuitive *and* completely consistent with "common knowledge" regarding the region and its people. In the *Saturday Review* feature, above, for example, author Karl Meyer points out the initial resistance to *The Mary Tyler Moore Show*'s proposed locale, noting, "who (so it was thought) would watch a program set in dowdy Minneapolis?"[35] As Grant Tinker himself recalled, for the series' pitch "all I had to start them off . . . was the premise of Mary being single and thirty and living in Minneapolis—which on the face of it is a pretty dull thought!"[36] If a midwestern setting seemed counterintuitive for prime time, the series' stars and the shows' brand of humor were promoted as iconographic of the same qualities of midwestern square, comfortable "middleness" as had been heralded for Minnesota in the *Time* feature, above. According to a *New York Times Magazine* essay from 1974, for example, in Mary Tyler Moore

one is reminded of other cultural entities millions of Americans will accept with 'practically no complaints'—*The Reader's Digest,* Norman Rockwell, Muzak, Hallmark Cards, McDonald's hamburgers. . . . She is a high school sweetheart who hasn't gone sour; an intelligent, highly polished, well-engineered product of the American dream that hasn't faded. She is a Republican; . . . America is still home for her; she has no desire to travel. Somehow Mary Tyler Moore has fended off the sixties without turning her mind or her life to mush.

The article also quotes Perry Lafferty, Vice President of Programming at CBS, who proposes, "she's the well-scrubbed, all-American girl that everyone likes. I think it's her vulnerability that makes her particularly appealing. . . . beautiful and all that without being threatening."[37] Similarly, Bob Newhart is hailed as "Mr. Mid-America in a crowd, Charlie Everybody, the American flag with a ribbon tied around him."[38]

If comedians were articles of clothing Bob Newhart would be a classic
navy blue blazer: not faddish, not flamboyant, hardly at the fashion
vanguard and yet an essential component of a man's wardrobe. Always
in good taste, . . . timeless.[39]

MTM Productions' series thus remained true to the spirit of pastoral associations with midwestern "values" while significantly revising the image of the Midwest as a setting. Each proposed quality that was comfortable, urbanity that was shimmeringly mod but not issue-oriented,
metropolitan life that was, after all, midwestern.

This ethic of equilibrium is important to write back into the history
of *The Mary Tyler Moore Show* because of its conscious and doubled
significance as an appeal that defused the potential threat of featuring a
single career woman over the age of thirty on TV, as it simultaneously
upscaled the midwestern life and culture that would factor into the program's content and address. *The Mary Tyler Moore Show* and *The Bob
Newhart Show* redefined the Midwest as both viably urbane and as a
site of touristic and consumer value. Both introduced the modern consumer-subject to the Midwest within the broader U.S. geographic imagination. That is, the Midwest, while still evacuated here of racial and
economic diversity, was also dislodged from a pastoral setting and redefined as *urbane* site of personal liberation through modern architecture,
art, fashion, labor, and consumerism. Here, the urbane disposition enables "survival" of the sixties, and a new 1970s liberation and redemp-
tion. This appeal can be examined best through an analysis of the opening titles sequence of *The Mary Tyler Moore Show* and its changes from
the premiere 1970 season through season five, after which the titles remained unchanged for the duration of the series.

Designed and executed by Reza Badiyi and David Davis, the opening titles posit Minneapolis as a glamorous, vibrant city wherein Mary
Richards can "graduate" (symbolized by the famous tam toss) to a "free
woman" of the 1970s, out from under her old familial ties and friendship bonds in small-town Roseburg, Minnesota. Badiyi had also designed titles such as those for *Hawaii Five-O* and his design scheme features bright, contemporary colors and title font, and a warm, rich, film
aesthetic matched, aurally, by Sonny Curtis's upbeat lyrics and dynamic
brass, woodwind, and guitar instrumentation. The premiere season's titles chart the narrative of Mary's transition from her previous job in

Mary Richards begins her new life in Minneapolis, in *The Mary Tyler Moore Show.*

Roseburg to her new residency in Minneapolis. While the title images and lyrics emphasize Mary's transition from small-town to big-city life and the need for her to take risks and to become more self-interested, subsequent season image and lyric shifts emphasize the success of her transition and her full integration into the life of the city, both professionally and socially, as well as her transformation into a self-possessed consumer.

The premiere season titles open with a royal blue background. A baritone saxophone, trombones, and other woodwind and brass bass instruments punctuate the appearance of yellow titles reading "Mary" then "Tyler" then "Moore." A solo electric guitar then plucks out the theme's harmony line as orange, red, purple, and blue "Mary Tyler Moores" emerge to fill the top and bottom of the screen from the yellow titles at the center. The letters zoom out toward the viewer, and inside a now "clear" letter "e" from the center title, we see Mary Tyler Moore inside a white Ford Mustang on the interstate. During the close-up of Mary at the wheel, looking somewhat anxiously, through the windshield to her right, we hear the query: "How will you make it on your own?" Our view of Mary then partially dissolves through the windshield to reveal her memory of her bon-voyage party given at her last job, where she is surrounded by friends, champagne, and a "Good Luck" banner. This scene dissolves back to an expectant-looking Mary gazing left through the windshield at the line, "this world is awfully big." Another incomplete dissolve shows Mary gratefully receiving a farewell bouquet from a co-worker. As Sonny Curtis sings, "Girl, this time you're all alone," Mary wags her finger at a male co-worker who tries to give her a farewell kiss. A complete dissolve on the words, "but it's time you started living" sends us back to Mary, smiling, head-on, through the windshield, with apparent new confidence as Curtis sings, "it's time you let someone *else* do the giving."

At this point in the opening season titles, the music and images take a significantly up-tempo, dynamic turn, with much heavier brass orchestration and punctuation and a remarkably dynamic flash-cut editing sequence that introduces Mary and her viewers to sparkling visions of Minneapolis–St. Paul. From this point, the titles move, rapidly, from a "macro" view of the city—emphasizing a touristic gaze of the skyline at dusk and featuring freeway and aerial shots—to a focus on Mary's gradually more quotidian movement through the city via neighborhood streets, parks, and downtown's Nicollet Mall. Underscoring the series' location, a superimposed freeway sign reading "Minneapolis–St. Paul" "floats" above Mary's Mustang as she enters the city by the interstate. Here, the viewer accompanies Mary, traveling with her through overpasses and moving from a head-on view of Mary's car to a profile shot and then tracking her from behind, as each sees Minneapolis at dusk for the first time. The camera pulls back to reveal a beautiful orange and purple sunset as the lyrics state that "Love is all around—no need to waste it." From the sun at dusk, there is a cut to what will soon be revealed to be Mary's new workplace, the WJM office building. A few floors of the building fill the entire frame, from which the camera pulls back to street level.

Now inside the city, the lyrics encourage that "you can have the town, why don't you take it?" Mary is shown in medium-long-shot, walking on a busy city sidewalk, looking up with some wonder. From this point, the titles feature a series of shots of Mary, integrated into—if still in awe of—the everyday bustle of the city. She is pictured in strolls along neighborhood streets and the river, featuring snowy and tree-lined sidewalks, and also making her way downtown, surrounded by bustling pedestrian and vehicular traffic. The final sequence of the titles is the famous tam toss which shows Mary at the corner facing Donaldson's department store, followed by three different quick zoom-in shots, after which she crosses the street to the corner facing Dayton's department store and begins her twirling turn and toss. Significantly, here, the lyrics still have a sense of wonderment and some caution, noting and then repeating that "You *might* just make it after all." The title sequence concludes with a freeze-frame and the credit "created by James L. Brooks and Allan Burns."

The first season's titles thus chart Mary's departure from her hometown and her expectant travels—interspersed with memories from home—to the "awfully big" world of the Twin Cities. Viewers move from a classic "postcard"-type overview of the city to a quotidian accompaniment of Mary as she walks through heavily peopled and trafficked streets, strolls along the river, walks downtown, and tosses her tam. The music and lyrics build in encouragement of Mary's *attempt* to "make it." By season two, the question of whether Mary would make it on her own had been answered. Now the final sequence lyrics state "You're *gonna* make it after all!" In the larger titles sequence, the images now shift from the premiere season's emphasis on entering the city to further detailing Mary's day-to-day, happy, full integration within the life of the city, emphasizing her familiarity with her neighborhood and daily joys with her co-workers and friends. The lyrics emphasize this transition, acknowledging Mary's ability to "turn the world on with her smile" and "take a nothing day and suddenly make it all seem worthwhile." New images in season two's version of the titles include an immediate transition from the title to shots of Mary driving in her neighborhood—already within the daily life of the city—wearing a big, bouncy grin. Her Mustang pulls up in front of the Victorian home within which she has an apartment. Mary is then shown in a neighborhood park alongside the river, waving to kids who are being pulled on a sled, underscoring the day-to-day rhythms of her life in the city. The second season titles also now incorporate other characters from the cast, featuring Mary and Rhoda together inside Mary's apartment, a laughing two-shot of Mary and Phyllis in Mary's living area, and each of Mary's male co-workers at the WJM office receiving a hug from Mary.

In season three the opening titles re-inserted a sequence from the pilot season that explicitly emphasized the "Minneapolis–St. Paul" location, by adding back the shot of Mary's Mustang going under an overpass, with the "Minneapolis-St. Paul" freeway sign superimposed against a profile of her driving, followed by the shot of the rear of the Mustang heading into downtown. In season three, then, the show opened on Mary driving in her neighborhood, as in season two, but then gave viewers an overview of the skyline and explicit locale, before returning to the shot of Mary's mustang pulling up in front of her home. While season two's titles arguably moved "out" of the city (other than for the tam toss) to emphasize Mary's day-to-day home and work rhythms, season three's titles bridged a significant transition that occurred, visually, for their revision in season four.

As Ernest Pascucci has noted, season four's

> opening credits announced the malling of Minneapolis, replacing the outdoor location shots that lead up to Mary's famous toss of her blue hat with a thoroughly majestic image of Mary reaching the top of the escalator in Philip Johnson's IDS Center. . . . A full two months before Philip Johnson proudly presented his recently completed project as Minneapolis's new indoor downtown in *Architectural Forum, The Mary Tyler Moore Show* enacted the transformation of downtown in front of a much larger audience than *Architectural Forum* could ever hope to attract.[40]

The opening titles for season four and season five (after which the titles sequence remained the same through the end of the series' run) truly reveled in public, urban, mod architecture, fashion, and the dynamism of city life, while they simultaneously idealized quotidian engagements at home and work with friends. Overall, by season five, the titles sequence had solidified, envisioning Mary's full integration within and command of the life of the city both as an accomplished career woman and as a now-practiced single head-of-the-household. Images, here, for example, point out that her work life is no longer defined merely in relation to her male co-workers. Mary is now seen out and about, bustling between offices with reams of work papers, and producing the remote location sound for a WJM feature. In her personal life, Mary is also now fully engaged in a spectrum of activities, as the titles images now also feature her engaged in mundane, everyday household chores such as grocery shopping and washing her car.

The titles "evolved" to offer a "balanced" view, portraying Minneapolis as a site of public liberation and private self-actualization. In this sense, the program promoted an idealized vision that suggested 1970s downtowns might be "reclaimed" (particularly for young, white, female professionals) as liberating, joyful spaces of tourism, labor, and consumption in an era post-1960s upheavals and political traumas. *The Bob Newhart Show*'s titles, visualized by David Davis, were similarly dynamic in their representation of Chicago and of the quotidian joys of home—here, featuring married bliss. The theme to the Newhart show was titled, "Home to Emily," and the titles track Bob Hartley's daily commute home to his Lincoln Park high-rise, where his wife, Emily, awaits with a kiss. Much more jazz-influenced and less poppy than *The Mary Tyler Moore Show* score and without lyrics (they were written for, but not sung with the theme), aurally, the "Home to Emily" theme moves from a very upbeat, brassy score—paced closely with visuals featuring quick zooms, dynamic staging, sharp contrasts in screen direction, and quick edits—to a wistful tone, as the sequence concludes in the warm embrace of home and romantic partnership.

"Our Realism Was of a Different Sort"

The opening titles sequences of MTM Productions' "quality" 1970s series were departures from titles sequences of the past, due to their dynamic, contemporary, midwestern newness. The production staffs at each show perceived of the titles sequences as an important means to grounding the series in a fresh "realism." According to Mary Tyler Moore, these were settings "that hadn't been seen to death on television already, . . . full of life and young people and old people; fat, skinny, tall, thin."[41] It is this merger of the counterintuitive and the quotidian— settings "hadn't been seen to death" *and* were also now seen through a stylishly urbane lens that still featured "everyday" people rather than just Hollywood stars—that encouraged MTM staff, critics, and the programs themselves to promote an ethic of "authenticity" that was closely hewed to setting and midwestern "values."

According to Moore, the program's "real," believable qualities "promised you *truth*."[42] For producers David Davis and Allan Burns, this "truth" came, largely, through the show's setting, which created plot points, as well as crafted the show's "intimate" aesthetic. According to Davis and Burns, respectively:

This is one of the things that was different about the show. With Minneapolis you have weather. And you've got snow. It was always the staging—Mary would come in to work and go right to the coat rack, hang up her coat, put her purse, walk down to her desk—actual business that was real.

And,

this is an interior show and we thought, let's have a reason to want to be inside and so that it looks cozy and, so if you have the seasons and weather outside there.[43]

Significantly, in this emphasis, the *program* text of MTM series' seems aesthetically impoverished by contrast to the shows' opening titles sequences. As John Caldwell has pointed out, MTM's producers "actually gained their fame by making shows that were visually uninteresting."[44] *The Mary Tyler Moore Show* and *The Bob Newhart Show* both typically featured only two sets, the office, and the home, rarely venturing to third locales which would typically be restaurants or other interior spaces. The setting in cities where, according to James Brooks, "the major industry is snow removal," encouraged this interiority for plot purposes.[45] Interiority translated into a style of production that production staff claimed as *qualitatively* superior to that of their competitors. Specifically, "intimate" settings translated into "gentle," "intelligent" comedy. The quotidian translated to "class and charm and wit."[46]

This strategy explicitly differentiated MTM Productions from Norman Lear's series which, though also "interior" shows, were the target of criticism for their "demonstrative" rather than "well-rounded" characterizations and execution. MTM director Jay Sandrich makes this distinction explicit when he notes that whereas Lear shows were shot like a stage play, with characters facing the audience as if on a proscenium and projecting as if in a theater,

I tried to do more of a *word* play, not scream the lines. There *are* mics . . . more of a conversational style . . . play more *to* each other . . . the writing was so good, so real . . . intelligent . . . the laughs would come out of character.[47]

Bob Newhart has drawn this distinction by arguing that his humor was deceptively radical, as it was never gag-oriented but always involved the audience's engagement to fill in the gaps. As opposed to "loud" joke-driven comedy, then, Newhart "always thought of [his] humor as subversive. It doesn't appear to be doing what it's doing, but it does, . . . It involves the audience. . . . It's not what's said that is funny."[48]

This idea of an MTM/Lear contrast was shared across the production staff and cast, with writer Treva Silverman noting the MTM series' "realism of a different sort," characterized by "insight into behavior" that was "very real, and not jokes as such." These were "things that couldn't be quoted because they were so in context with what was happening emotionally."[49] Indeed, while *The Mary Tyler Moore Show* has been analyzed in terms of its quality address and, therefore, its qualitative distinctiveness, much of the production team and critical promotion and reception of the show repeatedly emphasized that this quality was based in the series' contrast with Lear's comedies, as it was drawn by MTM's specifically *mundane* characteristics—a quotidian equilibrium that was often, explicitly connected to the show's midwestern setting and sensibilities.

This "everyday" strategy also reinforced the idea of *personal* synchronicity between lead character and "square" star. Indeed, while the mod titles sequences position Moore and Newhart as expertly urbane, the program text itself consistently underscores the "squarer, slightly uptight"[50] uncertainty and, in fact, conscious "whiteness" of each character. This characterization is drawn most sharply in the early seasons of *The Mary Tyler Moore Show* with Rhoda Morgenstern acting as Mary Richards' "ethnic," New Yorker foil and, in *The Bob Newhart Show,* by his reactions, as a psychologist, to patients and co-workers at his practice. Critical to Mary's and Bob's characterizations, here, is their ultimately endearing, self-deprecating embrace of their own "limits" as squares, and their relative happiness in being "midwestern" in relation to an "outside" imagined to be more worldly, diverse, and flexible.

The Mary Tyler Moore Show consistently drew contrasts between Mary's midwestern-native Protestantism and Rhoda's New York-native Jewishness. While Mary was drawn as an all-American pompom girl, Homecoming princess, and sorority girl who wears flannel pajamas and "never even had to stay after school," Rhoda was portrayed as a drum and bugle corps member, a Sharkette, and a native of "neighborhoods you're afraid to walk alone in." In an episode from season three, Rhoda tries to assure Mary that she can guiltlessly date a friend's ex-husband. "Not only do I think it's alright, the *whole world* thinks it's alright.

Lawrence Welk thinks it's alright!"[51] Being as square as Lawrence Welk was a position that Mary Tyler Moore herself embraced, in publicity that linked her off-screen identity to Mary Richards and Valerie Harper's to Rhoda Morgenstern. In a feature on "My Friend, Valerie Harper," Moore states:

> Val's a theater person; I'm not . . . Val's comfortable with social causes; I'm likely to be suspicious of them. Val's tendency in any uncomfortable situation is, as she puts it, "to shine on"; mine is to pull back. Val is last minute; I'm ahead of time and waiting. Val's open; I'm reserved. . . . Val instinctively takes the liberal position in political and philosophical discussions; I tend to be more moderate—even conservative. . . . As for our political differences, even if I'm a registered Republican and Val a registered Democrat, our hearts are pretty much in the same place; seeking social justice and leaders in whom we can really believe.[52]

Within the discursive world of the program, Mary and Rhoda's "differences" were always resolved through this shared commitment to liberal humanism and the defense of their familial community and its relationships against the "outside" world. Unlike the images with which Rhoda portrays her native New York, Minneapolis stands in as a support and analog for Mary's squareness. Notably *not* "worldly" in its portrayal, Minneapolis is frequently the butt of the show's gentle joking about its lack of diversity. Examples across the series include throwaway lines from Ted Baxter's WJM newscasts, such as "And, that's a look at the Filipino community in the Twin Cities. And weren't they three of the nicest people you'd ever want to meet?" Or, noting that a "field trip" would be required "to see hippies," that the Mexican population of Minneapolis is "one," and that the only Japanese restaurant within driving distance of the Twin Cities is "Chef LeRoy's Teriyaki." Other characters are "endearingly" naïve and not-worldly—especially Ted Baxter, the WJM anchorman, who believes that New York city is "somewhere there in the Middle East," that Rhoda is Mary's "Israeli friend," and that Gordy, the station's lone African American employee, must be the sportscaster when, in fact, he is the meteorologist.[53]

Although *The Bob Newhart Show*'s Chicago was notably more "worldly" than Minneapolis in terms of its incorporation of characters of different ethnicities and races, Bob's square white midwesternness is always comically amplified in such interactions. Established, throughout the series, as a rather inflexible, routine-oriented character—described by Newhart himself as "flawed" and sometimes "peevish and egotistical"—Bob is radically uncomfortable with change. An episode from the series' final season exemplifies this particularly well. In "Ex-Con Job" (CBS, October 1, 1977), Bob is asked to serve as the psychologist to a group of prisoners about to be released to resume "ordinary" life. Bob has an ongoing problem trying to wrest control of the group's attention away from their leader, Mr. Tatum, who is African American, and imprisoned for burglary. Bob's attempts to communicate are dismissed by Tatum as "jive," prompting the following exchange:

> *Bob*: You want to go with that, Mr. Tatum?
> *Tatum*: How you going to help us, Jack? You don't even speak our language!
> *Bob*: Well, I don't think that's true.
> *Tatum*: You a suit that's fat-mouthin' cause you ain't hip to what's cold in the joint or what's tight up in the street, man, you dig?
> *Bob*: [after a long beat and stunned reaction shot] I'll be darned. You *are* right.

Bob then fails to impress the group with his recounting of his "criminal" past—when he once "moved down to the better seats" at Wrigley field. Later, Bob's square discomfort is called out by a prisoner named Mr. Hawkins, whose sexually suggestive tale of what he will do upon his release (and with whom) causes Bob to cut him off. Bob's lack of "soul" is then foregrounded as Mr. Tatum asks him to join in on a song he's penned, "Hey Little Mama, I'm Coming Home to You." When the group leaves, Bob, self-satisfied, off-key, and out-of-rhythm, repeats the chorus to himself.

The episode sets up the idea that Bob's well-intentioned liberal humanism is simply not up to the task of preparing the group for the radical, structural, and institutional barriers that await them "outside." Bob, literally, has no way to communicate from his square, enfranchised world. However, the program "redeems" Bob's "coolness" in the end, by having Mr. Tatum come over to rob Bob and Emily. Knowing that Tatum is only there to seek help, using the stick-up attempt as an excuse, Bob gets him to engage in "rational" conversation instead. Tatum and Bob come to an agreement to reconvene the group as part of the new "everyday" of each prisoner. Bob "soul shakes" and claims to "dig

Bob Hartley embraces his "squareness."

it" when he and Tatum strike a deal: "OK, Doc. You teach me how to get a job, being a Black man with a prison record and no education, and I'll make you a big man with the group, dig it?"

MTM Productions' quality comedies embraced their "square," local, placidity, always resolving problems within the "family" and tightening or revising the borders of that circle when threatened by "outsiders." Mr. Tatum thus travels, across this episode, from being a recalcitrant threat to Bob's self-confidence and solid squareness, to being part of Bob's patient roster as a client who also reinforces Bob's "coolness" *as* a square. Both *The Mary Tyler Moore Show* and *The Bob Newhart Show* often featured episodes in which "outsiders" were deflated or expelled in ways that reinforced the value of *being* a square like Bob or Mary; of being exceptional at being mundane.[54]

Serafina Bathrick has argued on this count that Mary Richards' "middleness" is thrown into relief by her contrast with Rhoda *and* by her difference from Phyllis Lindstrom, her friend and landlord who, while native to the Midwest, seems "alien" to Mary's world because of her overtly "political" affiliations and stridently elitist pretensions.[55] Across the series, a sampling of Phyllis's activities, for example, included The Abolish Capital Punishment Dinner Dance, Women for Better Government, Group (therapy) Weekend Marathon, Sensitivity Group, Creative Movement Class, and the Concerned Democrats of Minneapolis. Phyllis was, thus, the most "current" of any of the show's stable characters, but her *faddish* attachment to "causes" and her overblown claims about her expertise and worth made her the object of the others' ridicule from the stable center.

Both Mary and Bob are, in this respect, positioned as "ordinary," believable, populist heroes in contrast to characters and organizations that are overtly elitist or political. Such characters, frequently, are affiliated with the arts or media within each series' narrative. In "The Critic" (CBS, January 8, 1977) and "We Closed in Minneapolis" (CBS, January 30, 1971), for example, Mary and her friends are allied with the "booboisie" of Minneapolis against critics who "hate everything." When WJM hires Professor Carl Heller to act as a "critic at large," Mary is forced to tap what the show's producers referred to as her inner "Presbyterian militant,"[56] finally upbraiding Heller, arguing that "we are supposed to appeal to the public, you know, not just to the intellectual elite. Just being negative isn't really constructive." Similarly, in *Bob Newhart Show* episodes such as "Mister Emily Hartley" (CBS, November 3, 1973) Bob encounters the condescension of the "High I.Q. Club." Bob assesses this thinly veiled encounter with MENSA as the worst night of his life since the Korean War, mostly for the offense he takes at the High IQ members' "straining to be 'regular guys.'" "You must admit," he says to Emily, "Beer Barrel Polka on the harp is a bit much."

Overall, the comic conceit of MTM's 1970s series was that their titular squares were the last sane, stable centers of a relatively insane contemporary world. After *The Mary Tyler Moore Show* and *The Bob Newhart Show* left the air, MTM Productions tried a new variation on the Midwest-set quality comedy with *WKRP in Cincinnati*. Airing only from 1978–1981 (doomed, in part, by a different time slot and day each season), the series featured key departures from its predecessors, though much of its humor was still rooted in location and "square" values that were, here, upheld in the context of a rock and roll station. Like *The Mary Tyler Moore Show* and *The Bob Newhart Show*, *WKRP in Cincinnati*'s opening titles were shot on-location and featured the downtown skyline, freeway interchanges, community landmarks, and office workers flooding onto city sidewalks. However, the *WKRP* titles sequence is shot on video and has an amateurish look, buttressed by its aural track, which features program snippets on a rapidly changing car radio tuner (alternating from a weather report, to a song, to news, to a classical refrain, before launching into the program's theme song, "Baby, If You've Ever Wondered").

The most "hip" characters in the ensemble at *WKRP* were, significantly, "closet" squares for whom Cincinnati and the station represented refuge from "mistakes" each had made in the 1960s. These included Tim Reid's Venus Flytrap and Howard Hesseman's "Dr. Johnny Fever." Venus, the station's lone African American DJ, whose exquisite couture and daily greetings of "what's happening, white folks?" suggested a flamboyantly unflappable cool, for example, was later revealed to have gone AWOL from the Vietnam War and to be in hiding in Cincinnati (wherein the station's co-workers become his protective and supportive "family"). For Johnny Fever, WKRP represented the last resort—fired elsewhere for saying "booger" on the air and for his general stoner affect, Fever is revealed to be a doting father and caring colleague.

Conversely, the most "radical" characters on the show are newsman and "Award Winning Farm Reporter" Les Nessman (Richard Sanders), local salesguy Herb Tarlek (Frank Bonner), and, crucially, the Cincinnati-area radio listeners *outside* the "family" feeling of the station, who seemed to pose the *real* revolutionary threat. In the show's premiere, for example, a group of listeners, adamant that the station format not change from easy listening to rock and roll, picket the lobby. Their spokesperson states:

> We're a small bunch, admittedly, but we're a determined fringe element that cannot be counted upon to do the sensible thing. . . . my group has petitioned the Federal Communications Commission to have your license revoked unless you immediately return to your previous format and apologize, live, on the air, to Lawrence Welk.

Indeed, much of the humor of *WKRP*'s short run, was rooted in a comedy of inversion, whereby the stereotypical "dumb blonde" receptionist (Loni Anderson's Jennifer Marlowe) was the smartest, most together character on the show and the white, male, "patriarch" boss (Gordon

Jump's Arthur Carlson) was, essentially, an endearing but blundering child. The Cincinnati "natives" and the station's senior-skewing sponsors (e.g., Rolling Thunder European Regularity Tonics, Shady Hills Rest Home, Bo Peep Safety Shoes), were notoriously nuttier than the new staffers who were the true squares—transplants and refugees from elsewhere "up and down the dial" who had finally found their home.

Heartland Tourism: MTM Productions and Civic Identity

Since the early 1980s, MTM Productions has not had another "midwestern" quality comedy on air (the company became primarily a distribution house in 1983 and was bought by the Family Channel in 1992, changing ownership several times through the 1990s) and yet, the televisual imaginations of the Midwest as urbane *and* mundane common to these series has taken on a new life off the edges of the TV screen. At roughly the same time that these series left the air, the post-industrial economic downturn—particularly in midwestern urban centers—encouraged a transition to a service-oriented economy bolstered, particularly, by a regional strategy to promote the Midwest as a tourist destination that would capitalize upon the region's presumptively "secondary" destination status (to coastal cities or foreign travel) by offering to reward travelers with its "safe," "comfortable," "cheaper" sensibility. [57]

Indeed, as industry and manufacturers left the Midwest and agriculture shifted in economic viability in the 1980s and 1990s, tourism and the service economy have become the leading revenue producers for a majority of midwestern states. The regional association of the U.S. Travel and Tourism Administration, the "America's Heartland Tourism" promotion group, has, thus, pushed travel to the Midwest (chiefly, to Minneapolis and to Branson, Missouri) as the ideal tour package destination. Simultaneously, tourism groups report a broader increase in travel based on television programming. Over thirty tour buses a day are reported to travel past Mary Richards' former "home" on Kenwood Parkway in Minneapolis. But "television tourism" has also succeeded in examples such as Southfork Ranch outside of Dallas, the Sopranoland Bus Tour, the *Sex and the City* Tour, "Kramer's" Tour of *Seinfeld* locations, the *Little House on the Prairie* Tour, and the annual Mayberry Days festival in Mount Airy, North Carolina.

With the exception of the Sopranoland, *Sex and the City*, and *Seinfeld* tours, it is notable that the majority of "television tourism" takes place outside of New York and Los Angeles. The relative rarity and, therefore, exceptional nature of such "secondary" locales within the national imagination is certainly one part of the appeal. Such cities are also much more dependent upon and deeply invested in such associations to "brand" their identity for tourism and convention business. With an economy of "saleable" and instantly familiar images with which to promote travel to the Midwest, "television tourism" has become increasingly important, and MTM Productions' talent has taken to this task seriously. Bob Newhart has served as a spokesman for the Illinois Tourism Bureau (in advertisements from the mid-1980s in which the Chicago native claimed: "No matter where you're from in America, Chicago is your hometown. Come home!"). Cast members of *WKRP in Cincinnati* routinely participate in special events and an annual "Turkey Drop" event (based on the series' infamous Thanksgiving episode). However, Minneapolis's identification with and through Mary Tyler Moore has been distinctive and merits further analysis of the extent to which civic identity and popular memory are beholden to televisual representations for their shape. Why make sense of civic identity and its broader national worth through these frames? In the case of *The Mary Tyler Moore Show* and Minneapolis, I would argue that the city has been able to promote itself as an accessible, secure, consumer-friendly space that is *not* associated with "political" action, voice, or conflict. It thus presents itself—as "read" through the series, its star persona, and the broader popular discourses around it that are then used as tourist appeals—as an idealized "safe" space for urban exploration wherein an "un-Mary-like" life is inconceivable for the tourist.

Indeed, Minneapolis's own urban resurgence and national "coming out"—including the dedication of Nicollet Mall and the construction of IDS Center and its heralding in the *Time* magazine cover, as mentioned above—took place just prior to and during *The Mary Tyler Moore Show*'s original series run. Thus, the actual and symbolic resurgence of the downtown district coincided with the success of the series that, weekly, depicted its possibilities for a national TV audience. When the series concluded its run, and into the early 1980s, Minneapolis continued to "twin" the ideas of urbanity and squareness in two key promotions: The early 1980s "Minneapple" campaign, and the early 1990s facelift to Nicollet Mall and expansion of the downtown skyway system, boosted by the opening of the Mall of America. Indeed, even though *The Mary Tyler Moore Show* went off the air in 1977, the city of Minneapolis has continued to imagine and promote its identity through reference to the program and its ideals.

From 1982 to 1992, Minneapolis engaged in a civic version of the "Mary-Rhoda" contrast, when the Chamber of Commerce adopted an advertising campaign that promoted the city as the "Minneapple," complete with a logo featuring an apple draped in snow. According to the *Star Tribune*, "the idea, of course, is to highlight the already sharp contrast between Minneapolis and New York City."[58] City residents were generally dismayed by the Minneapple campaign's definition of the city by what it was *not*, especially as it depended on such a chilling image. In the mid-1990s, Mary Tyler Moore returned to the Twin Cities to promote her autobiography, visiting each of the series' locations and being celebrated by local leaders and press. Indeed, no association has seemed so positively embraced by or productive for the city.

In May 2002, the cable television outlet, TV Land, and the City of Minneapolis commemorated Mary Richards' liberating tam toss on Nicollet Mall with the dedication of a bronze statue of "the toss," crafted by artist Gwendolyn Gillen. While criticisms emerged regarding the statue's root commercialism and its potentially bizarre recognition of a purely fictional "resident" of Minneapolis, the dedication drew thousands of attendees, live global coverage on CNN, and a round of civic appearances and speeches by Mary Tyler Moore who herself proclaimed that "she feels a connection to Minneapolis, 'more than I do to my real hometown of Brooklyn.'"[59] One of the stated goals of the statue's installation was its potential to increase Twin Cities' tourism. Indeed, by accepting and promoting TV Land's bronzed Mary Tyler Moore, Minneapolis has been able to position its downtown as a "must-see" destination for tour groups whose primary time will otherwise be spent at the Mall of America, which is now the number one travel destination in the United States, outstripping Disney, Graceland, and the Grand Canyon, combined. Minnesota tourism has grown over thirty percent since the Mall's opening (in 1992) with almost fifty percent of non-Minnesotan visitors claiming "shopping" as their primary travel activity.

Just prior to the statue's dedication, Minnesota native and journalist Jerry Haines reiterated the importance of Mary Tyler Moore and

Dedication of the Mary Tyler Moore statue in Minneapolis. Photo by Dawn Villella for the Associated Press, by permission AP Wide World Photos.

popular *cultural* expression to Minneapolis's civic identity shift, from "square" regional hub to newly, national "hip" credibility:

> To many people who grew up there, the state could be summarized as taciturn Lutheran elders and Spam casserole. To the nation at large we were known mostly for cold weather. We were indistinguishable from Iowa and the Dakotas . . . Then Sir Tyrone Guthrie founded a world-renowned theater there, Mary Tyler Moore set her TV program there, the Twins went to the World Series, and Garrison Keillor built a national radio program around us. . . . Formerly merely cold, now we were cool, sophisticated, enviable.[60]

Both during its prime time run and in its syndicated and statuesque afterlife, *The Mary Tyler Moore Show* suggests that while the central myths of geographic identity can be reimagined in certain ways (from pastoral to urbane, if not urban), there remain limits on the power to redefine the central myths themselves (the region remains characterized as "white," middle class, and mainstream). While MTM Productions' quality comedies were radical in their strides to "put things in a different light" by reimagining an urbane Midwest as shimmering and mod, these series could not alter the apparent lingering investment in the evacuation of race and political subjectivity from broader national "schemes of perception," which as yet kept such realities "unnoticed or relegated to the background."[61] Chapter 5 thus interrogates the challenge posed when the overtly *political* subject appears in the Midwest through the "interruptive" appearance of *queer* subjectivity.

5

"There *Is* No 'Dayton Chic'"

Queering the Midwest in Roseanne,
Ellen, *and* The Ellen Show

In the midst of the April 1997 media uproar surrounding
Ellen DeGeneres's coming out, playwright Paul Rudnick stated, "Here's
something I resent about coming out: It's an act demanded only of gay
people."[1] This chapter examines the ways in which, in controversial
prime time depictions of lesbianism during the 1990s, the "joke" is, in
fact, based upon a comedy of inversion regarding who must come out
or be outed. Specifically, in the infamous 1994 "lesbian kiss" episode of
Roseanne and in the post-coming-out final season of *Ellen*—epitomized
here by the 1997 episode featuring Emma Thompson—coming out is
an act demanded of midwesterners. The outed Midwest is, within each
program, abject in relation to the series' comparatively mobile, cosmopolitan, place-transcendent portrayal of lesbian identity. The effectiveness of these episodes—the judgment of whether or not they are funny
and whether they represent significant incursions within the prime time
status-quo—thus depends on the degree of success with which anxieties
about the "difference" of lesbianism are transferred to the national
viewing audience's presumed, consensual understanding of the Midwest
as a presumptively rural, white, and "straight," pre-modern, hermetically sealed land of hopelessly un-hip squares. Indeed, both of these episodes pose midwesternness and lesbianism as fundamentally incompatible identifications that cannot "logically" share the same space. Imagined as almost exclusively rural and rooted in place, midwesterners are,
by extension, entrenched in fixed ways of thinking and political conservatism. Geographic middleness is analogous to ideological middleness.
By contrast, both shows define lesbianism through its presumed, natural
alliance with urban life and culture on either coast, and with diverse
sex, race, and class affinities and identifications. Contra-mainstream,

lesbianism is marked as the epitome of what is cutting edge, hip, and culturally cool, mobile, and consumer savvy.

Roseanne and *Ellen* thus tread a tricky line. On the one hand, the series knowingly, purposefully appropriate the rhetoric of neoconservative voices that launched vitriolic attacks against the shows' perceived threats to "mainstream America" in order to turn those fears back upon themselves in a critical fashion. On the other hand, the economy of the sitcom—its brevity, the need for quickly recognizable types to propel the jokes and the story, and the need for the central characters to return "as is" the following week—also encouraged and, arguably, assured that each program accepted and reinstated the most abridged assumptions about both lesbianism and midwesternness. Bleakly politically significant here is that these programs' and their critics' share a "common sense" understanding that midwesternness and homosexuality are presumptively understood to be fundamentally irreconcilable identifications. And yet, the prime time friendly, apolitical twist enacted by these programs in posing this incompatibility is their evacuation of *sexual* identity from the episodes' primary concern. Instead, the episodes each propose that lesbianism and midwesternness are incompatible in terms of economic, social, and cultural capital. They are pitted as irreconcilable *taste* cultures.

Roseanne (ABC, 1988–1997), *Ellen* (ABC, 1994–1997) and Ellen DeGeneres's subsequent, short-lived sitcom, *The Ellen Show* (CBS, 2001–2002) each, arguably, empowered lesbianism through their lesbian characters' "capacity to draw the line between and around categories of taste"[2] via relational categories of style or cultural distinction. In each, the "politics" of lesbianism is portrayed as a common-sense orientation to good *taste,* against which déclassé midwesternness serves as comic foil. Thus inverting the expected coming-out narrative, the real cause of ridicule, shame, and subsequent loss of cultural acceptance in these programs is to be "outed" *as* midwestern. Such outing immediately forces the characters "to take account of their distribution in a socially ranked geographic space" within the nation-at-large and to recognize the limits that geographic position puts on the "economic, cultural, and social capital [she] can deploy."[3]

The *"Flyover"* Audience as Niche-Resistant?

Ron Becker's *Gay TV and Straight America* meticulously outlines the television industry's and political and cultural transitions during the late 1970s through the 1990s, which enabled "the rise of gay-themed programming on U.S. network television in the 1990s" and invigorated attention to market research, demographic targeting, and narrowcast practices that encouraged networks to focus their attention away from "mass and undifferentiated" audiences toward newly reconfigured "quality" audiences, "niche" programming, and sponsorship appeals. According to Becker:

> Although demographics had played a part in the business of network television for years, their influence soared in the mid-1990s . . . The interconnected growth of niche marketing and cable competition in the 1970s and 1980s drastically changed the context in which ABC, NBC, and CBS operated in the 1990s. The value of their historical strength— namely their ability to offer advertisers access to a mass and undifferentiated audience of consumers—was seemingly undermined by a social climate where differences among Americans appeared more relevant to their lives and to marketers.[4]

Among the key new niche demographic groups targeted in this period was what Becker has termed the "slumpy" demographic, defined as "socially liberal, urban-minded professionals."[5] Slumpys were "not just the 'genuinely affluent' but also the 'selectively affluent.' . . . the networks . . . envisioned this audience to be 'hip,' 'sophisticated,' urban-minded, white, and college-educated 18–49 year olds with liberal attitudes, disposable income, and a distinctively edgy and ironic sensibility."[6] The slumpy audience was, further, one for whom homosexuality "was actually becoming chic" in the 1990s for its new market viability, promoting a "cutting-edge allure dulled just enough by . . . assimilationist goals to appeal to a relatively broad base."[7]

This idealized niche was, thus, conceptually articulated with marketers' growing investment in a highly particularized imagination of the gay and lesbian "community" as, itself, an upscale, urban demographic.[8] Danae Clark has conceptualized this marketing address and consumer appeal as "commodity lesbianism," whereby:

> Once stripped of its political underpinnings, lesbianism can be repre-
> sented as a style of consumption . . . "the strategy is that gay images
> imply distinction and non-conformity, granting straight consumers a
> longed-for place outside the humdrum mainstream."[9]

Such markets are, however, also geographically defined. Demographic
research and market analysis map geographies of taste and economies
of cultural distinction.

As discussed in chapter 4, Detroit and Chicago have, since the 1960s,
been typically imagined—economically, culturally, and demographically
—as "extra-regional" to the Midwest. This excision holds for the television industry's broader conceptualization of the Midwest as a market. Of the top one hundred television markets, the only midwestern cities appearing in the top ten are Chicago (third) and Detroit (tenth). In
the "transitional zone" of markets eleven through twenty-six, only Minneapolis–St. Paul (fourteenth), Cleveland-Akron (sixteenth), St. Louis
(twenty-first) and Indianapolis (twenty-fifth) appear. These markets are
considered "transitional" for the fact that, in terms of market and media use, demographic and socio-economic composition, these areas fall
somewhere, in flux, between "the major urban media markets and the
smaller, more suburban and rural markets."[10] The "bottom" zone, from
market twenty-seven through one-hundred, skews "more to the heartland," capturing less populous markets, further inland and south from
the coasts. Markets one through twenty-five represent a small number of U.S. television markets, but almost fifty percent of the nation's
population. [11]

The top-ten urban niche markets, clustered on either coast in part depend upon the "mass" older, rural, square Heartlander market to define
their tastes and sensibilities as contrastingly young, urban, and hip. As
outlined in each prior chapter, the Heartland has, historically, been defined as a "mass" television market—both in terms of audience distinction (or, lack thereof), and in terms of economic value. Historically, that
is, the Midwest, as a television market, has been, presumptively, resistant to niche-ing—a resistance that is commonly referred to through the
"massifying," homogenizing term, "flyover." This term refers both to
the broad, multi-generational contours of the midwestern audience, as
well as to the broad rural-skewing map that could be drawn to identify the region as a market area. In the early to mid-1990s, as niche-
marketing was increasingly aggressive about targeting urban, coastal

consumers, contrasting advertising discourses embraced a consciously neo-traditional appeal to "flyover" audiences (or to the "flyover"-identified consumer lurking inside the slumpy). That is, *both* niche and flyover appeals were actively marshaled and energized in this period to express and sell competing "all-American" ideals. With niche, slumpy appeals organized to promise socially progressive market diversity, urbane mobility, and place-transcendence through consumption, and flyover appeals to social continuity, tradition, and the recovery of place-bound identity in a fast-moving era.

An example of such competing, concurrent appeals in these terms is the contrast between the mid-1990s Gateway Computer and Subaru Forrester campaigns. Gateway advertised its "friendly" personal computers through a campaign the company termed "prairiefication." Gateway's computers, in this period, arrived at consumers' doorsteps in boxes designed to look like cow-skins—white with a Holstein's black splotches. Gateway's television and print-ad campaigns featured homespun middlewesterners who occupied bucolic one-stoplight towns surrounded by cornfields. The ad copy for these promotions indicated that to "pursue your own happiness" and to "take time to live a little" one must live in such a locale (or escape there via consumption); once there, however, "it takes a mighty sweet deal just to get off the porch swing." Each advertisement concluded with the tagline that, "things are *different* in the country.*" So, Gateway encouraged consumers to question where "difference" really lived in the 1990s consumer market by promoting the myth of the Heartland and the middle-west as a site of "core values" that, in the current climate, are "othered" or "made different." The implication of this campaign was that the coastal niche consumers were, in fact, the uncritically homogeneous market, held in sway to "fads" and the relentless pursuit of the latest trend rather than following the true and simple path to peace and contentment.

Subaru, by contrast, contemporaneously embraced an audience it defined as "active lifestyle women" and targeted this consumer group through out lesbian tennis legend, Martina Navratilova. Set to a techno beat and featuring "extreme" game action photography of Navratilova's tennis, Diann Roffe-Steinrotter's skiing, and Juli Inkster's golfing interspersed with sexy driving shots, one of these televised ads featured the tagline, "Subaru: For women who kick butt." Specifically marketing "fun, freedom, adventure, confidence, and control," the "athletic-type woman" who is targeted by this ad is presumed to be figuratively and literally mobile, fluid, sexy, cool, independent, and urbane—she who, in contrast to Gateway's imagined target audience, would *not* be at home "down on the farm."

Popular press coverage regarding regional identity in this period reveals an awareness of a growing divide in marketing and also in market identifications, based on this niche versus mass contrast and its geographic, raced, and classed premises. This emerges, particularly, in features regarding the Midwest and its "core" values compared to trends on either coast. A *Forbes* magazine feature from 1990, entitled "You Can Go Home Again," states, for example, that square is the new hip:

> Get ready for the first shock of the Nineties: The new trendsetter is the heartland. The symbolmakers are fleeing from the cynical cities of the East and West coasts, and seeking sturdier soils in which to sink roots. . . . The uncluttered, unbridled lives of midwesterners will become the envy of the nation by the next century, says the trend-watching consulting firm Brainreserve. . . . Everything everybody wants—big family, good food, regular people, nothing hyped up—is all in the Midwest . . . basic values, family strength, the smell of homemade apple pie, oxygen so rich it makes one's lungs jump and quiver like a colt's flank, and a golf course ten minutes from home. . . . Many fast-trackers on both coasts are now asking themselves, "Why?" There is something particularly unnatural about the fast track. . . . The small-town Midwest still has time for fathers to go shooting with their sons and snowmobiling with their daughters. . . . Practically everybody knows how to fix things. . . . the return to favor of such values as home, family, church, and the work ethic.[12]

And, in a *Newsweek* feature plainly titled "The Flyover People," the Midwest is firmly located as an "authentic" contrast to either coast which is, itself, niche resistant:

> Anger dissipates between the coasts . . . a bastion of civility . . . Trends begin in the West, leapfrog East, then gradually creep back to the country's center. . . . filtering out what's trendy, retaining what has substance. . . . The Midwest's own hyperactives have fled for New York or Los Angeles. That's one reason our quality of life is so high. . . . This very dullness holds our population down. Trend seekers stay away in droves.[13]

Target asks: What if the best of the city were available everywhere in the country?

Notably, perhaps the most successful marketer and retailer during the 1990s and into the new millennium, was the Minneapolis-based Target Corporation, which cannily tapped both niche and Heartland appeals in order to position itself as the new "haute" spot of big-box retailers. An advertising supplement inserted in Sunday newspapers around the country in 2003 demonstrates this dual appeal. Designed to launch Isaac Mizrahi's fall fashion line, the eight-page portfolio asks, "Where Does New York's 5th Avenue Meet Main Street, USA?" Inside, each page features a contrasting photo of a female model in either New York or a Heartland setting. "What if the Best of the City . . . were available everywhere in the country?" queries the centerfold text, which features an image of Mizrahi arm-in-arm with three models crossing a New York city street facing a page with a young woman in an Audrey Hepburn-esque black cocktail dress standing in a highly stylized, set-bound cornfield. Promising "luxury for every woman everywhere," Target was hailed, particularly, as the anti-Wal-Mart:

> The best decision Target executives ever made, retail consultants agree, was to differentiate themselves from other discount chains by having

"cool stuff." . . . Why can't other mass merchants do the same thing? It's a bit of culture clash for many. Wal-Mart, for example, is price-focused, and designer names might not connect with its customers.[14]

Desire for the Midwest's perceived simplicity and droll, naïve square-ness thus coexists with its portrayal as unenviably pre-modern and lack-ing in consumer savvy. But, can the counter-practice to the nostalgic and typically neoconservative retreat to the myth of the American mid-dle only be imagined in market terms? Via the promise—to "knowing" viewer-consumers across the country—of national mobility and cultural worth accrued through the acquisition and incorporation of, specifi-cally, urban gay style, repositioned as mainstream desire?

Parental Discretion Is Advised: From Realism and Nothingness to Gratuitous and Political

Herman Gray has recently argued that television viewers are positioned as subjects in three ways: as cultural subjects, economic subjects, and political subjects.[15] Gray defines "cultural subjectivity" as that which invites viewers to identify with "traditions, practices, identities, and rep-resentations that are generated from and recognized to exist within a specific cultural tradition and social location." In the "controversial" episodes of *Roseanne* and *Ellen* analyzed below, midwesternness and lesbianism are represented as culturally incompatible, encouraging view-ers to identify as *either* oriented toward a midwestern *or* a lesbian sub-jectivity in relation to program address. "Economic subjectivity" consti-tutes TV viewers "as consumers whose desires and preferences are reg-istered in the structure of the marketplace organized by the television industry." As suggested above, the "lesbian kiss" episode of *Roseanne* and the post-coming-out season of *Ellen*, were, economically, sites of in-dustrial and market tensions that exposed the ongoing need to negotiate both "mass"/"flyover audience" market appeals and "niche"/"slumpy" market appeals, and to confront the potential market backlash of a per-ceived "erring" to one side or the other.

Sponsors who regularly underwrote time in each series but now ac-tively pulled ads from the "lesbian" episodes—or, were "not otherwise scheduled to appear" during those weeks—were also sponsors that had previously "hailed" the most "mass," multi-generational, cross-class, and cross-geographic audience with their advertising appeals (including Wendy's, Chrysler, Coca-Cola, McDonalds, JC Penney, Dominos, Ford, and GM). New sponsors who entered into these spots maximized their time within these "event" broadcasts by directing their messages toward much narrower, slumpy-identified demographics (e.g., E-Trade Group, Olivia Cruises, and the Human Rights Campaign).

For Gray, political subjectivity refers to "the ability of audiences to constitute themselves as political entities or, . . . interest groups, and to have their interests raised and represented to the industry and the state."[16] As Anna McCarthy has argued, specifically as regards *Ellen's* final season, the series' lesbian episodes shifted *Roseanne's* and *Ellen's* relation to their audience's standard expectations for each program and also actively shifted each program's relation to televisual seriality and flow. "Don't Ask, Don't Tell," and the post-coming-out episodes of *Ellen* adopted

> the signifiers of the 'must see TV' event as a form of *political* display. . . . a political moment in national culture, . . . a moment of extreme narrative development for the lead character in the show, . . . And, . . . a structural shift in the sitcom form.[17]

In these respects, much of the popular press and critical discourse surrounding the series' controversies expressed a sense that the programs represented a radical departure that betrayed the series' foundational appeals, and that this shift was located expressly in the transition from seriality to event, from quotidian concerns to political commitment, and from "mass" appeal to "niche" strategies. Both series were accused of jettisoning their "authentic" appeals for insincere, cynical market gain —particularly in contrast to popular series such as *Seinfeld* and *Friends*, which had historically been counterpoised to *Roseanne* and *Ellen* as symbolic of the industry's *overtly* "trend" and gag-oriented approach to comedy that was perceived to be "snide" and flip.

In the case of *Roseanne*, particularly, anticipation of and reaction to the "must see" kiss episode marked a stark departure from prior valorizations of the program's "realism" and also implied that, as an "event," disproportionate attention would be cast upon a single program from a series that had, arguably, always already "queered" critical expectations. *Roseanne's* weekly appearances had historically taken a feminist viewpoint and actively interrogated class and gender dynamics with a racially and sexually diverse ensemble cast that took key roles in that critique. Indeed, according to scholars such as Alexander Doty, Pamela Robertson, and Kathleen Rowe, Roseanne's "pre-kiss" persona, arguably, read and inhabited the world of Lanford, Illinois "queerly" from the program's inception, presenting a star persona that was "marked by contradiction and undecidability" that critiqued cultural norms "from a non- or anti-straight, albeit frequently non-gay position."[18]

And yet, in the seasons leading up to "the kiss" episode, *Roseanne* was not popularly perceived as politically threatening because of its very "ordinariness," grounded by its setting in a *place* that was presumptively apolitical. From the series' first airing, its star, production staff, and the critics who embraced the show hailed it as ordinary, real, truthful, and resolutely "non-urban, non-yuppie and non-upscale."[19] Roseanne and series creator, Matt Williams, ritually associated this realism with the program's midwestern setting and its working-class milieu. Significantly counter to the industry and market definitions of a "flyover" audience of unsophisticated tastes outlined above (though anticipating Target's corporate branding strategy), Roseanne told *The New York Times*, for example:

> I want to do a show that reflects how people really live. Telling the truth at any point [on TV] is really revolutionary. . . . When you tell the truth you don't insult the audience's intelligence. . . . I grew up with people in the Midwest and, in fact, they're as hip as anyone else. In fact, you grow up with more minority people in your neighborhoods in the Midwest than you do in L.A. or New York, because we're factory working-class people, generally. So, we grew up in the same neighborhoods. We're not so isolated. It's all kinds of colors of people in the Midwest. All that talking down to the audience stuff really drives me crazy[20]

This recognition of diversity and progressive savvy between the coasts—itself a counterintuitive, if not actually queered, reading in broader public discourse—was noted for its refreshing departure and overt challenge to the industry as "a revenge that Middle America could share" against perceived industry disrespect, and a proliferation of images replete with "designer clothing, upscale professions, and social posturing."[21]

The counterintuitive nature of this reading of the midwestern audience and its ostensible market value (considering the series' top ten rating for eight of its nine seasons), was not one that the industry and advertisers embraced in this period of waning broadcaster power and transition to narrowcast strategies. *Roseanne's* broad market appeal, in fact, was consistently reported as a rationale for why the series was destined to win People's Choice Awards rather than Emmys. Asked about the lack of Emmy Award recognition for the series and its star, ABC-TV President Ted Harbert, commented:

> The only speculation I would offer . . . is that this is a show about what it is like to live in mid-America on a lower income and facing all the struggles that may be unrelatable to the fortunate people who work in the entertainment business. Perhaps people think it is hipper to be represented by a "Seinfeld" than a "Roseanne" because of the upper-income, educated patina.[22]

Roseanne's appeals to authenticity and its Heartland audience were, thus, explicitly counterpoised to narrowcast address to "hip" coastal viewers and the prevailing trend toward "edgy," urban comedies emerging as the new industry standard. *Roseanne's* creators and proponents argued that the program was ideally crafted to appeal to a broad viewing audience, receptive to thinking of TV as a "cultural forum"[23] through which identity norms could be humorously interrogated in contrast to market-driven, "niche" audience appeal programs "about nothing."

So, how does a program hailed for its authenticity, its sensitivity to working-class life and culture, and its realistic portrayal of a midwestern community diversified in terms of race and sexuality, suddenly become attacked for a lack of credibility and for being demonstratively out-of-step with Heartland values? How does the "mass" appeal program that was always already invested in thinking "queerly" about identity become accused of "selling out" as a stunt? *Roseanne's* "kiss episode" and the post-coming-out season of *Ellen* licensed somewhat radical industrial, popular, and critical shifts in apprehensions of each programs' identity largely *external* to the programs themselves and, thus, suggestive of a much broader *national* perceived "threat" and debate over the "mainstreaming" of lesbianism that was *actively* re-contextualized and "contained" as a "midwestern" problem. This shift was predicated upon two key assumptions: that lesbianism was an inherently *political* identification that was now newly-valued as a hip consumer "niche";

and that the persistent association of a culturally "Middle American" audience's "more conservative" sensibilities and economically "mass" "flyover" market tastes proved the group's predisposition to be antagonized by such images and claims for lesbianism. According to *Newsweek*, for example:

> Viewers in New York, Los Angeles and San Francisco might not be fazed by a same-sex sitcom, but folks are a little more conservative in the part of America Hollywood types call "fly-over country." And Jerry Falwell is already fulminating against "Ellen Degenerate." [24]

Whereas the "safe for the mass market" *Roseanne* had been hailed for its realism, the "kiss" episode was charged with being "really gratuitous," insincere, and "another milestone in America's descent into narcissism—the notion that who we are is all that matters; identity is everything."[25] However, recasting *Roseanne*'s relevance as "unrealistic" once lesbianism enters the text can only be conceivable if lesbianism and ordinary, everyday, working-class midwesterners are posed as fundamentally irreconcilable identifications.[26]

Publicly, this was never an assumption that Roseanne or her program's production staff shared. Notably, Roseanne recently stated that the single most consistent source of conflict between her program and its network was the ABC executives' consistent "underestimation" of an audience "they used to always call 'the Bible Belters'—now they'd call them 'red state people' —but then it was always 'Bible Belters.' "[27] Indeed, ABC-TV—home network to both *Roseanne* and *Ellen*—licensed and actively encouraged interpretation of the "kiss" episode and post-coming-out season as threatening, politicized "exceptions" to the series' status-quo, which might "offend" broad cultural sensibilities. ABC initially refused to air the "Don't Ask, Don't Tell" episode of *Roseanne* as a "defense" of majority audience "standards," claiming—according to series producer Tom Arnold—that "the [kiss] scene is not the lifestyle most people lead."[28] In April, ABC compromised by attaching a parental advisory or viewer discretion notice to the episode. The entire post-coming-out season of *Ellen* was, likewise, prefaced by such a warning, as well as by a "PG-14" rating. In the midst of the growing uproar over the revised *Roseanne* air date, suburban-Chicago-based Kraft General Foods pulled all of its advertising for the *Roseanne* episode, while *Ellen*'s coming-out episode was abandoned by Ohio-based Wendy's and suburban-Detroit's Chrysler. The ABC-affiliate in Birmingham, Alabama, refused to run the episode. Notoriously, *Ellen*'s owner, Disney Company, was boycotted by the Southern Baptist Convention, which singled out the company's purported "homosexual agenda," while Jerry Falwell and also the Christian Coalition released statements respectively arguing that *Ellen* and its sponsor and viewer-supporters were "degenerates" who were "way out of the mainstream."[29]

The tension that these criticisms bring to the surface is one that locates the programs' discursive shift from an "ordinary" to an expressly political one. Lesbianism, here, is presumed to "raise and represent" politics to the industry, program sponsors, and viewers. The lesbian is presumed to be a "political subject," in Gray's terms. And, if one presumes that lesbianism and the Midwest are, indeed, incompatible subjectivities then it follows that if an "authentic," "realist," "Middle American" program incorporated lesbianism into the text, then that program's own realism would be brought into question. Significantly, however—consistent with Roseanne's expressed understanding of her audience, above—viewers did not follow the response patterns anticipated by the industry, sponsors, or outraged political action groups. Following the boycott, Disney's stock and viewership of *Ellen* both increased by ten percent. The "kiss" episode of *Roseanne* and the coming-out episode of *Ellen* garnered each series' highest ratings with over twenty and thirty-six million viewers, respectively. Indeed, as critic Matt Roush argued, the episode suggested that Roseanne "and her show continue to challenge an industry that assumes its audience can accept only so much truth."[30]

The somewhat more cynical take on this ratings popularity was that, in the most commodity-conscious nation in the world, "lesbianism now sells"—that, no longer countercultural, commodity lesbianism is hip and "hip *is* the franchise," having become "a consumer mandate."[31] Overall, however, while critics on the Right argued that *Ellen* and *Roseanne* veered "sharply away from both the common sense and moral intuition of Heartland Americans,"[32] the programs countered with the charge that the most palatable Middle-west is a queered Midwest. They suggested that "maybe lesbianism has become a lifestyle that squares can dig, too."[33] Thus, *Roseanne* and *Ellen* embraced and represented, exactly, the fears of Jerry Falwell and his ilk, while having the satisfaction of calling those critics out as culturally insignificant, tasteless squares.

Outing the Midwest in Roseanne *and* Ellen

The April 30, 1994 episode of *Roseanne*, titled "Don't Ask, Don't Tell," chronicles Roseanne Connor's and her sister Jackie's trip from their hometown of Lanford, Illinois to Elgin for a Friday night on the town at a gay bar with their friend Nancy (played by Sandra Bernhard) and her partner Sharon (Mariel Hemingway). While Roseanne begins the episode demonstratively vocalizing her "coolness" with the trip and her wisecracking ease around her lesbian and gay friends, when Sharon kisses her at Club Lips, she becomes threatened and confused. The remainder of the episode explores Roseanne's attempt to examine her own fears and desires, and to recuperate her "cool" status within the group and for viewers, thus enabling her return to "unruly" form the following week.

In this episode, the audience is clearly encouraged and, indeed, presumed to identify sympathetically *with* Roseanne's "uncool" reaction even as, early in the episode, it is meant to ally with the still-cool Roseanne's pronouncements: that lesbians have better taste in women than straight women do in men; that most straights are really uncool and puritanical; and that lesbian couples can be just as fuddy-duddy traditional as any straight middle-American couple. However, the fact that Roseanne and her friends must relocate to the nearest urban outpost to openly enact their identities, in combination with Roseanne's and her husband Dan's reactions throughout the program concerning what constitutes sexual "norms"—specifically, their expectations and hopes for the "normative," "straight" behavior of their children—make it clear that there is really no place for a sustained lesbian presence in Lanford.

For the first third of the episode, Roseanne promotes a familiar liberal humanist line that lesbians are "just like us" by transferring clichés about homosexuality and outing onto straights. When Nancy reluctantly introduces Sharon by stating that she hasn't introduced her to *any* of her friends, Roseanne counters, "Oh, you mean any of your *straight* friends, right? Because you've never been able to accept our alternative lifestyle. Well, it isn't a choice you know!" Roseanne also teases Jackie about her forthright trepidation regarding the club trip, pretending to be Jackie's partner while at the bar and teasing, "you don't have to hide our love." Roseanne's affinity with lesbian "culture" is, further, signified by her enthusiastic dancing and "teaching forty people to do the monkey." Lesbian chic is, here, explicitly allied with bodily expression and popular cultural conversance. As Roseanne notes, "I studied [dance]. In my living room, with the *Solid Gold* dancers."

However, while Roseanne's character starts out with great bravado about how "cool" she is, in the aftermath of a same-sex kiss, she is, figuratively and literally, made into the episode's comedic "straight woman." Thus, in "Don't Ask, Don't Tell," Roseanne Connor and star Roseanne's weekly "unruliness" is put to its limit.[34] Lesbianism is, within the rules of this episode's narrative, posited as inherently more indeterminate, challenging, demonstrative, and *interesting* than Roseanne's comparative "squareness." The morning after the kiss, Roseanne's distress is signaled by her diligent scrubbing of the Lunch Box diner. Now, Jackie gloats, "it's not so awful that the kiss freaked you out; you're just not as cool as you thought you were." In attempting to save face, Roseanne transfers her anxiety back onto Jackie ("Oh, I'm not cool? You're the one sitting there at the bar telling everyone you're from PBS doing research!") and then onto her husband, Dan, claiming that *he* will be threatened and jealous and might, potentially, act out on Sharon. When Jackie presses Roseanne on this point, Roseanne snaps, yelling "I am *not* gay!" just as Nancy enters and then quickly leaves the room. In the climactic scene, Roseanne apologizes to Nancy and attempts to reestablish the new limits of her "coolness."

Roseanne's feelings of indeterminacy and threat finally force her to admit that she's really hip only within the rather circumscribed context of Lanford, stating, "I'm still pretty cool you know, for a forty-one year old mother of three that lives in Lanford, Illinois. I like that Snoopy Dogg Dogg." Roseanne's mistaking Snoop Dogg for "Snoopy Dogg Dogg" is not only funny, but politically purposeful, as it reinscribes her midwestern heterosexuality and whiteness *as* uncool markers of that which lacks of contemporaneous cultural fluency, while also positing African American culture and homosexuality as analogous, "hip," urban, minoritarian social and cultural voices. Roseanne thus explicitly invokes tropes of Blackness (*as* cultural currency allied with hip hop) to begin to recuperate her "cool" credibility, while also "safely" circumscribing her unruly potential for the audience (in familiar, consumable, market terms).

The program's epilogue fully reinstates Roseanne's unruly coolness by intimating that she is (hetero-)sexually accomplished and voracious, and by transferring any residual "issues" from her onto Dan. As Dan begins to fantasize about Roseanne's and Sharon's interaction, Roseanne turns the tables by invoking the image of "a lot of men there, too, with hard bodies, kissing." Thus provoking Dan's "common sense" threatened revulsion, Roseanne stands, restored, in judgment of him. However, lesbianism becomes the limit-test of Roseanne's capacity for cultural critique. In relation to lesbianism, Roseanne Connor is truly *not* unruly.

The November 19, 1997 episode of *Ellen,* entitled "Emma," takes the question of where queerness may "logically" reside as its comic conceit, specifically skewering broader cultural clichés regarding the British (as necessarily affiliated with "high culture"), Hollywood (as thoroughly gay and comfortable with that), and the Midwest (as squarely affiliated with "low" culture and that which the queered must flee). The episode features Emma Thompson in an Emmy Award–winning guest spot wherein she plays herself—the famed British actress, Emma Thompson—but with a fictional twist or two. Early in the episode, Ellen happens upon Emma in a passionate same-sex kiss. Ellen comes out as a lesbian to Emma, hoping that it will encourage her to come out herself. Thompson finally agrees to come out publicly at a Hollywood awards dinner, but is soon dissuaded by the thought that, once out in the open, *all* of the secrets of her life will soon be divulged by the Hollywood press and a gossip-hungry public. Thompson perceives that this would lead to the most horrific possible revelation, causing the immediate end of her career. But what could possibly be more disastrous than the renowned public figure's admission of homosexuality? That which is more ghastly—that which, within the episode, leads to Thompson's immediate, precipitous, career-killing slide down a descending scale of professional and social value—involves her "outing" her true geographic alliance and, therefore, her abject cultural, economic, and social worth. The revelatory scene plays as a coming-out confession, with Emma confiding in Ellen as they sit on the sofa in the actress's hotel suite:

> The truth is, there is something highly explosive about my past that I don't want anybody to know about, ever. . . . The fact is, I'm not, technically, British. If you must know, I was born in Dayton, Ohio. . . . Say something—please! I see the way you're looking at me—you find me disgusting. . . . Oh, I can't come out to the world tonight—I can face telling them I'm gay, you know, Hollywood people can deal with that. But there *is* no "Dayton Chic!"

Emma comes out . . . as a native midwesterner.

Ellen's previous encouragement turns to wariness, as she notes, "You know, maybe you're right—maybe the world isn't ready for this."

In this episode, the comedy of inversion at play is compounded by Thompson's "known" identity as an Academy Award–winning British citizen with associated affinities for all things high-cult (particularly, notes Ellen, projects "based on the novel by Jane Austen, and one based on a short story by Jane Austen, and then . . . "Jane! The Musical"). Emma's "naturally" classy affinities make her outed, midwestern fall from grace twice as fast and twice as hard. In fact, up to the point of Emma's admission of her true identity, Ellen is flustered and in awe in the face of the actress's native high-cultural cache, formal carriage, and attire. As a lesbian *and* a Brit, Thompson represents, to Ellen, the pinnacle of high style and chic. When Emma agrees to come out at the lifetime achievement awards dinner, Ellen rationalizes that her professional achievements and alliance with the capital that accrues "naturally" to Britishness should protect her, arguing that "English people are [after all] smarter than regular people." Being British is innately linked with both high culture and with homosexuality, in Ellen's imagination (or, at least, with strategic modes of silence around homosexuality). Says Ellen, to Paige, her friend who works for a studio's public relations department, "I'm sure they'll support her. I mean, it can't be a very homophobic country with all those men running around named Terry and Vivian."

But, Emma's real "explosive secret" *will* guarantee that she never works in the film industry again. As soon as Thompson's native midwesternness is revealed, she rapidly descends the slippery slope of cultural, occupational, and sartorial hierarchy. Emma now drinks Thunderbird instead of gin, admits to expertise at square dancing, and is soon wearing the modest attire that her new waitressing career expects and affords. The program thus balances between a very thinly masked critique of the dangers of coming out in Hollywood—as experienced by DeGeneres herself six months prior to this episode's airing—and the relatively easy, consensual laughter brought about by the audience's understanding that "the industry" does not value the "flyover" audience or its presumed tastes and cultural proclivities. The implicit argument made here, then, is that the so-called "liberal media elite" is no more accepting of or enlightened about sexuality than any other business. But *Ellen*'s critique of industry homophobia is transferred, here, onto a more broadly consensual flyover phobia. It is, after all, only Emma's outing as a "Daytonite" that guarantees her descent from heralded Oscar winner to hounded waitress.

Elayne Rapping argued, shortly after *Roseanne*'s "Don't Ask, Don't Tell" episode aired, that the program was "politically audacious because it did *not* lecture the vast majority of Americans who are, yes, queasy about homosexuality." Notably, this was the most watched episode in *Roseanne* series' history, presumably by a lot of "Middle America." Says Rapping:

> It presented [this audience] with a mirror image of their own confusion and anxiety and led them to a position of relative comfort about it all, by sympathizing with their very real concern about radical social and sexual change.[35]

In this light, it is likely the greatest strength of the episode that Roseanne does "play it straight." Similarly, *Ellen*'s post-coming-out episodes were marked by knowing invocation and play with the most conventional, "common sense" clichés regarding presumed gay sensibilities and cultural affinities as these were *expressly* opposed to a presumed midwestern disposition. The final season demonstrated a newly energized "institutionally critical and self-aware" mode of address that, now structured its comic conceit as a performance of "gay panic" in relation to heterosexuality, Baptists, midwesternness, and "low," déclassé cultural activities and investments. In order to cast Ellen's lesbianism as "something potentially assimilated into the repertoire of romantic and personal situations replayed weekly on the prime time sitcom," midwesternness was "queered," positioned as an "interruptive force," "illogical" as a home to or shared subjectivity with lesbianism.[36]

Niche Identities in a Flyover World

Ellen DeGeneres's return to television in the fall of 2001 with the CBS series *The Ellen Show* (2001–2002) extended, if softened, this conceit. *The Ellen Show* placed Ellen at the center of an ensemble of sweet, simple squares, in relation to whom she was the lone stylish, consumer-savvy, urban-identified character—a lesbian slumpy among Heartland flyovers. According to DeGeneres, viewers do not want to see "educational and funny . . . I think people want to sit at home and turn on their TV and just laugh." With this in mind, DeGeneres set out to make lesbianism a non-issue in the program, as far as political expression was concerned, though, as detailed below, the program casts the character's lesbianism as her "difference" from the show's other characters, based in Ellen's comparative consumer savvy and cultural fluency.

DeGeneres promoted the series as a throwback to the MTM sitcoms of the 1970s, explicitly invoking *The Mary Tyler Moore Show* and *The Bob Newhart Show,* which respectively, at their core, featured a single woman who did not have much of a romantic life (something DeGeneres insisted upon for the character, following her last series' experience), and a sane protagonist surrounded by a group of kooky characters. Critics promoted the show in these terms, noting that Ellen's character "might as well be named Mary Richards, . . . She is just a very nice person with a wry sense of humor . . . There is nothing daring, stylistically innovative or breakthrough about *The Ellen Show,*" and, identifying the program as "closer still to one of Bob Newhart's hit comedies."[37] While linking DeGeneres's star persona with Moore and

Newhart, critical reviews of the program also linked the program's setting as integral to its "gentle" "retro" appeal: "Clark is frozen in time, a newfangled Mayberry. . . . The townspeople are so clueless and nonchalant about diversity, they look and act like liberals."[38] And, *The Ellen Show* sets its wonderland in some Midwest small town . . . we didn't realize we'd missed so much . . . a gentle sitcom . . . these characters don't overthink things—a welcome change of pace after so many sitcoms peopled by snippy, conniving slicksters."[39] States DeGeneres:

> Clark is this fantasy town that I wish existed. Everybody kind of congratulates her. Nobody has a problem. Nobody is shocked by it. It just is what it is and they accept her for who she is. And that's sort of what I love about small towns—there's just this kind of, everybody accepts everybody and it's not a big deal.[40]

Intriguingly, because of these characteristics, in critical press and interviews with DeGeneres, the program was presumed to be set in the Midwest, even though the town of Clark is never explicitly identified as midwestern, and according to any available cues within the program itself, it could not actually *be* in the Midwest. Expressly located "eighteen hours from L.A. on the 10-freeway," the closest Clark would come to the region is somewhere between El Paso and San Antonio, Texas. And yet, critics persisted in labeling the show midwestern due to its small-town setting, its "decidedly non-political," "non-issue-oriented" subject matter (read: Ellen's lesbianism is not and never will be the focal point of any episode), and its supporting characters' profoundly straight, white, square, place-bound, lack of "taste" and consumer savvy.[41] The program was also described as Middle American due to its "old-fashioned," "bland and nonthreatening," "quaint" character, and for its "down-home warmth and naïveté," which is "comfortably entertaining" and not at all "sarcastic" or "mean-spirited"—characteristics presumed to be common to slumpy-skewing urban sitcoms. Following 9/11, CBS executives and DeGeneres additionally spoke of the program as a televisual equivalent to "comfort food." And, indeed, the program's highest ratings were earned in November and December of 2001, when it was the second-highest rated program for adults aged eighteen to forty-nine years old.[42]

While *The Ellen Show* was a "fish out of water" narrative—which focused on "Ellen Richmond's" return to her native Clark after failing

as a dotcom administrator—Ellen is, here, notably *not* a fish out of water because of her sexuality (though she is one of only two lesbians in
Clark—the other being the high school gym teacher), but because she is
the only character who is fluent in contemporary urban life and culture.
Ellen is also the only Clark resident who has traveled much at all outside of the city limits. Bluntly, Ellen is the only Clark resident with consumer clout, savvy, and good taste. Ellen's lesbianism is rarely referenced, but is cued visually, through popular cultural references to out
celebrities and gay icons: The room Ellen grew up in is adorned with
posters of Wonder Woman, Charlie's Angels, Billie Jean King, and work
by Georgia O'Keefe in the pilot episode. Later episodes feature posters
of k.d. lang, Melissa Etheridge, and Martina Navratilova.

Ellen's real "distinction," however, is established by her relationship
to urbanity and to the market. Ellen's urban chic is invoked, as in *Roseanne,* by her references to popular African American cultural expression, particularly as cued through reference to hip hop and soul music.
Such references bolster Ellen Richmond's "cool," "outsider" status in
relation to Clark residents. As in the *Roseanne* episode, invocations of
African American expression here also, in stereotypical fashion, underscore Ellen Richmond's comfort expressing herself bodily, and are used
to indicate a self-confidence and knowingness about the broader world.
This remarkably clichéd "way in which race, though itself a maligned
category on the contemporary political scene . . . can still function to
provide this kind of legitimacy to other forms of oppression when necessary"[43] both marks Ellen's lesbianism as qualitatively "different" and
is invoked to throw into relief the ways in which Clark is, resolutely,
"white space."

Visually, this "whiteness" is established during the opening credits,
which are animated and feature textured cut-out roadside images, in
bright teal, pink, yellow, and green color-schemes, suggestive of post-
cards from the 1950s. The titles track Ellen's drive east from Los Angeles to Clark, with characters from the show featured on the side of au-
tos, billboards, or buildings en route. The final images feature Cloris
Leachman (Ellen's mother, Dot) made into a roadside diner sign, holding a cherry pie. The titles close on the image of a sunset, American flag
and white picket fence, at the mailbox to Ellen's childhood home. The
titles thus visualize the small town as a pre-integration era, Rockwell-
meets-pop-art fantasy. Within the program itself, the starkest contrasts
to Ellen's own "hip" characterization also represent her "whitest,"

squarest foils: Ellen's former prom date Rusty and her co-worker Pam, the home economics teacher. Rusty's face adorns a Wonder Bread–type delivery truck in the opening credits sequence and he is a character who is completely out of touch with contemporary culture and, blankly, with himself in the program's diegesis—"being myself, that's just not my thing," he states.

As a knowing consumer extraordinaire, Ellen is consistently frustrated by Clark residents' comparatively simple desires and motivations, to comic effect. In "Muskrat Love" Pam, taunts, "Well, it looks like the city girl has found that life isn't all mochaccinos, bell-bottom pants and fancy sunglasses," to which Ellen replies, "I don't think that's what life is. It's also nice cars and full-body scrubs." While all of Ellen's co-workers shop at "Folksy Fashions" and "Fun Casuals," Ellen balks, claiming such outfits would make her "feel like John Lithgow in *The World According to Garp*." "Ellen's First Christmas" features a trip to the local mall with her visiting Aunt Mary (Mary Tyler Moore), with whom Ellen commiserates that in Clark "the Gap is just a space between two stores."

Of course, the potential problem with constructing lesbianism, coastal consumerism, and cultural production as analogues is that such representation embraces and reifies stereotypes of the materialistic, trend-driven gay consumer, and of a bi-coastal "media elite" out to deconstruct, undermine, or permanently overturn Heartlander mores. As seen above, in fact, a central theme running through the reams of popular press coverage of the *Roseanne* and original *Ellen* series' episodes—both positively and negatively—coalesced around questions of regional and cultural distinction. The felt *threat* at stake in calls for boycotts of Disney or the expressed "outrage" of groups such as Focus on the Family would appear to be an insecurity regarding the point at which midwestern viewers might be queered by such programs—made over as a newly indeterminate population, receiving "outside" ideas and values through these series' market-driven cultural politics. In debates about the consensual ideals that define (or should define) America, forged around these television programs, the Midwest became iconic of one of the two, competing, irreconcilable myths of the American Dream—that which imagines an America made up of Edenic small towns with Main Streets featuring church steeples and populated by nuclear families with homes, yards, and picket fences—indeed, this is how *The Ellen Show* imagines Clark. Lesbianism, by contrast, became iconic of the other competing myth of the American Dream—that which imagines the success of individual self-actualization, self-awareness, and spatial, economic, and cultural mobility—that which could not conceive of Rusty's claim that being himself just "isn't him" and wouldn't dare shop at Fun Casuals.

In October of 2003, an episode of *South Park* titled, "South Park is Gay," imagined the final extension of the "threat" implied in *Roseanne, Ellen,* and *The Ellen Show.* The episode suggests that, through televised exposure to "HBC's" *Queer Eye for the Straight Guy* (based on the Bravo series, 2003–2007), the nation would be destroyed from within, effectively turning America's "rugged, manly" men into "whiny little wusses" through the trickle-down of "metrosexual" style from its "natural" home in gay enclaves to its new availablity at South Park Mall's Express for Men. Indeed, when the residents of South Park "buy in" to metrosexuality, they lose their "core" identity and authentic claims to civic responsibility. For example, the first (and, presumably last) "Metrosexual Pride Parade" ends in a disastrous fire that threatens to destroy Main Street.

South Park's "metrosexualization" leads to a crisis of identification, particularly for Kyle and for Mr. Garrison. Kyle loves to be a "dirty boy" and has a terrible time giving up football and his ear-flapped hat. The gay Mr. Garrison is outraged at how "his" culture has been co-opted and depoliticized through the straights' new consumption practices. Both characters thus turn to Chef, their "natural" ally and expert counsel to resolve their identification dilemma. As the community's arbiter of cultural authenticity and co-optation, by virtue of being African American, Chef articulates the program's theme that, from a consumer perspective, "gay is the new Black," Chef knows a new fad when he sees one.

> *Kyle*: Oh my god. This is not a fad—this is who we are.
> *Chef*: No it's not. Last year you children were all trying to be Black, now you're all trying to be gay. . . . don't buy into this fad, Kyle. Be who you are—not what's cool.

Later, when confronted by Mr. Garrison, who asks, "What did *you* do, when white people stole *your* culture?" Chef responds, "Oh, well, we Black people just always try to stay out in front of them."

Here, Chef states what remains implicit in *The Ellen Show*—that "authenticity" is not faddish or cool but is, instead, reflective of a core stable inherently "white" identity, and that "gay" and "Black" are, conversely, cool, but unstable, faddish, and, generally, "unfit" modes of identification outside of the urban coasts. In classic *South Park* fashion, all political "sides" here are skewered evenly. And yet, the program exposes the problematic "politics" of each of the earlier incursions of lesbianism into prime time. Here, in the parodic program, and elsewhere in the "controversial" TV event, gay and lesbian life and culture can only be imagined as frivolity and "style," while "authentic," self-actualized citizenship is "removed" from fashionable conversance— it is square, but "straight."

As Becker argues, into the early 2000s, "anxious to uncover new markets and more effectively build brand loyalty, marketers and commercial media outlets have tried to translate cultural differences into a panoply of consumer identities . . . In the process, such media have worked to erode a sense of cultural unity,"[44] in large part by reinforcing the idea that consumer choices mark one's civic identity and political commitments. As exemplified in the previous chapters—from Welk's "blue hair" fans opposed to a New Frontier elite to Minnesota's image as the "girl you'd want to marry" pitted against California's "flashy blonde you'd take out"—the Heartland midwesterner has, historically, functioned as a marker of "low" to "mid-cult" tastes and social capital, while also representing the level-headed ballast between the "exceptional" desires and ever-changing behaviors characteristic of either coast. As a *market* construct, therefore, the midwesterner has functioned as that which must be shunned to be truly fashionable *and* as iconographic of steady, pragmatic, "mass," majoritarian or mainstream tastes, typical to the "average" American.

As suggested in the previous pages, by the 1990s, such market constructs and allied consumer "choices" were increasingly promoted as having a *politics*. The "slumpy's" social liberalism, urban identification, and "edgy," stylish tastes, were—in public rhetoric from the Right—now allied with highly individuated, "elite," Clinton-esque, and Boomer-identified "special interests" that were focused on "difference." Such political rhetoric seemed supported if not stoked by marketers' portrayal of a contrasting "average" American, "mature" and rural-identified, whose mainstream tastes and class standing suggested a transhistorical subject, self-actualized, and invested, instead, in a "politics of social unity."[45] Imagined as resistant to "niche-ing" and highly individuated appeals, the midwestern consumer-subject was portrayed as focused on community and sincere bedrock U.S. values, whereas the slumpy consumer-subject embodied a historically contingent *anomaly*, in sway to playful performance of fads rather than commitment to choices that mattered.

While much recent scholarship on the "postwar emergence of neoliberal thought" has argued that "self-gratification is no longer defined in opposition to civility," as "consumers . . . can—and do—build civic identity and virtue through their consumption practices" (and corporations are encouraged to do the same),[46] the public, corporate, and industrial discourses surrounding "controversial" incursions of "lesbian" identity in prime time offered politically conservative voices the opportunity to, *rhetorically,* deny this seamlessness, arguing instead for an imagined political order that was *only* "at home" in a Heartland portrayed as *transcendent* of the market. Such rhetorical moves relied, of course, on effacing both the market realities of the Midwest and its diversity of consumer types, as well as on obfuscating any connection between the neo-liberal civic-consumer bond and its historical promotion through policies fostered and supported, in large part, by "new Right" legislation and presidential leadership. As outlined in detail in the epilogue, the traditional "Big Three" broadcasters appropriated this consumer-identity-as-politics logic, allying themselves along a continuum, with ABC and NBC claiming to offer "programming with 'edge' "[47] speaking directly to the slumpy-identified niche of the 1990s and early 2000s, while CBS proudly claimed to be the last "mass" audience broadcaster, evoking earliest broadcasters' claims to follow a "moral obligation" to program for "underserved" audiences in the face of new market and industrial realities.

Across these texts' rhetorical, political, consumer, and industrial appeals, what is at stake in the larger unwillingness to imagine lesbian and gay life and culture *beyond* the urban coastal (or at least slumpy-identified) market and the performance of style? How might we, further, interrogate the apparent inability to conceive of lesbianism at home in the Midwest, or, critically, to even imagine "middle-America" as being a viably progressive cultural or political entity? What are the politics of stasis, invisibility and retreat that are rationalized by these myths of identification and place and how do they limit our ability to think "queerly" about those myths? What larger, real, political impact have these market constructs of commodity lesbianism or "metrosexual" style and this

insistent mythology of the desired and disdained Heartland and its endearing *and* abject squares encouraged? If the "flyover" audience is presumed not-niche-able and, therefore, unidentifiable or "invisible" in an
era when, arguably, "citizenship becomes an effect of market incorporation," whereby "only consumer-citizens are truly enfranchised,"[48] then
a good deal of the "threat" of these programs and their presumptively
"niche" appeals (especially considering *Roseanne*'s historic claims to
quality and relevance based on critiquing such niche-strategies) might
be located in their audience's felt isolation from the *market,* expressed
as a politics of resentment in a political climate where "straight panic"
remains, broadly, "acceptable" discourse.

A key dilemma here is that, through market tropes, institutional and
critical discourses assert that homophobia is a problem of incompatible
style or taste cultures, rather than of institutional disenfranchisement
and intolerance. Further, these discourses propose that homophobia
is, in any event, neatly contained, demographically, as it appears—in
broader popular and market discourse—to be "safely" symbolically circumscribed within the Heartland and geographically at home in the
Midwest. As Becker notes, "shifting political sensibilities and identifications that coalesced during the 1990s" were expressly identified and
gained traction *as* a "divide between cosmopolitan liberals and heartland conservatives—between the 'us' that apparently control the media
and don't have a problem with two dudes kissing, and the 'them' who
feel disenfranchised by mass media and do have a problem with two
dudes kissing."[49] Jon Kraszewski has succinctly identified the danger in
such vivid "common sense" and yet perilously simplified conflations of
cultural geography and political ideology. His argument—a reading of
The Real World's use of rural conservatives to expose racism—applies
here, positing that lesbianism is commodified in these discourses to encourage slumpy identification and ego-gratification, while simultaneously absolving

> the audience of any implications in [homophobia] by blaming rural
> conservatives for the problem . . . by using discourses about the rural
> United States and conservatism to construct [homophobia] as a prob-
> lem of individual opinions, the show as well as the channel overlook the
> systemic nature of [homophobia] and the way it operates in liberal ur-
> ban environments.[50]

The "niche" versus "flyover," "divided America" discourse energizing debates over these programs, their intended audience, and their broader cultural and historical significance, was not monolithic during the 1990s, however. While this "divide" was frequently at stake in entertainment appeals, news events of the period forced a reassessment of Heartland value to the nation-at-large similar to that which occurred in the 1970s.[51] Indeed, while comedies of the 1990s and early 2000s frequently "played" with gay and lesbian identity as slumpy capital and performance of style at home in glamorous urban coastal milieu (if, increasingly, "sold through" to Target shoppers elsewhere), *news* coverage of traumatic national events overtly disdained niche-address to appeal to "mass" viewing audiences and to posit national values as native to "flyover" country and definitive of shared U.S. ideals. Specifically, chapter 6 explores television and broader popular discourses of the Heartland as these informed news, documentary, and anniversary coverage of the April 19, 1995 Oklahoma City bombing. These discourses encouraged an idealized notion of national unity that was rooted in the Heartland and revivified through "norms" based on heterosexual, familial reconstitution. While the "mass" flyover viewer might momentarily identify as "slumpy," the "commodity lesbian" could *not*, such discourse implied, be recuperated or restored to Heartlander status.

6

Fertility Among the Ruins
Reconstituting the Traumatized Heartland

While previous chapters have focused on populist media address and aesthetics and on the documentary as a genre, this chapter merges these concerns by examining "anniversary journalism" coverage of the Oklahoma City bombing of April 19, 1995. Barbie Zelizer defines anniversary journalism as a distinct genre of news story, "generally organized around anniversaries" in the interest of commemoration. Such programs are telling with regard to the culture at large as "the tone and content of televised recollections" reflects "larger moods and concerns at the time of each anniversary." [1] Anniversary journalism is closely analyzed here as a category of news and documentary programming whose narratives and images are conventionalized from anniversary to anniversary. These conventions vary between sites of celebration or trauma, however, according to broader mythologies of place. That is, anniversary journalism draws heavily upon geographically based myths and values that are presumed to define the place impacted by triumph or trauma in order to contextualize and explain the event's broader symbolic value to a national audience.

Specifically, this chapter examines anniversary coverage of the Oklahoma City bombing as aired in a five-year period that represents a discrete moment between the initial horror of the event itself and the events of September 11, 2001—a day which has recast all subsequent coverage in comparative terms (e.g., the Oklahoma City bombing is now often mentioned as a "precursor to 9/11" and anniversary coverage since 2001 has focused on the bombing through this lens). Anniversary coverage of the Murrah Building bombing was the first to work through and to establish formal and narrative conventions for representing the domestic impact of terrorism. Thus, this chapter provides a template for thinking through and interpreting current and future commemorations of subsequent national traumas such as 9/11, but also disasters such as Hurricane Katrina. These events, when commemorated, will be most productively read for their continuities and contrasts with the conventions initially established in the Oklahoma City programs.

While anniversary coverage is characterized, broadly, by a "populist" attention to "ordinary" people who rose to extraordinary heights and sacrifice in service to others during a disaster and in the resurrection of community thereafter (e.g., the heroic tales of "first responders" characteristic to each of these anniversaries), pre-9/11 Oklahoma City coverage also drew upon and reiterated conventions, established in previous chapters, that posited an additional, particularized "Heartlander" *difference* from coastal and demonstratively diversified urban areas. This "difference" is based, across these programs, in the imagination of Oklahoma City as a place that is presumed to be sacred and innocent in the face of terror. In other words, Oklahoma City anniversary journalism positioned the city as sacred and innocent, as opposed to previous disaster sites that were, comparatively, "profaned" by their worldliness. The events of 9/11 have now shifted this view, primarily through an energized discourse regarding the everyday exceptionalism of individuals in response to the day's events in a broadly regional, "shared" context (from New York to the District of Columbia to Pennsylvania). That is, a comparison of anniversary narratives from 9/11 comes much closer in tone to Oklahoma City coverage than, for example, the coverage of the World Trade Center bombing of 1993. However, while coverage of Oklahoma City always connects individual heroism and character *to* place as innately related to one's native Heartlander status, this is not the case in coverage of New York's "first responders," whose heroism is, instead, typically posed in terms of *class* logics and work ethic, independent of regional nativity.

Oklahoma City anniversary journalism is thus informed by a particularized fantasy of exceptionalism, based in place, which is notable for that which is *absent* from its story of the bombing and its representations of the community. Anniversary journalism, thus, recounts a powerful "preferred narrative" articulated through regional mythology. This allows televised specials to remain commemorative in honoring the victims of the bombing and restorative in recounting the survivors' stories and the community's resurrection. And yet, in doing so, they encourage a particularly selective representation of community and collective memory—one that is, additionally, problematically, raced and heteronormative.

Edward Linenthal, whose *The Unfinished Bombing: Oklahoma City in American Memory* analyzes the history of the event and the development of the Oklahoma City National Memorial, notes that narratives of "innocence" are particularly tenuous in the context of the "Buckle of the Bible Belt" where "the notion of human innocence goes against religious teaching" (given the Christian doctrine of original sin).[2] Additionally, anniversary coverage left out news events surrounding the bombing and its aftermath that would have incorporated the early, local, "rush to blame Muslims for the bombing."[3] Thus, the consistent positioning of Oklahoma City and its citizens as *innately* innocent occupants of a newly violated safe space forces the question that, considering "significant portions of our citizens"—particularly African Americans (especially in light of Katrina and its aftermath)—"have long known that there is no zone of safety, that there are no innocent spaces,"[4] who is at "home" in the Heartland? And, to what extent is its reconstitution *as* such also a rush to reconstitute the white nuclear family as iconic of "all-American" safety and innocence?

Anniversary Journalism in the Heartland

During the third week of April from 1996 to 2000, cable and network news series turned their cameras on Oklahoma City, in specials that commemorated the April 19, 1995 bombing of the Alfred P. Murrah Federal Building. These programs encouraged and buttressed shared national outrage at the event by "localizing" Oklahoma City's image—inscribing the metropolitan capital as the epitome of the imagined pastoral Middle-American Heartland. Although it has been proposed that the "major category of television is time" and that television's "insistent 'present-ness'" allows it to jettison the past to deal with "the potential trauma and explosiveness of the present," these bombing anniversary programs re-contextualize national tragedy in terms of residual notions of local community and traditional geographic mythology.[5] In anniversary journalism the major category of television is, in fact, *place*. Televised commemorative accounts each contextualized the shock to Oklahoma City in terms of its rupture of the illusion of an idealized American middle landscape and worked to reconstitute the Heartland as an imagined rural American safe space, untouched by the contemporary, "worldly" strife *expected* to be visited upon the country's primary coastal urban centers.[6]

Anniversary coverage of the bombing and its aftermath imagine Oklahoma City to be a residual touchstone—a sacred place rightfully separated from modern traumas due to its spatial isolation from America's centers of culture, finance, and politics. This geographic separation is represented as having fostered shared time- or tradition-bound community values "massively linked with the rural aspects of regional life and hence with the past and with a kind of cultural nostalgia for old folkways, values, and customs."[7] Anniversary coverage thus uses television's space-binding technological capabilities (uniting a shared, national audience in simultaneous viewing, across different time zones and variegated continental and extra-continental locales) to recall a "pre-televisual," place-bound community.

In anniversary programs, Oklahoma City represents the national dream of the "American sublime": A frontier "virgin land and a life of peace, serenity, and community;" a site characterized by balance between nature and humankind, resistant to being drawn into the modern machinery of the more "Faustian and rapacious" side of the American character—"the desire for power, wealth, productivity and universal knowledge, the urge to dominate and remake the world" presumed to mark the metropolitan centers on either coast.[8] Prior to the bombing, it is implied, Oklahoma City had "insulate[d] itself from technology's more destructive consequences by projecting a zone, a spatial place, outside of and independent of the destructiveness of industrial society. . . . It remained the middle landscape, the zone of peace and harmony."[9]

Oklahoma City's catastrophe of April, 1995 thus threatened to point out the exceptionally tenuous nature of the myth of the American sublime. This national desire for a safe, revered, residual place, and the fear induced by the exposure of this desire's impossibility are illustrated in two articles in an April 24, 1995 edition of *The New York Times*. While President Clinton's memorial service remarks characterize Oklahoma City as a uniquely pastoral place where everyone is on a first-name basis, living in a town of "neighbors and friends . . . the church and P.T.A., . . . civic clubs and the ballpark,"[10] an article entitled "New Images of Terror: Extremists in the Heartland" acknowledges that the bombing proves that America's sacred, as well as "profane," spaces are now vulnerable and, by extension, the defining national myths that constituted them as such. According to Douglas Simon, a political scientist at Drew University and consultant to the *Times,* "any place can be targeted. After all, this wasn't New York or Los Angeles. It was the Heartland of America."[11] Equally, *The Minneapolis Star-Tribune* warns, "If it can happen on a street in Oklahoma City, it can happen in Minneapolis or Fargo, Madison or Duluth."[12]

Thus, in anniversary narratives the inconceivability of the bombing hinges, in part, on the fact that April 19, 1995 now represents the day the "outside world" of destructive technology and overt political agendas came to the Heartland—wreaking terror and havoc upon the last safe American space, destroying the pastoral equilibrium, and unjustly adding Oklahoma City's name to a list of sites such as Los Angeles and New York, which were already understood to represent worldly targets with established histories of trauma from both domestic and external perpetrators. The Heartland's unique status here is grounded in two specific, central distinctions from the metropolitan locales with which it would otherwise be lumped as "American site of terrorist attack." First, Heartlanders are presumed to be innocent in their loss: The threat to the Heartland community is explicitly understood to have come from outside its borders, generated by individuals who do not share the values of Oklahoma City's citizens and do not take part in these citizen's everyday routines. Second, Oklahoma City rebuilds differently from America's metropolitan centers—its recovery is rooted in specific, place-bound, residual cultural ideals focused on family, church, and community self-sufficiency.

Popular press coverage of the bombing reinforces the Heartland's exceptionalism in relation to America's metropolitan centers. Typical is a story in *Time* magazine wherein author Nancy Gibbs' "The Blood of Innocents" argues that Oklahomans are familiar with trauma in the form of *natural* disasters, "those ugly storms that arrive across the prairie," but human-made, technologically wrought tragedy is foreign or, explicitly, "incomprehensible" in this apparently pre-modern, residual, rural place.[13] Barry Tramel of the *Daily Oklahoman* concurs, noting:

> We didn't have the Yankees or the Metropolitan Museum of Art or a 24-hour night life, but we had a place to fall in love and raise children and grow old. A place where the people were gentle and kind, and the living was easy and slow. . . . This [the bombing] made you wonder if

throwing a ball or bouncing a baby, chasing a pup or grilling a burger would ever be the same.[14]

Unlike America's bustling modern metropolitan, coastal centers, everyday life in the Heartland is *uniquely* characterized by pre-modern, Rockwellian American values of local continuity, "family values," a clear Protestant work ethic, and a corresponding staunch religious faith. Within this context, the technology that rebuilds Oklahoma City and its people, *within* the boundaries of traditional values and the local community is accepted as a common good (as that which returns the city to its essential character). However, rebuilding technology or strategies that would *revise* this Heartland ethic or local character are disdained as disruptive, unwelcome, outside forces.

To emphasize this distinction, post-traumatic coverage of events *outside* of the American Heartland were, until 9/11, strikingly, not reconstituted according to these same residual, local, communal ideals. I reference these events, specifically, not to conflate civil unrest and acts of terror, but rather to underscore the significant difference and relevance of cultural mythology regarding *place*—and a presumed innocence based in residual, rural, pastoral values—in subsequent anniversary coverage of traumatic events. For example, events such as the uprisings in Los Angeles in 1992 have been revisited only very quietly—primarily by local L.A. rather than national broadcasters—and have subsequently been discussed in terms of the city's reconstitution as a viable site within the national *marketplace*. As indicated by the mid-1990s publicity slogan, "L.A., It Works!," Los Angeles's post-uprising identity was inscribed as a corporate achievement. The city's identity was couched in *publicly*-oriented appeals to getting back to work and to profit in the world of things, rather than in terms of intimate human costs and shared community losses. Los Angeles and pre-9/11 New York City healed through innately mobile, public, market solutions or the triumph of finance capital, rather than through the place-specific, privatized Church, family, and face-to-face community solutions proposed to be the key to both Oklahoma City's "rebirth" and to the nation's sympathy and collective interest in that process. Non-Heartland traumas were localized and public, *not* simultaneously national and intimate. Through anniversary narratives, Oklahoma City literally becomes a place defined by recognizable faces and knowable victims who were not "complicit" in their trauma and loss.[15] As with Los Angeles's traumas, the 1993 World Trade Center bombing in New York City did not seem to have required the same attempts at community reconstruction as those made in Oklahoma City, presumptively because of its "limited" and innately more "international" character. Pre- and post-9/11, coastal metropolises and their citizens are presumed to live everyday life on "high alert" in harm's way. This sensibility is particularly stark in the now-common reference to "targeted" versus "non-targeted" areas (in spite of the lesson of Oklahoma City). Coastal, urban residents are thus, on some level, seen as culpable for choosing to live in such potentially dangerous locales.

The triumph of Oklahoma City in anniversary narratives is, thus, its unique commitment to "reaching back" as it rebuilds—its unwavering adherence to explicitly place-bound Heartland values of community self-sufficiency, church, home, maternity/family, and the prioritization of a mundane, quotidian existence rather than facility with or any interest in the world of things, individual aggrandizement, and/or mobility outside of Oklahoma City. One survivor has called this style of commemoration "a new standard, the Oklahoma Standard."[16] By 1998, this "Oklahoma Standard" had migrated into fictional prime time series programming where Oklahoma City continues to serve as the exemplary Heartland locale: A place-bound and thus necessarily time- and tradition-bound touchstone that all Americans are presumed to desire, but with which they only actually affiliate on ritualized memorial dates through the momentary shared community imagined via televised travel.

This chapter thus analyzes anniversary coverage of the bombing on TV, in dialogue with newspaper and magazine accounts of the event, to outline the often hyperbolic ways in which Oklahoma City is "located," or firmly emplaced, to become the *tangible* image and place-bound site of the mythic American Heartland ideal. Specifically, anniversary specials remake the capital, from a modern, metropolitan hub into a residual, rural prairie town defined by and sanctified through its striking homogeneity: Oklahoma City thus becomes uniformly emblematic of pastoral American ideals of "small-town" life and traditional community ties—residual community based on face-to-face relations, forged at Church and across families. Good citizenship is understood as: fealty to the community as a self-sufficient entity and, correspondingly, disdain for movement outside of Oklahoma City; regular church attendance; and good parenting—particularly mothering—in the context of a stable, nuclear-family home. What is underscored here is the apparent national investment in this imagination of a Heartland home and its "more traditional" values rooted in intimate institutions and face-to-face, everyday relations forged through family, community, and faith. This is particularly significant when considering shared strategies and important contrasts in news and documentary specials regarding 9/11 and also Hurricane Katrina anniversaries.

A "Sacred Place . . . Burned Into the American Prairie"

Cultural geographer Kenneth Foote has recently argued that whereas "not so long ago" annual recognition of the Oklahoma City bombing and, especially the construction of a memorial at the site "would have been considered improper, almost an affront to a community's self-image. Now such a memorial is viewed as reflecting respect for the victims and their families and paying tribute to the community's ability to constructively respond to adversity."[17] The community's response is characterized by Foote as "convergence behavior" wherein, following a disaster, it vigorously reasserts a shared "sense of identity based on civic pride, ethnic or religious affiliation, and occupation that encourages" residents "to view the disaster as a loss to the group as a whole rather than as losses to isolated individuals and families."[18] Such convergence and sanctification are only possible in "those few situations where disaster inspires a sense of communal, collective loss" and is therefore limited to "small," "self-identified" communities that are "relatively homogeneous, socially and economically."[19] Thus, for the ritual commemoration of the Oklahoma City bombing to continue, and for it to have significant meaning, requires that the city itself be conceptualized as a limited, unified place that exhibits consensual values.

Paradoxically then, it is Oklahoma City's representation as a typical, mundane, self-sufficient, rural small town that allows for its annual inscription as an exceptional, nationally symbolic site—as *the* idealized Heartland. Televised anniversary specials and fictional representations of Oklahoma City thus have to actively *work* to inscribe the metropolitan center of the state as innately "rural"[20] and to portray its diverse body of citizens as, in fact, relatively homogeneous. By undertaking this work, televised anniversaries serve as the route for ritual, public, formal consecration of Oklahoma City as a sacralized site and for the communication of a shared national understanding of the city through the lens of the Heartland. Characteristic of anniversary journalism, the city's unique, sacralized status is primarily imagined through "pictorial repetitions" of key images, and is embodied through the repeated telling, in *each* commemorative special, of a few representative citizens' narratives.[21] These narratives are characterized by an overwhelming sameness that contributes to their identity as, unmistakably, one communal group that conforms, time and again, to a particular paradigm of "Oklahoma City resident." Exceptions to this sameness are thus thrown into high relief, underscoring what is shared and, thus, what remains "outside" of the bounds of accepted community behavior.

In five years' worth of anniversary specials aired on ABC, CBS, NBC, and CNN, Oklahoma City is consistently visually represented as a singularly rural locale. Because these specials primarily emphasize interior settings and medium close-ups of individual interviewees, the choices that are made for the representation of the external city-at-large seem particularly significant. Specifically, exterior shots of the city are selected so as to efface urban culture by emphasizing the capital's frontier, prairie-bound affinity with nature and with the residual, self-sufficient pioneering ideals that accompany such a milieu. For example, during a segment devoted to the reconstruction of the city's main downtown access artery, Robinson Avenue, *CNN Presents: Legacy of Terror* (CNN, April 14, 1996) explicitly imagines Oklahoma City to be an outpost of the American pastoral, self-sufficient community, symbolic of God's good earth. Reporter Tony Clark, introduced by program anchor Judy Woodruff as "a native Oklahoman," is dispatched "to his hometown to see how the city and its people rebuild after terror." Clark's segment, titled "Robinson Avenue," investigates the physical and emotional difficulties in rebuilding the area bound by this thoroughfare. The segment focuses on two primary locales: St. Paul's Methodist Church and the entire city block where the Murrah Building once stood.

Post-bombing, but prior to the ground-breaking of the Oklahoma City National Memorial, this block has, here, been returned to "prairie." The lot is completely flat, dusty, and grown over in spots by wheat-colored wild grasses. The church is itself riddled with scaffolding, but is primarily, visually represented as a successful, fully functioning "sanctuary for the community" as the camera lingers on shots of its stained glass windows and parishioners attending services, rather than on the labors of its reconstruction. Throughout the segment, each time

Clark's narration returns to the Church, the change in locale is prefaced by shots that feature stained glass windows, portraying a cross which appears to emit colorful rays of light and an image of Jesus extending open arms to those who enter the building.

Clark acknowledges other locales' stories as he guides the audience in a walk along Robinson amidst the remaining shells of shattered businesses. One stop is the Journal Record Building which had housed the accounting offices of interviewees Ken and Gail Klingenberg. Dating to the late 1800s, the Journal Record Building's "total loss"—combined with the bomb sites "return" to the range—literally represents Oklahoma City's alignment with a pre-modern America. While the bomb forced this condition on an unwitting community, it is Oklahoma City's innate frontier ethic and residual values that are simultaneously inscribed as its key to success in the rebuilding effort. The bombing has thus forced the city's physical return to a spirit that it had never lost: Oklahoma City's residual ethic makes it the best equipped American site to survive and thrive in the bombing's aftermath.

Indeed, the entire "Robinson Avenue" segment reads much like a cinematic western in the tradition of John Ford: Oklahoma City is the outpost community poised between civilization (represented by the Church, its family of parishioners, individual businesspeople of Oklahoma City, and visitors to the bomb site) and frontier/lawlessness (evidenced by the dust-bowl-evocative vistas and remnants of destruction up and down Robinson Avenue) between fences/streets and the expanse of wide-open range; between the good town-folk—determined to stick together as a community filled with safe daycare centers, churches, and workplaces that front Main Street/Robinson Avenue—and the evil bad men whose terror rained down upon the community from *outside* its borders. As if to make this analogy explicit, the segment opens with a long-shot of two unidentified men in ten-gallon hats walking amidst the Robinson Avenue rubble.

At the heart of this segment, Clark walks the audience down Robinson Avenue to "the bomb's beginning" where the Murrah Building once stood. Two balancing, slow-panning shots (the first from right to left and the second from left to right) reveal the bomb site. The second of these shots is dynamically framed, as jagged walls of reddish-brown, desert-evocative rubble fill the left-hand foreground while, in the upper-right-hand corner of the screen, St. Paul's steeple rises into the prairie sky. The church steeple, symbolic of the community that survives and remains self-sufficient, is now the tallest structure on this block. As the image track refocuses on the bomb site's flat, dusty lot, speckled with brush-like grasses, its sacralized status is literally underscored: The congregation of Methodist St. Paul's church sings the Doxology[22] on the soundtrack as the camera vertically tracks down the chain-link fence surrounding the bomb site, lingering on mementos that have been left in memory of victims and in tribute to their families (including a strand of pearls, bouquets of flowers, and then a single rose). Next, a man holding an infant in his arms is seen standing at the fence, as the infant reaches out and kisses an item left among the links, indicating the lasting, communal resonance and the event's multi-generational legacy.

A close-up of a Psalm affixed to the fence accompanies Clark's final address to the audience.[23] In this closing statement—punctuated by St. Paul's congregation's final resounding "Amen"—it is clear that Oklahoma City's successful recovery will inscribe the city as the apotheosis of the American dream of balance wherein Nature/the prairie is coequal with Culture/the capital. It is this achievement which promises to allow Oklahoma City's exemplary "local" identity to transcend to nationally sacred status as the epitome of the Heartland. As a shot of a U.S. flag flapping over the site slowly bleeds into a shot of the plains' sunset, Clark concludes, "It's a sacred place . . . a new national shrine burned into the American prairie."

In other anniversary specials Oklahoma City's frontier identity and prairie locale are similarly inscribed. For example, in *ABC News Turning Point: Rebirth—The Untold Stories of Oklahoma City* (ABC, April 18, 1996), the city's morning commute is photographed from the prairie outskirts—cars are surrounded by fields of grain at dawn (again, the wide-open range evokes a pre-modern America as it is bathed in sienna hues) as their progress into the city is accompanied by the sound of a mournful train whistle. Other programs such as *CNN Saturday Morning* (CNN, April 19, 1997) and *The Today Show* (NBC, April 19, 1996) focus on the frontier appearance and pioneering ethic of the center of the city by featuring footage of the remains of the Murrah Building and its demolition, and by underscoring the surviving community's "Day of Remembrance" with the pealing of church bells.

Most significantly, in all of the anniversary coverage during a five-year span, there is only one brief shot of the Oklahoma City skyline and this shot is itself contextualized as being somewhat unrepresentative of the community's identity—as potentially inauthentic in its iconographic reference to the modern, urban, "outside world." The skyline shot appears, ominously, at the opening of a segment of *CNN Presents: Legacy of Terror* titled "Murder and Mystery," wherein anchor Judy Woodruff and reporter Susan Candiotti question whether or not those in the world outside of Oklahoma City have the same sense of and capacity for frontier justice. "Outsiderness" is represented here by both the bombers, who traveled from elsewhere to wreak havoc upon the city, *and* by a federal government understood to have systematically disregarded what is important "out here in the hinterlands."

In *CNN Presents: Legacy of Terror* (CNN, April 14, 1996), the pre-titles opening montage features Oklahoma City resident, bombing widower, and newly single father Lyle Cousins asserting that, without a doubt, in spite of his solid commitment to the Church, "I don't think Tim McVeigh would survive with me in the same room." This sentiment is implied to be shared by the community-at-large as it is followed by video footage of McVeigh being led from a holding facility in Oklahoma City while flanked by almost a dozen FBI agents. All members of this entourage are wearing high-collared flak-jackets. Later in the same program, Regional FBI Director Bob Ricks comments that, locally, the Waco inferno and its anniversary (which shares the same date as the Oklahoma City bombing) had always been taken very seriously. Says Ricks, with obvious frustration and anger, "We tried to explain, it may not be important to Congress and the Beltway people have moved on to other issues in D.C., but out here in the hinterlands it [the anniversary of the Branch Davidian Compound's burning] became an extremely important issue." Woodruff and Candiotti, respectively reiterate: "Is another suspect still out there? Is the government doing enough to prevent *another* Oklahoma City?" and, "could there be others out there, still not caught?" The program's explicit critique of the national (mis-)handling of the bombing, coupled with local residents' forceful testimonials regarding their resolute *lack* of indecisiveness in punishing the bombing suspects, buttresses the portrayal of the "local" Heartland as a contrasting, sacralized, populist, unified, homogeneous site.

"People Who Worked in Cubicles"

The pioneering prairie-dwellers of Oklahoma City are thus conjoined in their necessarily rural, residual, insular self-sufficiency. Unlike Americans who live outside of the Heartland—particularly city-dwellers aligned with cosmopolitan mobility and with the material success of the world of things—the citizens of Oklahoma City are devoted foremost to the spiritual and human world of church, family, and community. In the Heartland, occupation is not definitive of one's identity or even necessarily expressive of one's expertise. It is, instead, simply a way to provide for one's family by making do, with little to no fanfare. It is an explicitly mundane, quotidian, even endearingly mediocre way of life. Combined, these recurring depictions of Oklahoma City's ordinariness —embodied in its citizens' daily attempts to just make do in order to get back home to the family and the Church—bolster the image of the Heartland's incontrovertible innocence in the bombing itself.

According to a *U.S. News and World Report* article published the week after the bombing, for instance, the attack was "a strike at the very heart of America," envisioned as a Middle-Landscape wherein

> the bomb landed among the people who served [the] government at its least exalted, most familiar level; people who worked in cubicles and stuck to their lunch hours, who made best efforts, modest livings, and small splashes. People whose real lives lay far away from the Alfred P. Murrah Federal Building. They were mothers . . .[24]

Paradoxically, this account and others like it overtly localize or intentionally distance the bombing's victims from the nation-at-large while simultaneously holding them up as a national ideal. That is, in spite of their status as, largely, federal employees, victims are described as people marked by their lack of investment in public life (as underscored also by the above critiques of the lack of federal awareness prior to the bombing and of the response in its aftermath). These are people who lead locally circumscribed, private lives, distinct and separable from these jobs or from attendant governmental concerns—people whose look toward home is also a reaching back to residual American traditions of self-sufficiency on the frontier.

Anniversary programs establish Oklahoma City's residual, quotidian life to underscore the violence and shock of the bombing, to emphasize its citizens' innocence in relation to the act, and to valorize the community's post-bombing re-inscription of "normalcy" according to privatized ideals. If representations of Oklahoma City as a rural, frontier community borrow conventions of the classical Hollywood western, the capital's exemplary mediocrity (its "least exalted," "most familiar" citizens who make "small splashes" and lead their "real lives" far away from the Murrah Building) and its pre- and post-bombing portrayal as Heartland idyll seem particularly indebted to the disaster film genre.

Across anniversary coverage, pre-bombing Oklahoma City and its citizens are established as representative of a mundane, everyday mediocrity and privatized turn toward home which is presented as characteristic of the Heartland way of life. Next, the bombing and its twenty-four-hour aftermath represent the extraordinary, unpredictable disaster that has been wrought by a force which is alien to the community. Finally, the post-bomb community is shown struggling to reconstitute normalcy with a renewed spirit of togetherness. The tragedy and "un-Americanness" of the bombing is, in this light, explained as the act's destruction—if, at best, only momentary—of the Heartland way of life constituted by private, heterosexual, reproductive family values. Specifically, the bombing left children without mothers and fathers and parents without children. Anniversary coverage is thus consumed with the reconstitution and reassertion of traditional family structure (and the resumption of gender-appropriate duties within that structure), maternal wholeness and successful pregnancy—in other words, the return to the roots or foundations of the quotidian Heartland's insular rural community and church bonds.

Anniversary programs visualize and authenticate the pre-bombing Heartland's way of life as residual, privatized, and mundane by featuring home videos, family photos, and survivor accounts of the day before and the day of the bombing. In particular, maternal voices are held in the highest esteem as the most trustworthy and the most heartfelt. That is, rather than foreground professional journalists' voices, or compete with one another by offering a particularly distinctive "visually-based . . . aesthetic based on an extreme self-consciousness of style,"[25] these programs exhibit an overwhelming sameness based on developing the national viewing audience's intimacy with the distinctly unexceptional, Heartland-specific "Oklahoma Standard," featuring local citizens' own voices and self-authored images.[26]

Each of the networks and CNN, in both prime time and morning specials, feature medium-close-up framing of one-on-one interviews with bombing survivors and family members that take place in these citizens' homes or in their churches. Each special features the same set of families and individuals, creating a storehouse of repeated images and, therefore, shared narratives of the bombing and its aftermath. Specifically, the programs analyzed here each seem to have made the conscious choice to pare down their technical capacity to dazzle audiences with the "bells and whistles" of news programming (flying graphics, elaborate titles, modern set design, etc.) to instead feature more ostensibly quotidian, populist forms of expression, and to shift the authorial voice within each program onto the survivors and their stories. These choices are exemplified by featuring Heartlanders' amateur home videos and family photographs, by letting citizens appear to speak for themselves without audible "guidance" by professional journalists, and through program segments briefly introduced and connected by reporters speaking from spare sets, or on-location from Oklahoma City itself.

ABC News Turning Point: Rebirth is exemplary of this spare, non-televisual, "amateur" aesthetic. In its opening title "Rebirth" is spelled out in Old English calligraphic script, pointing to both the Heartland as a sacred space (recalling as it does the typeface in the King James Bible) and to its impending fertile reconstitution. From a spare set, drenched in blue light, anchor Forrest Sawyer sits on a stool, flanked by acrylic blue walls that feature photo collages of the citizens of Oklahoma City. Sawyer introduces the program by asking, "What happens when *ordinary* lives are shattered by an extraordinary event? When ordinary people are caught in the glare of the national spotlight?" The program proceeds to reconstruct the evening and early morning just prior to the bombing by featuring home videos, family photographs, and point-of-view shots of the morning commute down Robinson Avenue into downtown. This pre-bombing section of the program features the stories of Edye Smith and her sons Chase and Colton, Erin Almon and her daughter Baylee, and Glenn Seidel, his wife Kathy, and their son Clint.

Home video of child victims Chase and Colton Smith and family photographs of victim Baylee Almon reconstruct their carefree innocence and playfulness in the hours before the bombing. Home video of Edye Smith's children features them at play at home on their way to school at the Murrah Building's America's Kids Daycare Center, and at play at the daycare center itself. It is implied but never explicitly stated (and it is doubtful) that the home video footage is synchronous with the program's chronology, representing Chase and Colton on the evening prior to and the morning of the bombing. Forrest Sawyer and mom Edye Smith both underscore the quotidian nature of the video images in voice-overs grounded in the everyday realities of the kid's behavior— "they were just running and romping through everything," Edye recalls. Erin Almon's story is introduced by comments by Sawyer that overlay Polaroid photos of Mom and daughter Baylee, face full of cake, on her first birthday. Says Erin Almon, "I was running after her the whole time trying to clean her off."

The pre-bombing segment proceeds to the morning of the bombing, reconstructing the commute and daily routine of a representative of the "more than five hundred employees" who worked in cubicles at the federal building. This segment features a sunrise shot of Oklahoma City's prairie outskirts, as commuter traffic drives by bound for downtown and a train whistle whines in the background. A family photo of victim Kathy Seidel, a secret service agent, is displayed on-screen. Next, Kathy's husband Glenn Seidel directly addresses the audience. Framed in medium-close-up, against the background of a waving grain field, Seidel recounts his banal pre-bomb morning discussion of Kathy's plans for after work. Next, a studio-portrait of Kathy and her son Clint fills the screen as Clint matter-of-factly says "she gave me a kiss and a hug. She went to work and I went to school." This sequence ends with more home video of Chase and Colton Smith in the car on the way to daycare and then inside the America's Kids Daycare Center itself. Sawyer's voice-over repeatedly returns to the totally typical nature of the day of the bombing with phrases such as "like most mornings," and "on a typical day," and "Colton was always happy to see two-year old Rebecca Denny."

CNN Saturday Morning constructs a similar vision of Oklahoma City's mundane, everyday, pre-bombing life as it recreates the morning of the bombing by intercutting different survivor's interviews recounting the moments before the bombing and their accounts of the explosion itself. This segment primarily features the voices of the mothers and wives of victims, interspersed with the commentary of Oklahoma City Fire Chief Jon Hansen, an expert emergency response professional who is yet undeniably localized and put on an equal plane with his "civilian" cohorts due to his expressed shock at the completely unexpected event.

In an interview conducted in a church meeting room, Caye Allen, wife of victim Ted Allen, recounts the totally typical morning prior to the bombing. Flanked from behind by stained glass windows and heavy, oaken woodwork, Allen's narrative of the couple's last goodbye connects her husband's persona with the frontiersman ethic of the Heartland featured across all anniversary programming. Caye laughingly describes Ted as a laconic, modern-era cowboy whose pick-up truck has replaced a trusty horse:

> He leaned over and said "I love you," and I said "I love you too." And he said, "Don't hit any curbs with my tires." And I said, "Ted! I *swear* you love this truck more than you love me." He just kind of started laughing and shook his head and kind of turned around and said "Geez, Caye" and walked into the [federal] building.

Next, Edye Smith, Jim Denny, Jon Hansen, and Marsha Kight each describe their reaction as they heard the explosion itself. Each witness describes the otherworldly and therefore alien quality of the event and their resolve to now "just make the best of our lives and go out and try to help other people make the best of their lives."[27]

According to these narratives, given that no one would have ever predicted that the bombing could have happened in the Heartland, Oklahoma Citians' grounding in everyday, quotidian values of the human world of family, church, and local togetherness has prepared them exceptionally well to reconstruct their lives in the event's aftermath. In an interview with anchor Joie Chen on *CNN Saturday Morning*, Veterans Administration psychologist Dr. Paul Heath, now president of the Oklahoma City Bombing Survivor's Association, calls this process of reconstruction and return "reaching a 'new normal.'"

> That . . . really means that we come to a place in our lives where we can fit all of the events, including April 19, 1995 and everything since into our lives without being distracted from our *everyday reality.* We call it "reaching a new normal." And that's our goal. We're not thinking in terms of never being able to remember it. [But rather] being able to fit it in to our new normal.

And yet, paradoxically, reaching this "new normal" often requires near-miraculous intervention—both divine and medical/technological—in order to reinstate mundane, residual cultural ideals of maternity, nu-

clear family, God and Church, and self-sufficiency to the newly victim-
ized Heartland.

Technology and Its Limits: Toward the "New Normal"

As indicated above, the "Oklahoma City Standard" of recovery takes
the form of shared, collective prioritization of *privatized* ideals of participation in Protestant church groups and the assumption of one's con-
ventionally expected roles within the traditionally defined heterosexual
nuclear family. Oklahoma City as Heartland is, thus, a site that is es-
teemed in anniversary coverage for its distinctive and envied turn toward home—historic American ideals of the hearth and Main Street, reinscribed for the 1990s as "the sphere of discipline and definition for
proper citizenship in the United States [which] has become progressively
more private, more sexual and familial, and more concerned with personal morality."[28] It is this style of citizenship that Oklahoma City epit-
omizes in television coverage that valorizes the Heartland as repository
of strong community tradition and bedrock "family values"—a rare site
of idyllic heterosexual reproductive sexuality, devout spirituality, and
traditional home life. The bombing thus literally *engenders* and locates
national outrage through the imaging of the privatized Heartland's vio-
lation and its struggle for familial-communal reconstitution and rebirth.

Four of the recurring family narratives throughout the anniversary
coverage most clearly exemplify the apparent desire to reconstitute quotidian Heartland life and domestic ideals, by almost any means necessary, in order to achieve the "new normal." The stories of recovery
which focus on Dana Bradley Bruce, Glenn and Clint Seidel, and Lyle
and Corey Cousins each contextualize their survivors' "rebirth" through
the intervention of locally and domestically circumscribed technology.
Technological intervention is, in these cases, "humanizing" and communal—the technology emerges from, and is used within, the bounds
of Oklahoma City itself, or is explicitly "domesticated" as a home-
based aid. These survivors' successes depend, equally, upon their fealty
to Church and their faith in the institution of marriage and in life-long
nuclear family ties. Alternately, accounts of Edye Smith's recovery serve
as cautionary tales of technological exceptionalism. Edye is portrayed as
having strayed outside the bounds of the Heartland community. She has

thus exceeded domestic propriety by flirting (if only momentarily) with the self-aggrandizement of public celebrity and mobility which inhere in trafficking in the world of things. Having slipped the bonds of the Heartland community, Miss Smith's public reconstitution positions her as an "outsider" in the bombing's aftermath.

In combination, across each of the anniversary programs, the crucial, recurring function of these stories is that they suggest a particular politics of "the normal" that is held up to be revered by the larger national viewing audience as a shared cultural fantasy of the ideal, mythical American middle-landscape that is located in the Heartland—an idealized "normal" of devoutly religious, privatized citizenship based on traditional, residual gender-roles within the "proper" nuclear family. The "new normal" of Oklahoma City would thus be the restoration of the American Pastoral—the self-sufficient, self-contained community and residual, familial ideals of a time-prior to the bombing. While necessarily aided by technology, then, the Heartland's "rebirth" must observe the ethic of the "middle landscape"—the proper balance between technological assistance from the "world of things" and the moral, spiritual, familial "human world" of the quotidian Heartland.[29]

By featuring the case of Dana Bradley Bruce, *CNN Presents: Legacy of Terror* illustrates the "appropriate," localized use of technology in the interests of maternal reconstitution. In the "new normal" Heartland, Mrs. Bruce literally embodies the hope that recovery can be achieved through the medical restoration of "wholeness," the sanctity of marriage, and new pregnancies that will guarantee the nuclear family's reconstitution. In Dana's case, "wholeness" is achieved through the provision of an artificial limb to replace the one she lost in the bombing, at the same time that her children and her mother were each killed. The program features footage of a press conference with Dana and local doctors at Oklahoma City's Sabolich Prosthetic & Research Center who provided the prosthetic leg, free of charge, to assist what correspondent Bonnie Anderson calls Dana's "tentative steps toward recovering her life." Here, technology emerges from the Heartland itself, in the service of familial restoration.

For Dana, marriage and a new pregnancy follow shortly on the heels of this surgical intervention, promising to rewrite some of the loss experienced as a result of her family's deaths. The program's report is, in fact, structured to indicate a fairly direct correlation between Ms. Bruce's successful adaptation to her new body—illustrated via a montage of physical therapy sessions and meetings with doctors—and her ability to "look to the future" in her embrace of a new marriage and pregnancy. Amateur video of Dana's wedding to "her high school sweetheart," Gabriel Bruce, in December of 1995 plays as the reporter acknowledges the couple's expectant parenthood. Ms. Bruce's physical restoration is thus made allegorical of Oklahoma City's own restoration of its maternal, familial, insular community ideals.

On the other hand, when Edye Smith required surgical intervention to allow her to once again become a mother after the loss of her two sons in the bombing, she came to represent "rebirth" in the technological and commercial extreme and, as such, suggested the potential limits of insider- versus outsider-status within the Heartland community. In *ABC Turning Point: Rebirth* Edye is singled out as a post-bombing anomaly. Says anchor Forrest Sawyer, explicitly comparing Mrs. Bruce with Mrs. Smith, "Edye and [ex-husband and current fiancé] Tony Smith were also trying to put their lives back together again, but in a *very public way.*" The next image is of Edye and Tony during their appearance on the *Leeza* talk show on which Tony proposed to Edye for the second time. Next, in a whirlwind montage featuring flash-cuts, quick-edits, and fast-motion photography—self-conscious stylistic choices that are absent from the rest of the program (or any of the other anniversary programs, for that matter)—Edye is shown trying on designer dresses, accepting *The National Inquirer*'s offer to pay for her wedding including travel to Hawaii, and at a Dallas press conference wherein a doctor announces his donation of his services to reverse the tubal ligation she had had after the birth of her sons, Chase and Colton.

Within Oklahoma City, Ms. Smith's public grief, growing celebrity, and increasing material gain following the bombing (including her for-profit sale of posters of her children, called "Edye's Angels") was seen as overstepping the bounds of local propriety, as being self-centered rather than communally or familially concerned. While gravitating toward Ms. Smith as an obviously photogenic and cooperative interviewee, anniversary programs tend to adopt this tone as well. Flatly, Ms. Smith's travels and extraordinary surgery to produce "kids that look like Chase and Colton," are portrayed as excessive and misguided in their transgression of Heartland values and mores. Ms. Smith's campaigns for remarriage, rebirth, and personal happiness are portrayed as appealing to personal gain in the "outside world" rather than to communal, familial local responsibility.[30]

In this context of both successful and more compromised narratives of maternal restitution, the newly single fathers featured in anniversary journalism seem to represent the magnification of tragedy and the extraordinary difficulty faced by Heartlanders in reconstituting everyday, mundane community and family life post-bombing. The success of these men, while overwhelmingly convincing and touching, also underscores the expectation that the Heartland "norm" should, ideally, conform to the traditional nuclear family model of breadwinner father, mother who may work outside of the home but also maintains the house, and children who are well-schooled and well-churched. Now that these dads must be "moms" too, they each have different coping strategies but both stay well within the bounds of local community for their support system. Pioneers on the "new normal" frontier, they turn inward, respectively, to the time-worn institution of the Church, and to the core site of family restitution—the home.

In a segment entitled "Forgive and Forget," reported by Bonnie Anderson, *CNN Presents: Legacy of Terror* features the story of newly single Dad, Lyle Cousins, his son Corey, and their survival through devotion to the Church. Home video of Lyle and Kim Cousins' wedding further cements the family's central connection to this community institution—it is where "Lyle met Kim at adult Sunday school." However, "even for the most devout," Judy Woodruff's introduction intones, "the tragedy [of the bombing] is a test of forgiveness and a test of faith." In the absence of a traditionally conceived maternal presence in the home, Lyle and Corey Cousins have turned to their church groups and church activities to keep them occupied and to remind them of their moral and spiritual grounding when faced with the upcoming trial of Timothy McVeigh. This traditional community within the community appears, in this segment, to be the rock upon which the Heartland itself is built, and upon which it will be rebuilt.

Featured in *ABC News Turning Point: Rebirth*, Glenn and Clint Seidel have, instead, turned to the home and hearth to focus on rebuilding their lives on the terrain of the mundane, everyday routines that used to be handled, unnoticed, by Kathy Seidel, but now keep Glenn in perpetual motion. An ideal frontier-type, Glenn Seidel is portrayed as at one with nature and as a patriotic entrepreneur—framed in interview segments against a flowing field of grain, he wears a "U.S.A" baseball cap throughout the segment and is established as having his own business as a plumbing contractor. Thus, the daily domestic routine he and Clint are seen struggling through is characterized as foreign to his masculine, Heartlander upbringing. Says Glenn, "I've never washed so many clothes in all my life as in the last seven months, you know."

The segment follows Glenn and Clint on a "typical day"—from their early morning trip to the grocery store to balancing the checkbook in the evening. Clint explains the cooperative domestic arrangement that is the pair's "new normal": "I vacuum, he makes the beds; I mop." And Glenn acknowledges that traditional domestic technology has saved him and made him into a satisfactory Mom. Describing the roast he makes every Sunday, Glenn sighs, "Thank God for Crockpots," while Clint chimes in, "him and that Crockpot are just like that." Glenn's struggles, as Lyle Cousins's above, are thus aligned with a privatized ethic of balance between technological aids and self-sufficiency. Community restitution and healing take place in accord with traditional ideals of local community and familial good.

Of course, the problem with these portraits of the placid, upstanding Heartland is the fact that the convicted perpetrators of the bombing are, arguably, products of that same "Heartland"—an America that might, alternately, be defined by alienation, extremism, paranoia, and obsession. Television coverage of the rebirth of Oklahoma City thus has to expressly position Timothy McVeigh as an outsider—a lone individual who came to Oklahoma from elsewhere and who, in any case, does not fit the community profile. For example, *CNN Presents: Legacy of Terror* graphically depicts McVeigh's outsiderness by contrasting amateur video of Easter services at the Church of the Servant with footage of the route that McVeigh presumably drove that same day, ominously underscoring footage of interstate and urban traffic at dusk and at dark. The intercutting of this material portrays the contrasting worlds of McVeigh's lone travels in the "getaway car that left downtown on Sunday" and Oklahoma Citians' presumed communal attendance at Easter Sunday services during that same time, "three days before the attack." There are real, authentic Oklahoma Citians, this logic implies, and then there are the outsiders in the form of the Timothy McVeighs of the world. The real Heartlanders are identifiable by their solid connections to, and literal circumscription by, community, church, and family. The McVeighs, by contrast, are mobile drifters who exist at the margins— radically disaffected in relation to any community. We as an audience, it is implied, will choose to identify with the ethic of the American pastoral Heartland ideal.

Oklahoma City's Rebirth: From Promised Land to "Non-targeted City"

The CBS TV series *Promised Land* (1996–1999) was the first fictional, continuing prime time series program to devote episodes to commemorating the anniversary of the Oklahoma City bombing. *Promised Land,* created and produced by Martha Williamson, followed the nomadic travels across the American Midwest, South, and rural West of Russell Greene (Gerald McRaney) and his family. Greene is a Vietnam veteran and former Navy Seal who has been laid off from his manufacturing job and now works on an itinerant basis, depending on where the family relocates from week to week. His wife Claire works, similarly, as a substitute teacher. They also travel with Grandma Greene, the Greene siblings —a teenage boy and girl—and with a nephew who is in their care. Periodically, the family parks their Winnebago and pick-up truck, and stays for a duration with their long-time friend, Erasmus (Ossie Davis).

Promised Land began each week with Russell's pre-theme-song address to the audience—a prologue which is telling for what it presumes its audience *should* prioritize and, by extension, what values it assumes its regular audience shares:

> My name is Russell Greene. Maybe you've passed me and my family out on the highway. Maybe you were driving some fancy sports car or an old beat-up four-door. Maybe you had some place to be. Or, maybe, like us, you're living out your dream, with your house hitched up behind you and America the Beautiful up ahead. And whoever you are, you be sure to give us a wave the next time you drive by. Cause we're your neighbors, and we're all on the road together!

If not immediately obvious in the prologue itself, it becomes obvious in the program's address that those presumed to share its interests are those viewers who identify with the more mundane pleasures of everyday life and diligent labors (rather than rushing to be somewhere or having one's priorities out-of-whack). The wheat-field vistas that accompany this opening monologue, as the Winnebago travels along the interstate, clearly contextualize the concerns of the program as those of the Heartland.

On May 7 and May 14, 1998, *Promised Land* focused on the anniversary of the Oklahoma City bombing to argue that the Heartland is a touchstone for any American who values God, family, and America the Beautiful.[31] Here, the Heartland is amorphous in the sense that it is aligned with certain presumably shared values rather than with, necessarily, a particular location on the American map. Thus, essential to this special two-part program is the message that the bombing should never be forgotten because, Grandma Greene argues, "What happened here—in the middle of the country—really happened to *all* of us." Attempting to convince the family's reluctant teen, Josh Greene, of the purpose of visiting the Murrah bomb site (shot on-location in Oklahoma City) Grandma gives an impassioned speech which clearly articulates the broadly *national* resonance of Heartland values:

> Is three years ancient history to you? This was an outrage! It was the worst attack on this country in its history. And you know why? It was against *ordinary people* earning their daily bread and taking care of their families. And they mustn't be forgotten. Not in three years or three-hundred. You see, what happened here really happened to *every* state in the Union.

Gradually overwhelmed by the loss evidenced at the site, Josh later breaks down at the base of the Survivor Tree—a tree that burned during the bombing but subsequently lived to bloom again—as he comes to understand the strength of Oklahoma Citians who, like the tree, "refused to give in to the worst men"—opposed to Heartland values—"could offer."

Significantly, in the program's final season, the Greene family moved permanently to Denver—a site which shares with anniversary coverage of Oklahoma City an image as a place whose true identity is aligned with the rural frontier, residual tradition, and rugged self-sufficiency, in spite of its ostensible alliance with modern, urban culture. It can, thus, remain emblematic of the Heartland. Denver was also the site of the McVeigh trial. The decision to move the trial to Denver led the *Daily Oklahoman* to rationalize that the frontier city's jurors would apply the same values to the case as would be used in Oklahoma. Quoting Robert Crawford, a jury consultant in the Denver area for twenty years, regarding the McVeigh jury pool, "it doesn't have some kind of regional bias or something that makes them skewed . . . It's just a good, middle-American group of men and women" who "insist that the media behave and that Hollywood"—the outside world—"stay away."[32]

One week before the Murrah Building bombing, in April 1995, *TV Guide* published a feature story called "TV Heads for the Heartland," in response to what author Jacquelyn Mitchard identified as a growing trend toward "a whole new America" featured in prime time series programming. While the article vaguely defines the geographic location of the Heartland as the rural, small-towns of the American "midcountry," it is much more specific when it outlines the qualities and values that inhere in this place and therefore explain the Heartland's contemporary "chic" for the American viewing public. In opposition to the classic centers of television's attention "on either coast," the Heartland is "comfy," "safe, secure," and "hardy." It is, above all, the site of "strong tradition and family values" where people live "solid lives . . . on common sense foundations." The article concludes, thereby, that even though ideals of Heartland life are largely imaginary ideals, most Americans "want to feel they are part of" a Heartland "hometown, even if that's not where they're really from."[33] The Heartland is thus clearly less about bounded geographic location than it is evocative of a symbolic geography of a certain American pastoral ideal—a traditional, residual, "innocent" communal sensibility and privatized ethic of church, family, and citizenship.

Paradoxically, as the national awareness of Oklahoma City and the memory of April 19, 1995 recede from public discourse, the Heartland as geographic home and imagined repository of core U.S. values has been revivified. In spite of Oklahoma City's own National Memorial Institute for the Prevention of Terrorism's reportage regarding active hate groups and the continuing problem of domestic terrorism, following the events of 9/11, the region and its presumed values, have been reiterated as "opposed" to those of the more worldly and dangerous coasts.[34] Such accounts frequently invoke the belief in the region's innate safety and innocence. "The September 11 terrorist attacks . . . altered perceptions such that the East Coast suddenly seems dangerous, not exciting; the Midwest safe, not dull."[35] And, "a North Dakota address now feels like less of a punishment."[36] Between the coasts, the Heartland is comparatively "affordable, family-oriented, safer," and "value-oriented."[37] As summarized by a recent transplant from the Silicon Valley to Ft.

Wayne, Indiana, "I just felt better that my children are going to be in a non-targeted city."[38]

What are the politics of imagining a contemporary pastoral America whose perceived geographic/spatial separation has ostensibly fostered time-bound, residual values of emplaced community, church, and family? How does the privatized ethic of citizenship portrayed as the Heartland ideal in fact translate into a "cultural politics of . . . the normal . . . [that] has concrete effects"?[39] Overall, anniversary journalism coverage of localized national traumas suggest that community is reconstituted, literally, through rebirth and the rededication to maternity and to the church and that, in this respect, everyday American citizens might be best advised that the proper response to political conflict and to violent tragedy is to seek "normalcy" in the bedrock of localized "family values." That, when met with challenge, the solution lies in retreat to the home and hearth, no matter how impractical or unsustainable that retreat may have become. In the contemporary moment it seems particularly important to consider the ways in which maintaining an imagination of a United States divided between "targeted" and "non-targeted" areas has encouraged and strengthened broader public and media discourses of a "divided" nation and polity, and has emboldened a considerably selective understanding of history, identity, and place. Specifically, we should query how such narratives evacuate regional diversity and political complexity and be reminded that such commemorative events are also the occasion for intense forgetting.

Epilogue
Red State, Blue State, Purple Heartland

On November 9, 2000, *USA Today* published a map of the United States that was based on television news graphics produced for election coverage. This map, and its reproductions across television and other print media, coded presidential electoral votes according to two primary, patriotic colors: red for Republican-voting "Bush states" and blue for Democrat-claimed "Gore states." While color-coding of electoral maps had been used in magazines and on television prior to this time, the 2000 map became so prominent across media platforms during that chaotic November, as to now, firmly, represent *the* common sense visual—and, increasingly, linguistic, vernacular shorthand—for the politics of regional identity within the United States. The maps represented the nation as a stable Heartland unified by Bush red values, pitted against a fringe "blue" liberal, urban, intellectual class located on either coast and in the metropolitan islands excised from the Heartland core.

By the summer of 2004, the election-specific, political, journalistic phrase, "red state America," had broken the frame of talking-head shows to become a broadly colloquial catch-phrase that condensed a chain of complex ideological associations into a coherent, distinctly bordered cognitive map. Some red state references from just the past few years in the popular press, for instance, include protests over "red-state bashing," reference to country music written in a "red state of mind," and description of "red state Bush voters" as "inland" folk from "small-town America" representing, in short, "every county in America with a cow in it."[1] More specifically, however, recent television industry discourse has explicitly invoked the red state reference for two key strategic uses: as an appeal that is increasingly employed in network branding strategies and business practices by broadcast and cable outlets that claim to be home to "family-friendly," "classic" television address, and to promote the "authenticity" of reality programming featuring the "average," exemplary ordinariness of the Heartlander character.

Communications historian Carolyn Marvin has argued that "the introduction of new media is a special historical occasion when patterns anchored in older media that have provided the stable currency of social exchange are reexamined, challenged, and defended."[2] The neo-network, multi-platform, conglomerate-family focused context of the current television industry is, clearly, such an occasion. While television content delivery platforms have proliferated since passage of the 1996 Telecommunications Act (e.g., you can now receive TV content on your computer, PDA, cell phone, or iPod), if, as scholar David Morley has proposed, we imagine full inclusion in "cultural citizenship . . . as a graduated incline," then television still forms the media entry-point or base.[3]

The Telecommunications Act—with its support for a significantly deregulated marketplace encouraging conglomerate ownership and concentration—effectively urged corporate media interests to revalue or, at least, attend anew to markets beyond the top twenty-five, as "new" venues for expansion and market cultivation. Arguably, while certainly not solely market-driven, the "red state, blue state" narrative's prominence at this juncture is significant.

Heightened media attention has recently been devoted to consumers located in relatively "small" U.S. markets, "but who account for half the nation's population."[4] In the same period that the Midwest was experiencing an economic and housing boom, suggesting a strengthening of secondary and tertiary media markets, there was also a marked decline in "prized" viewer attention to television—specifically "adults 18 to 49 with annual incomes of $75,000 plus," who, notably, tend to be clustered within the top twenty-five media markets on either coast.[5] In this climate, increased attention has now been focused on branding networks and network content as "destinations" for midwestern viewers and their presumptively different tastes—positing the "traditional" medium of television as a site that was now, reliably, "eschewing an edgy, urban tone in favor of a heartland sensibility," featuring programming with "not a 'Friends'-style Central Perk coffeehouse in sight."[6]

If we, then, consider the "red state, blue state" maps as they inform a neo-network "turn to the middle" in certain network branding, audience address, and program content appeals, we are reminded that the two key, recurring tropes through which the Midwest and midwesternness typically have been imagined for national broadcast audiences are through lenses pastoral and populist—highly conventional and traditional interpretive screens that further excise or render invisible a diversity of viewers and dispositions therein. That is, in key "new" media branding and content appeals outlined briefly below, neo-network strategies that continue to imagine the Heartland as a "comforting," red-state preserve, suggest that business practice's "equation of public interest with an unregulated marketplace," post–Telecommunications Act, "has resulted in disconnecting social consequences from the cultivation of the marketplace."[7]

The excisions from Heartland discourse are, I posit, particularly important *because* of the relative unevenness with which modern encounters with new media environments are experienced. As Morley argues, for the majority of media users, the "paradigm of mobile deterritorialization" is not apt:

> It is, as Tomlinson argues, in the transformation of localities, rather than in the increase of physical mobility (significant though that may be for some groups), that the process of globalization perhaps has its most important expression. . . . "for most people, most of the time, the impact of globalization is felt not in travel but in staying at home." . . . their experience of locality is transformed by the now banal and routinised process of "consumption of images of distant places" which, paradoxically, become familiar in their generic forms (the streets of New York, the American West, etc.) . . . as they are normalized in the mediated life world of the television viewer.[8]

In the consumption of popular images of the Heartland, a now-familiar chain of raced, gendered, sexed, and politicized associations regarding American citizenship emerges. The cognitive map of the Heartland is, in this sense, both a market investment and also a field of power, enabling or encouraging particular subjective allegiances and dispositions in everyday life, while offering no recognizable "place" to others.

"Feel Good" Nets and Heartland Branding

In a multi-mediated context frequently theorized to be hostile to conventional, national broadcast networks then, some networks have counterintuitively achieved striking success by reconfiguring and cannily branding themselves as throwbacks to a "classic" network era of "mass" appeal TV and "shared" broadcast culture. Rather than follow the economic and programming logic of narrowcasting to a niche audience of focused demographic range, key broadcasters have capitalized on programming to a multi-generation family audience that is, in their vision, ideally midwestern. Rhetorically positioning themselves as corporate "uniters" not "dividers," engaged in public service over sheer profit motive, recent network strategies promote broadcast and cable outlets in exceptionally "classic" terms—as consensus markets poised to counterbalance "fringe" services and as outlets that "revalue" the culture and people of the American middle.[9]

In the mid- to late 1990s, stalwart CBS and the former PAX-net (now ION), initiated institutional strategies to mine this perceived larger public desire for a localized Heartland "hometown." Such rhetoric has, more recently, been taken up by other networks—particularly those whose viewership skews heavily toward television markets number twenty-five and below and, therefore, "perceived as skewing more to the heartland," including, for example, Country Music Television, Hallmark Channel, and Outdoor Life, but also networks such as the "nostalgic" TV Land, which programs "classic" TV series such as, currently, *Roseanne* and, periodically, MTM's 1970s comedies.[10] While proponents of myriad new technologies have, for over twenty years, argued that network television was rapidly facing extinction, CBS and PAX presented models for securing continued competitiveness *as* broadcasters by counterintuitively reconfiguring themselves as the sites wherein Americans could engage *residual* culture via a "classic" postwar technology that was (rhetorically, at least, in contrast to "new media" promotions and promises) "democratic" and "populist" in its availability and address.

These networks presumed to speak to what they considered to be an otherwise "forgotten" audience within the contemporary TV landscape. Exemplified by CBS television's mid- to late 1990s publicity campaigns which touted "America's Nights of Television" on a network where "The Address is CBS—Welcome Home!," or, PAX-Net's original pitch that it would be "the anti-network . . . a haven for alienated viewers because it is the only national family entertainment network"[11]—such programming and network branding strategies took advantage of and, arguably, magnified "divided" national rhetorics in the broader political and media landscape. In the same period as Ellen's coming out, CBS and PAX-TV invoked the imagined particularities of place—of the Heartland as a repository of residual American values—to position themselves as the two remaining sites defined by the voice of the traditional American middle. Featuring programs that imagined insular, shared community; that explicitly referenced the pioneering, frontier cultural past; that proposed and embraced overt, devout evangelical spirituality; and that, weekly, exemplified relative unawareness of urban life and urban populations, these networks and their schedules were promoted as lone sites wherein the language of "ordinary people" was spoken outside of the loop of the rapid changes and "alternative lifestyles" proposed by the more urbanely defined, younger, hipper networks. Indeed, on this count, PAX-Net's start-up was marred by an uproar over its explicitly conservative promotions in major news and industry trade papers, which condemned the major networks for "promoting 'alternative lifestyles,'" a phrase understood to refer to gay and lesbian populations. Perhaps only adding fuel to the fire, then PAX President and CEO, Jeff Sagansky, responded to the criticism by arguing that while "PAX-Net wouldn't shy away from featuring gay characters in its programming . . . that 'we are not here to promote a gay lifestyle.'"[12]

PAX Television was launched in 1998 and met its demise in November of 2006—by which time PAX's original programming and market appeal had been taken up and, arguably, better realized and capitalized by competitors such as those "feel good" networks noted above (especially Hallmark, Country Music Television, and Outdoor Life Network). During its lifespan, PAX became the seventh over-air broadcaster, joining ABC, CBS, NBC, FOX, UPN, and WB.[13] PAX was founded by "Bud" Paxon, who had previously owned cable TV's Christian Network, The Home Shopping Network, and multiple radio stations. While most early press surrounding PAX-TV referred to it as a "Christian network," Paxon considered his stations, instead, to represent a non-denominational yet spiritually uplifting "haven" for viewers presumed to feel alienated by mainstream media. In spite of its "anti-network" focus, however, PAX-TV succeeded largely due to strategic alliances with traditional networks that allowed it to marshal capital, extend its market penetration, and procure programming. PAX started broadcasting in 1998, for example, with programs that, while clearly fitting its professed brand ethic, were also almost exclusively former CBS program fare. Such programs included *Touched by an Angel, Dr. Quinn Medicine Woman, Diagnosis Murder, Christy, Dave's World, Life Goes On,* and *Promised Land.* In its first year, PAX's entire weeknight prime time schedule consisted of series that had aired or were concurrently airing on CBS (i.e., syndicated on PAX while in first-run on CBS). Further, PAX-TV's day-to-day operations were overseen by former CBS Entertainment executive Jeff Sagansky (who resigned in 2003). By the year 2000, PAX expanded its original programming to include a range of dramatic series, reality-TV, and game shows. Examples included *Doc* (featuring country and western singer, Billy Ray Cyrus), *The Ponderosa* (a prequel to *Bonanza*), *Miracle Pets, Supermarket Sweep* and *Next Big Star.* In 1999, Paxon sold thirty-two percent of his company to NBC. In November of 2005, NBC-Universal bought out Bud Paxon's remaining stake in the company, and by May of 2006, the network had been renamed iNetwork, and, soon thereafter, ION, and had begun the process of reconfiguring its brand identity.

While PAX was one of the first networks to capitalize on an arguably growing "Heartland media" "flyover" audience niche, its demise has not slowed such branding and audience appeals by broad- and cablecasters. Indeed, such appeals have accelerated as television viewership declines among higher-income and larger market consumers while it remains steady in smaller markets.[14] A new network, The America Channel, is currently set to enter cable competition on these terms. The America Channel's promotional materials claim that its sole purpose is to "show real American life *between* the East and West coasts . . . [it] will focus on 'real reality and real storytelling' about the nation and its people . . . highlighting the achievements of ordinary people." Here, again, the Heartland is the presumed repository of the "real"—the apparent antidote or corrective to the cynicism perceived to be rampant in the current reality TV cycle and in appeals to coastal viewers.

Though there are "ordinary people" living on either coast—as well as, likely, some flashy social climbers in the Midwest—in attempting to reclaim or revalue a "mass" audience, much industry discourse has located the "family audience" firmly in the Heartland as the imagined storehouse of nostalgia for a shared national TV culture—that "close-knit community where things are eminently manageable."[15] The Heartland is, in this sense, also as much a sensibility as it is a locale. A clear appeal of network branding and programming in these terms thus calls to viewers "exiled" from the Heartland on either coast, who are now able to "travel" via TV to momentarily occupy a Heartland subjectivity, through the flip of the television remote.

CBS has continued to be chief among traditional broadcasters in such appeals, though the network now claims both "hip, urban, edgy" programming and audiences *and* to be the Heartland home among the former "Big Three." CBS is, in fact, the most "mass" broadcaster currently on the air—attracting the greatest generational range of viewers to a single network as well as rating as the number one network with both African American and white viewers. While CBS is currently the number one network in the top twenty-five demographic markets, it also, currently, skews highest for viewership in smaller markets (those markets below the top twenty-five).[16] Regarding CEO Les Moonves' branding strategy, Nina Tassler, CBS's current entertainment president recently stated, "From the beginning, Les's mantra has been 'We are a broadcaster,' . . . We want all viewers. In that goal, if we get adults 18 to 49, that's a bonus and that's a good thing."[17] In this sense, CBS's strategy of playing to the middle has been a tremendous success and has freed the network up to allow its corporate siblings, MTV networks and the CW, to target more urban and youth-skewing audiences, which are understood, industrially, to be much more diversified in terms of race and class. Lloyd Braun, chairman of ABC Entertainment television group has also recently stated that his networks' (now-defunct) "TGIF" line-up succeeded most because it had a "Heartland sensibility." This is a sensibility which Braun allies with "real" Americans in a curious statement, arguing that: "I'm a New York Jew who moved to West L.A. I'm not America. And you better learn that real fast when you have this job."[18]

The Real America?

The Los Angeles Times recently ran a feature story discussing the problems with—and solution for—finding "real people" for reality programming. Mickey Glazer, producer of *Fear Factor,* had turned his program's cast recruitment to red state territory, focusing, particularly on Joplin, Missouri and Omaha, Nebraska. In these locales, he said, "instead of . . . aspiring models, actors and actresses, . . . [he] met . . . sales managers, [and] stay-at-home moms. They didn't have bottle-blond hair and 'Baywatch' bodies, but split ends and beer bellies. Many even wore shapeless flannel shirts." The Heartland is thus imagined as a site of guileless authenticity, as "proven" by its occupants' professions, appearance, and apparent lack of coiffure or fashion savvy. Glazer adds, in this respect, that his "dream cast is even better when found in Middle America."[19] Comedian Jeff Foxworthy recently supported this association of Heartlanders and an authentic, anti-Hollywood disposition, arguing that "reality shows have 'knocked the gloss off' the medium, . . . adding 'You don't have to be slick or suave to be on TV anymore.'"[20]

Heartlanders are also, in this sense, perceived to be the ideal subjects for reality TV's promised transformations that take the ordinary participant from her or his "low" cultural orientation and make her or him over to occupy a new status, allied with heightened cultural value. The premiere episode of Bravo TV's *Queer Eye for the Straight Guy* (2003–2007) is significant in this respect. A show which was initially clearly set in New York City and its surrounds—extending in its first two seasons only geographically so far as suburban Long Island—the premiere featured the Queer Eye collective's "recuperation" of midwestern refugee, artist Butch Schepel, to "proper" conversance with urban couture and self-presentation. Those who flee the Heartland, the program proves, can be recuperated for cultural capital due to their geographic relocation and improved style-consciousness. Post-makeover, one of Butch's New York friends notes that he "might have to start calling him Brian; I'm not kidding. Like, Butch was that big mountain-man guy, you know, like Butch went back to the Midwest and" Brian appeared in his place.

I propose that the imagination of "red state" unanimity, and the connection of its presumed, conservative politics to the traditional Heartland ideal, taken up by popular media as the repository of all that is "really real"—if "taste"-challenged—within U.S. culture, can have impact in the real social world. A Kellogg Foundation study of "perceptions of rural America" conducted in 2002, found that the three most common images of rural America were: farms and crops, pastures, and animals, even though today less than a quarter of all rural counties—primarily clustered in the red state region—depend on farming for their primary source of income and less than two percent of all rural residents earn their primary living from farming.[21] In these respects we might consider how the common sense imagination of the Heartland may, in effect, function to encourage that the region itself carry the costs of the national investment in its myth—mitigating against viable strategies that address less easily visualized realities of red state life, off the edges of the TV screen.

Rather than accept the red and blue rhetoric as visual culture's common sense representation of political realities in the contemporary United States, I urge further critical examination of the apparent ease with which both "official" culture and popular discourse have embraced a shorthand narrative about national identity that insistently asks us to accept as "natural and universal" realities that are, in fact, contentious, "selected, partial, and incomplete."[22] Indeed, while there were, in 2004, and 2006, pockets of "true" electoral red (e.g., in a streak that traveled, roughly, south to north along Highway 83 from the Texas panhandle to the South Dakota border, and in an S-curve from southwestern Utah, at the base, through Idaho's eastern border over into northeastern Wyoming), the Midwest was—and historically has been—thoroughly pocked and shaded by "purple."[23] The purpleness of the region is particularly striking as it also underscores a broader racial, ethnic, class, and educational diversity to the region than is often visualized or colloquially understood. For example, purple reigns: along both sides of the Mississippi River, with its concentrations of African American populations following post-Emancipation migratory patterns from the South to the North through Illinois; in regions of Iowa, Wisconsin, Minnesota, and the Dakotas populated, particularly, with Native-American communities; as well as in urban cores and ex-urban "ideopolises," home to academic and postindustrial metropolitan high-tech hubs (such as Columbia, Missouri, Lawrence, Kansas, and Madison, Wisconsin).[24] There were, also, importantly, "100 per-cent red" counties in New York state, Florida, and California, while the "urban elite" enclaves of Texas skew red, not blue. While certainly the "bluest" blues were to be found in Massachusetts, New York City, Los Angeles, and San Francisco, they were matched in Milwaukee, Minneapolis, Chicago, Cedar Rapids, Sioux City, and many other midwestern communities.

Though the intensity with which culture has become politicized has, arguably, accelerated from the 1960s onward,[25] *Heartland TV* demonstrates that the association of geography with predictable political allegiance—as further codified and defined through market and taste cultures—has actually been encouraged from the 1920s to the present. Indeed, historically, broadcast media and markets are prerequisite to and partly generative of such discourses. Television programs, advertisements, and network branding appeals represent the central sites for

imagining and struggling over this red and blue continuum in everyday life. We should consider these sites as invitations and opportunities to interrogate what popular mythologies of regional identity have encouraged us to excise from scholarly and popular analysis and how these erasures encourage institutional, cultural, and economic decisions about who is visible and what counts in the real social world.

In film, television, and media studies—particularly within the U.S. context—it is, thus, critically important to consider policy, industrial imperatives, market functions, and intended audience, as well as programming (scheduling and genre) and formal, textual characteristics, and audience response each in tension and relation to each other, as a matrix of interests that intersect with and inform broader social and political discourses regarding media and national identity. Across these discourses, disarticulating the common sense articulation of red states to Heartland to midwesternness to social and political conservatism takes work, but is intended as a strategic maneuver that troubles ritually energized conventional media discourses regarding regional identity *throughout* the United States. Ideally, this work exposes the power *and* vulnerability essential to the process of selective tradition, opening up possibilities to assess the real political impact that such chains of association have.

While several popular figures and critics (such as Garrison Keillor and Thomas Frank, for example) have begun to focus critical attention on regional mythology and the ways in which it informs both popular knowledge and "official," political discourse, academic scholarship has been somewhat reluctant to examine this myth. This reluctance, I would argue, has to do, in part, with the very issues of capital that are at stake in any such investigation. Television history and critical theory has, for example, often neglected the study of texts and genres that may win People's Choice Awards but never be nominated for Emmys (though, certainly, the earliest work in television studies, particularly by feminist scholars, was groundbreaking for its attention to "degraded" TV forms such as the soap opera and its disproportionately female fans). Currently, such a skew is understandable, as analysis of such "low," "mass," popular objects is not, typically, institutionally rewarded (a phenomenon that thus replicates the issues of taste and social value from the popular realm within that of academia). However, while I believe that rhetoric of cultural and political division has radically exaggerated actual conditions, I would still posit that the address and appeal of popular "Heartland" programming (such as, for example, long-running series including *JAG, NCIS, Seventh Heaven,* or series featured on ION, Hallmark, or ABC-Family) begs for further analysis as regards both institutional appeals and the real affective bonds and pleasures found therein. Failing to study such objects for "preferred" texts not only replicates the rhetoric of division itself but contributes to the notion that academic study is disconnected from everyday engagements with media and politics.

I hope that this book has encouraged and challenged readers to raise regional mythology to a shared level of attention within critical discourse to those categories of identity and capital relations (race, class, gender, sexuality, generation) with which it crucially intersects and each of which it critically informs. In the preceding, I have attempted to make visible typically unseen, but commonly accepted, discourses of geography and power that have been regularly re-energized in postwar American life and culture in ways that have far-reaching "real world" ramifications. Such mythology allows for entire populations and sites within the Midwest, for example, to remain invisible within national discourse. Such mythology sets the terms of political debate in election cycles, which capitalize upon both notions of "divide" and the politics of resentment only to betray those ideals and voters once the elections are concluded. Such mythology ratifies broader public assumptions regarding presumed political allegiances in ways that explicitly discourage or actively reinforce the apparent, historical impossibility to think or imagine *otherwise,* as regards place, nation, and identity. In this sense, the project hopes to have entered into cultural studies' tradition of interrogating and deconstructing the cultural common sense—a common sense that, here, encourages each of us to invest in divided rhetoric rather than to interrogate the broader market and political functions such investments support with their active mystification of the radical *overlaps* and shared values and ideals within and between such categories.

Appendix

In the archival collections at the State Historical Society of Wisconsin (SHSW) in Madison, Wisconsin, I consulted the papers of:

Harry R. Bannister (NBC Vice President for Station Relations, 1952–1960; papers from 1952–1965)

David Brinkley (NBC correspondent and news anchor, 1943–1981; papers from 1960–1969)

Benjamin Burton (CBS news producer from 1957; papers from 1967–1977)

William Hedges (NBC Vice President in charge of station relations and traffic, 1937–1948; NBC Vice President in charge of integrated services, 1949–1959; papers from 1941, 1948–1950)

Lee Loevinger (FCC Commission Member, 1963–1968; papers from 1965–1966, 1971–1972)

NBC Files (Central Files, 1926–1950; Station Relation Files, 1950–1951, 1956, 1960; Advertising Files, 1950–1959; and Office Files, 1940–1959)

Newton Minow (FCC Chair, March 1961–May 1963; papers from 1961–1964). Folders in Minow collection are alphabetical within the boxes, not numeric.

Edwin H. Newman (NBC radio and television news commentator from 1952–1984; papers from 1968)

Ernest Pendrell (Television writer and documentary producer from 1951–1978; papers from 1964, 1968, 1972)

Perry S. Wolff (Producer of documentary programs for CBS News and Public Affairs Department, 1950s–1990s; papers from 1963–1964, 1970–1971, 1977–1978, 1989)

Notes

NOTES TO THE INTRODUCTION

1. In spite of radical changes in the media landscape from its introduction to the present, commercial television remains the primary medium with which U.S. citizens engage on a daily basis, across age, gender, race, class, and geographic categories of measurement. Daily time spent with television outstrips its nearest competitor (radio) by over twenty-five percent in all groups, ages twelve to sixty-four. Television use is also significantly higher than that for competing media (radio, internet, video games, newspapers, and magazines) in rural markets—markets which are also overwhelmingly located in the Midwest. See, for example, Joe Mandese, "Video Games Emerge as 'No. 4' Medium," *Media-Post's Media Daily News* (5 April 2004); "Market Track: DMA Household Universe Estimates: May 2004 Cable and/or ADS," retrieved 30 July 2004 from http://www.tvb.org/rcentral/markettrack/Cable_and_ADS_Penetration_by_DMA .asp and, U.S. Census Bureau, "Information and Communications," in *Statistical Abstract of the United States* (Washington, D.C.: Government Printing Office, 2001), 705.

2. David Morley, *Home Territories: Media, Mobility and Identity* (London: Routledge, 2000), 246.

3. John Landgraf, FX President of Entertainment (quoted in Doug Halonen, "FCC Is Now 'Pvt. Ryan's' Battleground," *Television Week* [15 November 2004]: 22).

4. Les Moonves, Co-President and Co-CEO of Viacom and Chair of CBS, in interview by author, Chapel Hill, North Carolina, 18 February 2002.

5. Pierre Bourdieu, *Distinction: A Social Critique of the Judgement of Taste*, trans. Richard Nice (Cambridge: Harvard University Press, 1984), 124.

6. Janice A. Radway, *A Feeling for Books: The Book-of-the-Month Club, Literary Taste, and Middle-Class Desire* (Chapel Hill: University of North Carolina Press, 1997), 389.

7. Examples of historical narratives which imply a smooth, uniform progress of TV networking toward national, universal service, include: Ken Burns' 1991 documentary for PBS-TV titled *Empire of the Air: The Men Who Made Radio* (Prod./Dir. Ken Burns; PBS/Paramount, 1991); one of the most widely used

214 I Notes to the Introduction

introductory textbooks, Erik Barnouw's *Tube of Plenty: The Evolution of American Television,* 2nd rev. ed. (New York: Oxford University Press, 1990) also implies the inevitability of national networking, as well as its rapid, unobstructed standardization. William Boddy has interrogated this "monster blanket" mythology in " 'Spread Like a Monster Blanket Over the Country': CBS and Television, 1929–1933," in *Screen Histories: A Screen Reader,* eds. Annette Kuhn and Jackie Stacey (Oxford: Oxford University Press, 1998), 129–138.

8. Bradley Johnson, "Money Mapped: The Coasts Boast Most," *Television Week* (11 April 2005): 14.

9. John Leland, "How the Disposable Sofa Conquered America," *The New York Times Magazine* (1 December 2002): 86–92.

10. Herman Gray, "Television, Black Americans, and the American Dream," in *Television: The Critical View,* 5th ed., ed. Horace Newcomb (Oxford: Oxford University Press, 1994), 178.

11. Work in this area has especially emphasized local audience activism in response to network programming, local affiliate tensions with networks, and local, independent stations' distinctive identity within network-affiliate dominant markets. See, particularly, Steven D. Classen, *Watching Jim Crow: The Struggles Over Mississippi TV, 1955–1969* (Durham: Duke University Press, 2004); James Day, *The Vanishing Vision: The Inside Story of Public Television* (Berkeley: University of California Press, 1995); Mark Williams, *Remote Possibilities* (Berkeley: University of California Press, forthcoming); Mark Williams, ed., "U.S. Regional and Non-Network Television," Special Issue, *Quarterly Review of Film and Video* 16.3–4 (1999): 221–438.

12. For example, if we consider, proportionately, the active, broad, daily public engagement with television as it far outstrips engagement with any other communication medium, it helps to put into perspective the exceptional outcry when events such as the Janet Jackson and Justin Timberlake "scandal" take place (Super Bowl XXXVIII [2004]). On the one hand, the event seems to have been blown radically out of proportion, while, on the other hand, the event lingers in broader social discourse at the level that it does, in large part because it represented an increasingly rare example of a *shared* site of national cultural engagement, centered around, and made possible by, television.

13. A compelling argument for the waning power of network television in terms of socio-political voice in representational culture is made, for example, in Herman S. Gray, *Cultural Moves: African Americans and the Politics of Representation* (Berkeley: University of California Press, 2005). See also analysis of the transition to niche-marketing as industry imperative as outlined in Ron Becker, *Gay TV and Straight America* (New Brunswick: Rutgers University Press, 2006), and Amanda D. Lotz, *Redesigning Women: Television After the Network Era* (Urbana: University of Illinois Press, 2006).

14. John Caldwell, *Televisuality: Style, Crisis, and Authority in American Television* (New Brunswick: Rutgers University Press, 1995), 9.

15. Stuart Hall, "Culture, Community, Nation," *Cultural Studies* (December 1993): 354.

16. Gray, *Cultural Moves*, 6.

17. I am influenced in my focus, here, by scholars such as George Lipsitz, whose historical analysis of the working-class, urban, ethnic sitcom in the 1950s troubles popular memory's dominant understanding of that period of television history as represented by the white, middle-class, suburban sitcom. Similarly, this work is informed by John Fiske's early call to think about television in terms of "totally typical" programming—the most popular, mainstream, most commercially-valued programs. Janet Staiger's study of wildly popular and often critically disdained programming has been informative, as it takes up this call. Lynn Spigel's analysis of the "fantastic family sitcom" of the 1960s underscores the need to think critically about programs that often are dismissed as "low," "escapist" anomalies amidst "quality" TV appeals. John Caldwell's work on "zero-degree" aesthetics is crucial to theorizing the regionalist appeals of the programs central to this work. I am also inspired here by Christopher Anderson's study of Warner Brothers' "B-genre" television of the 1950s, Marsha Cassidy's work on audience participation genres in the 1950s and Anna McCarthy's study of *Candid Camera* and appeals to realism, as well as her study of television in public settings, which challenges scholars to think more broadly about TV beyond its domestic uses, and to query its local functions and the ways in which audiences engage (or disengage from) the medium as a fundamentally social relation. See Christopher Anderson, *Hollywood TV: The Studio System in the Fifties* (Austin: University of Texas Press, 1994); Caldwell, *Televisuality*; Marsha F. Cassidy, "Sob Stories, Merriment, and Surprises: The 1950s Audience Participation Show on Network Television," *Velvet Light Trap* (Fall 1998): 48–62; John Fiske, *Television Culture* (New York: Routledge, 1987); George Lipsitz, "The Meaning of Memory: Family, Class, and Ethnicity in Early Network Television Programs," in *Private Screenings: Television and the Female Consumer*, eds. Lynn Spigel and Denise Mann (Minneapolis: University of Minnesota Press, 1992), 71–109; Anna McCarthy, *Ambient Television: Visual Culture and Public Space* (Durham: Duke University Press, 2001); and her " 'Stanley Milgram, Allen Funt, and Me': Postwar Social Science and the 'First Wave' of Reality TV," in *Reality TV: Remaking Television Culture*, eds. Susan Murray and Laurie Ouellette (New York: New York University Press, 2004), 19-39; Lynn Spigel, "From Domestic Space to Outer Space: The 1960s Fantastic Family Sitcom," in *Welcome to the Dreamhouse: Popular Media and Postwar Suburbs* (Durham: Duke University Press, 2001), 107–140; Janet Staiger, *Blockbuster TV: Must-See Sitcoms in the Network Era* (New York: New York University Press, 2000).

18. Radway, *A Feeling for Books*, 259.

19. See Erika Doss, *Benton, Pollack, and the Politics of Modernism: From Regionalism to Abstract Expressionism* (Chicago: University of Chicago Press, 1991); Radway, *A Feeling for Books*; Spigel, "From Domestic Space to Outer Space"; Caldwell, *Televisuality*.

20. Radway, *A Feeling for Books*, 259.

21. See, particularly, "Radicalizing Middle America," in Laurie Ouellette, *Viewers Like You? How Public TV Failed the People* (New York: Columbia University Press, 2002), 23–67.

22. Michael Curtin, *Redeeming the Wasteland: Television Documentary and Cold War Politics* (New Brunswick: Rutgers University Press, 1995), 11.

23. Herman Gray makes this point in an interview segment included in Marlon Riggs's documentary video project, *Color Adjustment* (Prods. Vivian Kleinman and Marlon Riggs; Dir. Marlon Riggs; California Newsreel, 1991).

24. Stuart Hall, *The Hard Road to Renewal: Thatcherism and the Crisis of the Left* (London: Verso, 1988), 142, 154, 163.

25. Thomas Frank, *What's The Matter with Kansas? How Conservatives Won the Heart of America* (New York: Metropolitan Books, 2004), 15.

26. Raymond Williams, *Marxism and Literature* (Oxford: Oxford University Press, 1992), 115, 116.

27. Ibid., 115.

28. Stuart Hall describing Foucault's theorization of "discourse," in Hall, "The Work of Representation," in *Representation: Cultural Representations and Signifying Practices,* ed. Stuart Hall (Thousand Oaks: Sage Publications, 1997), 44.

29. Ibid.

30. This definition of the region also conforms to the U.S. Census Bureau "Census Divisions and Regions." The states included in the "Midwest" are, from east to west and north to south: Ohio, Michigan, Indiana, Wisconsin, Illinois, Minnesota, Iowa, Missouri, North Dakota, South Dakota, Nebraska, and Kansas. The border states of Kentucky and Oklahoma are also often included in this regional categorization in popular discourse, though both are considered part of the South by census definition. Areas of Kentucky, Arkansas, and Oklahoma claim "Midwest" as their regional affiliation, while sections of Illinois and Missouri, for example, claim both midwestern and southern identifications. When "on the border" in my own examples (e.g., in Chapter 2's Springfield, Missouri-originating *Jubilee, U.S.A,* or Chapter 6's inclusion of Oklahoma City), I have opted for an expansive understanding of the region, in accordance with the explicit "Heartlander" identity claims made in popular press and television programming discourses about these sites.

31. James R. Shortridge, *The Middle West: Its Meaning in American Culture* (Lawrence: University Press of Kansas, 1989).

32. Ibid., 16.

33. Ibid., 21.

34. The region was "comparatively settled" in relation to the "frontier" Northwest of this period and the "culturally different" Southwest—a point of distinction that becomes even more important in the mythology of midwestern-ness in the post–World War II era as the region becomes increasingly homogenized in popular discourse, identified with "whiteness," excising, particularly, images of Black midwesterners and burgeoning Southeast Asian and Latino migrant cultures from popular imaginations of the region.

35. Shortridge, *The Middle West*, 9.

36. Gilbert B. Rodman, *Elvis after Elvis: The Posthumous Career of a Living Legend* (New York: Routledge, 1996), 20.

37. This is, arguably, the distinction between the "square" and the popular conceptions of the "geek" and/or the "nerd." Though the "geek" and "nerd" are often the butt of jokes in popular discourse, these terms are also invoked with some regard for (typically and significantly, *his*) technological expertise or educational capital (as usually seen in the linkage to "computer geek"). Additionally, uber-geeks such as Microsoft founder Bill Gates are "redeemed" culturally by their coastal emplacement (allied with values of urban mobility) and by the economic capital that is presumed to accrue to their fields of knowledge (positioned as progressive in their forward look) as specialized fields of expertise, available for mastery to few.

38. While binary oppositions (e.g., hip versus square, urban versus rural, elite versus populist, etc.) are theoretically problematic for their over-simplification, it is nonetheless important to acknowledge how deeply embedded binary modes of thinking are within U.S. popular culture and how powerfully binary oppositions function as short-hand in visual representation. What seems most important here is to consider the ritual return to these binaries in new contexts, as what Derrida called "repetition with change." See also, George Lipsitz, *Time Passages: Collective Memory and American Popular Culture* (Minneapolis: University of Minnesota Press, 1989), 29, and Richard Dyer, "White," *Screen* 29.4 (Autumn 1988): 44–65.

39. See, for example, Leland, "How the Disposable Sofa Conquered America," above, Fabio Cleto, ed., *Camp: Queer Aesthetics and the Performing Subject* (Ann Arbor: University of Michigan Press, 1999), and Andrew Ross, *No Respect: Intellectuals and Popular Culture* (New York: Routledge, 1989).

40. George Lipsitz, *The Possessive Investment in Whiteness: How White People Profit from Identity Politics* (Philadelphia: Temple University Press, 1998), 72.

41. John Fiske, *Media Matters: Everyday Culture and Political Change* (Minneapolis: University of Minnesota Press, 1994), 42, 44.

42. Ibid., 140.

43. Ibid., 41.

44. Ian F. Haney López, *White by Law: The Legal Construction of Race* (New York: New York University Press, 1996), 120. Also, we might consider here the way that, in visual culture, barnyards stand in as iconic in the popular imagination of the Midwest, but *not* necessarily of agricultural upstate New York, western Pennsylvania, or of the San Joaquin Valley in central California.

45. Lauren Berlant, *The Queen of America Goes to Washington City: Essays on Sex and Citizenship* (Durham: Duke University Press, 1997), 10.

46. Ibid., 20.

47. Lauren Berlant, "The Theory of Infantile Citizenship," *Public Culture* 5.3 (Spring 1993): 399.

48. My interpretation of presumed audience and reading practice points to understandings developed, particularly, by Robert C. Allen, ed., *Channels of Discourse, Reassembled* (Chapel Hill: University of North Carolina Press, 1992); Aniko Bodroghkozy, *Groove Tube: Sixties Television and the Youth Rebellion* (Durham: Duke University Press, 2001); Charlotte Brunsdon and David Morley, *Everyday Television: Nationwide* (London: British Film Institute, 1978); Steve Classen, *Watching Jim Crow*; Fiske, *Television Culture*; Herman Gray, *Watching Race: Television and the Struggle for 'Blackness'* (Minneapolis: University of Minnesota Press, 1995); Wendy Kozol, *Life's America* (Philadelphia: Temple University Press, 1994); Horace Newcomb and Paul M. Hirsch, "Television as a Cultural Forum," in *Television: The Critical View*, 5th ed. (New York: Oxford University Press, 1994), 503–515; Lynn Spigel, *Make Room for TV: Television and the Family Ideal in Postwar America* (Chicago: University of Chicago Press, 1992).

49. For a full listing of archival collections consulted, please see Appendix. The majority of the collections cited here are housed at the State Historical Society of Wisconsin Film and Television Archive in Madison, Wisconsin.

50. Stuart Hall, *The Hard Road*, 154.

51. See Dan Marcus, *Happy Days and Wonder Years: The Fifties and Sixties in Contemporary Cultural Politics* (New Brunswick: Rutgers University Press, 2004) and Staiger, *Blockbuster TV*. On the uncanny possibilities or science fiction readings of *Green Acres*, see Spigel, "From Domestic Space to Outer Space."

52. An earlier version of this chapter's section on *The Lawrence Welk Show* appeared as Copyright 1997. From, Victoria E. Johnson, "Citizen Welk: Bubbles, Blue Hair, and Middle America," in *The Revolution Wasn't Televised: Sixties Television and Social Conflict*, eds. Lynn Spigel and Michael Curtin (New York: Routledge, 1997), 265–285. Sections reproduced appear here by permission of Routledge/Taylor & Francis Group, LLC.

53. Stagier's *Blockbuster TV* explores this paradox through the specific example of *The Beverly Hillbillies'* tremendous popularity concurrent with critical assessments of TV in the period as a "vast wasteland"—a term that, taken from an address given in 1961 by President John F. Kennedy's FCC Chair Newton Minow (1960–1962), set the tone for popular critiques of TV throughout the decade. See also, Michael Curtin's *Redeeming the Wasteland* for value judgments of the audience of popular programming in this period—often imagined, specifically, as midwestern—as complacent and dangerously isolationist in the face of Cold War threats.

54. An earlier version of the textual analysis of anniversary coverage featured in this chapter appeared as Victoria E. Johnson, "Fertility Among the Ruins: The 'Heartland,' Maternity, and the Oklahoma City Bombing," *Continuum: Journal of Media & Cultural Studies* 13.1 (1999): 57–75. These segments appear here, permission of Taylor & Francis (UK) Journals, http://www.tandf.co .uk/journals.

55. Exemplary close readings of "southernness" and regional identity in relation to national, popular television programming, include L. Clare Bratten, "Nothin' Could Be Finah: *The Dinah Shore Chevy Show*" forthcoming in *Small Screens, Big Ideas: Television in the 1950s*, ed. Janet Thumin (New York: St. Martin's Press, forthcoming); Allison Graham, *Framing the South: Hollywood, Television, and Race During the Civil Rights Struggle* (Baltimore: Johns Hopkins University Press, 2003); Tara McPherson, *Reconstructing Dixie: Race, Gender, and Nostalgia in the Imagined South* (Durham: Duke University Press, 2003); Horace Newcomb, "Texas: A Giant State of Mind," in *Television: The Critical View* 4th ed., ed. Horace Newcomb (New York: Oxford University Press, 1987), 221–228; Janet Staiger, *Blockbuster TV*.

56. Dee Davis and Tim Marema, "A Rural Perspective: The American Image of Rurality," *Center for Rural Strategies*, http://www.ruralstrategies.org/issues/ perspective1.html

57. James R. Shortridge, "The Persistence of Regional Labels in the United States: Reflections from a Midwestern Perspective," *The New Regionalism,* ed. Charles Reagan Wilson (Jackson: University Press of Mississippi, 1998), 60.

58. Lynn Spigel, "From the Dark Ages to the Golden Age: Women's Memories and Television Reruns," *Screen* 36.1 (Spring 1995): 16–33.

NOTES TO CHAPTER 1

1. Benedict Anderson, *Imagined Communities* (New York: Verso, 1991), 145.

2. Andrew Ross, *No Respect: Intellectuals and Popular Culture* (New York: Routledge, 1989), 53.

3. Leo Marx, *The Machine in the Garden: Technology and the Pastoral Ideal* (New York: Oxford University Press, 1964), 149, 188.

4. For this concept of networking as a reorganization of space and time toward nationally integrated cultures of production and consumption, I am indebted to work by Sharon Zukin, *Landscapes of Power: From Detroit to Disney World* (Berkeley: University of California Press, 1991), 29; and Michael Curtin, "Unraveling the Network Nation: Spatial Logics of Media History," Plenary Address to Society for Cinema Studies Annual Conference, West Palm Beach, Florida, 1999.

5. James Carey, *Communication as Culture* (New York: Routledge, 1992), 155. Here Carey is summarizing scholar Harold Innis's theories of space-binding media versus place-bound interests.

6. David Morley, *Home Territories: Media, Mobility and Identity* (London: Routledge, 2000), 176.

7. James R. Shortridge, *The Middle West: Its Meaning in American Culture* (Lawrence: University Press of Kansas, 1989), 16, 6–7.

8. Andrew Cayton and Peter S. Onuf, *The Midwest and the Nation: Rethinking the History of an American Region* (Bloomington: Indiana University Press, 1990), 117–118.

9. See, for example, Irving Dilliard, "What Is the Middle West Thinking?" *New Republic* vol. 103 (23 December 1940): 863–864; R.M. Lovett, "The Future of the Middle West," *New Republic* vol. 101 (8 November 1939): 54–56; Arville Schalaben, "This Is America," *The Nation* (17 June 1939): 690–693. Shortridge also notes that, in this period, themes of "maturation," balance, evenness, and representative Americanness are associated with the Midwest in the literature of the period from 1880 until the United States' entry into World War I.

10. Raymond Williams, *The Country and the City* (New York: Oxford University Press, 1973), 1.

11. Shortridge, *The Middle West,* 9–10, 55–56.

12. Christopher Anderson and Michael Curtin, "Mapping the Ethereal City: Chicago Television, the FCC, and the Politics of Place," *Quarterly Review of Film and Video* 16.3–4 (1999): 293.

13. For support of the idea that broadcast law and policy remain essentially unchanged from the mid-1960s to the mid-1990s see, for example, Anderson and Curtin, "Mapping the Ethereal City," 221–238; Patricia Aufderheide, *Communications Policy and the Public Interest: The Telecommunications Act of 1996* (New York: Guilford Press, 1999); James Baughman, *Television's Guardians: The FCC and the Politics of Programming, 1958–1967* (Knoxville: University of Texas Press, 1985); William Boddy, *Fifties Television: The Industry and Its Critics* (Urbana: University of Illinois Press, 1993); Michele Hilmes, *Hollywood and Broadcasting: From Radio to Cable* (Chicago: University of Illi-

nois Press, 1990); Thomas Streeter, *Selling the Air: A Critique of the Policy of Commercial Broadcasting in the United States* (Chicago: University of Chicago Press, 1996); Mark Williams, "Issue Introduction: U.S. Regional and Non-Network Television History," *Quarterly Review of Film and Video* 16.3 (1999): 221–228. Cable homes do not outnumber over-air broadcast reception until 1990, when, according to Nielsen Media Research, the percentage of cable homes first rises to 56.4 percent. The paradox of national TV becoming increasingly localized on either coast is addressed in Anderson and Curtin, "Mapping the Ethereal City," which closely analyzes "the demise of Chicago as a national center for broadcasting" and the resulting FCC hearings regarding network service to the region (conducted during the spring of 1962).

14. "Announcing the National Broadcasting Company," advertisement reproduced in Erik Barnouw, *Tube of Plenty: The Evolution of American Television* 2nd rev. ed. (New York: Oxford University Press, 1990), 55.

15. Ibid. WEAF was AT&T's former outlet in New York City whose ownership and operation was assumed by RCA in 1926, enabling its flagship status as an NBC outlet in New York City.

16. David Nye, *Electrifying America: Social Meanings of a New Technology* (Cambridge: MIT Press, 2001), 296.

17. Ibid., 287.

18. Ibid., 297.

19. Ibid., 300.

20. Ibid., 304.

21. Pierre Bourdieu, *Distinction: A Social Critique of the Judgement of Taste,* trans. Richard Nice (Cambridge: Harvard University Press, 1984), 124.

22. "President and Other Officials Laud NBC at Dedication of New Studios," NBC Press Release (23 July 1937), SHSW. NBC Collection, Central Files, Television Files, Box 103.

23. "1940 Report of the Television Survey Conducted at the NY World's Fair," SHSW. NBC Collection, Central Files, Television Files, Box 103, Folder 21.

24. Memo on television promotion, from Major L.R. Lohr to Clay Morgan (24 July 1939), SHSW. NBC Collection, Central Files, TV Files, Box 103.

25. "Television Report Prepared by RCA & NBC," (30 October 1939), SHSW. NBC Collection, Central Files, TV Files, Box 103, emphasis mine.

26. "NBC TV Master Plan, 1948," SHSW. NBC Collection, Central Files, TV Files, Box 106, Folder 7.

27. "1945–1950 Timetable of Completion," SHSW. NBC Collection, Central Files, Television Files, Box 105, Folder 17.

28. *Statistical Abstract of the United States, 1961* (Washington, D.C.: Government Printing Office, 1961), 516.

29. "NBC TV Master Plan" (emphases mine).

30. To paraphrase Harold Innis's theory of the frontier's relation to "back-tier" interests, as summarized in Carey, *Communication as Culture*, 155.

31. For the text of these laws and regulatory statements, I have turned to the government documents themselves and also to their reproductions in Frank J. Kahn, *Documents of American Broadcasting*, 4th ed. (Englewood Cliffs, NJ: Prentice-Hall, 1984) and Patricia Aufderheide, *Communications Policy and the Public Interest*. I have also examined the papers of Newton Minow and NBC executives related to these topics, at the State Historical Society of Wisconsin, Madison, Wisconsin.

32. Streeter, *Selling the Air*, 8, 15.

33. See, especially, Michele Hilmes, *Only Connect: A Cultural History of Broadcasting in the United States* (Belmont, CA: Wadsworth/Thomson Learning, 2002), and Mark Goodman and Mark Gring, "The Radio Act of 1927: Progressive Ideology, Epistemology, and Praxis," in *Connections: A Broadcast History Reader*, ed. Michele Hilmes (Belmont, CA: Wadsworth/Thomson Learning, 2003), 19–39.

34. Hilmes, *Only Connect*, 18.

35. Reprinted in Kahn, *Documents of American Broadcasting*, 46.

36. Reprinted in Kahn, *Documents of American Broadcasting*, 41. Ohio and Michigan, the other states of the "twelve-state" census definition were assigned to Zone II, with the "far Western" states of the Founder's Period, Pennsylvania, West Virginia, and also Kentucky and Virginia.

37. Ibid., 89, emphasis on "as nearly as possible" mine.

38. Ibid., 57.

39. Though "profit power" companies were certainly not above "spite-lining" practices in communities where cooperatives were seen as a competitive threat. See, Nye, *Electrifying America*.

40. Susan J. Douglas, *Listening In: Radio and the American Imagination from Amos 'n' Andy to Wolfman Jack and Howard Stern* (New York: Times Books, 1999), 39.

41. "FRC Interpretation of the Public Interest, Statement Made by the Commission on August 23, 1928, Relative to Public Interest, Convenience, or Necessity," 2 FRC Ann. Rep. 166 Reprinted in Kahn, 60. See also, Fritz Messere on the FRC, the Davis Amendment, and public interest, at http://www.oswego.edu/~messere/FRCdavis2.html See, Title 47, Chapter 5, Subchapter I., Section 151.

42. Kahn, *Documents of American Broadcasting*, 60.

43. Ibid., 62.

44. From text of "Allocation of Radio Facilities," 74th Congress, 2d Session, Senate Report No. 1588, http://www.fcc.gov.

45. Notably, following "The Interpretation of Public Interest" (1928) and "The Great Lakes Statement" (1929), the District Circuit Court of Appeals in

Washington, D.C. announced the "first judicial affirmation of the FRC's right to consider a station's past programming" when determining license renewal in the interest of the listening public over that of "the sender" of the broadcast message. In *KFKB Broadcasting Association, Inc. v. Federal Radio Commission* 47 F.2d 670 (D.C. Cir., February 2, 1931), the court concurred with the FRC's revocation of Dr. John R. Brinkley's license to broadcast as KFKB in Milford, Kansas on the grounds that his "uninteresting, but also distasteful" programs were serving only Brinkley's personal interests with their singular focus and profit motives (proffering "medical" cures by mail), rather than that of his listeners. See, Kahn, *Documents of American Broadcasting,* 76, 78.

46. The Communications Act of 1934, as reprinted, unabridged, at http://www.law.cornell.edu/topics/media.html.

47. *National Broadcasting Co., Inc., et al. v. United States et al.* (10 May 1943) as reprinted in Kahn, *Documents of American Broadcasting,* 124. See also James Baughman, *Television's Guardians,* 10.

48. Federal Communications Commission, *Public Service Responsibility of Broadcast Licensees* (New York: Arno Press, 1974), 38.

49. Ibid, 14, emphasis mine.

50. Ibid.

51. Ibid.

52. Though, ostensibly, phonograph recordings could include a broad range of presumptively "high" cultural program material such as recitations of poetry, opera, or symphonic performances.

53. Frank J. Kahn, *Documents of American Broadcasting* (Englewood Cliffs, NJ: Prentice-Hall, 1973), 160.

54. Ibid., 217.

55. Ibid., 219.

56. Federal Communications Commission, 38.

57. Ibid., 55.

58. Ibid., 174. In 1949 this principle was reinforced with the FCC's statement, "The Fairness Doctrine," which stated that it is the responsibility of the individual licensee to determine "what percentage of the limited broadcast day should appropriately be devoted to news and discussion or consideration of public issues," and to balance the dominant interests of the community with voice to "highly specialized," limited concerns. See also, "In the Matter of Editorializing by Broadcast Licensees," 13 FCC 1246 (1 June 1946) as reprinted in Kahn, *Documents of American Broadcasting* (1984), 167.

59. Kahn, *Documents of American Broadcasting* (1973), 202.

60. Ibid., 209.

61. Kahn, *Documents of American Broadcasting* (1984), 191.

62. Ibid., 201.

63. The FCC reinforced the importance of ascertainment in 1971, with a sig-

nificant revision. Now, "primary emphasis was placed on programming responsive to community 'problems' rather than 'tastes, needs, and desires.'" (Ibid., 191–192). By 1981, the ascertainment requirement was eliminated for radio broadcasters and, in 1984, it was repealed for television stations. As recently as 2004, the FCC's *Notice of Inquiry in the Matter of Broadcast Localism* stated that "Even as the Commission deregulated many behavioral rules for broadcasters in the 1980s, it did not deviate from the notion that they must serve their local communities." According to this "NOI," the FCC embraces and promotes digital television as the new technological solution to "provide service to all segments of the community in markets where multiple broadcast stations are available to satisfy the specialized needs of certain groups." In dissent, Commissioner Michael J. Copps asked, "What if we get to the end of this new proceeding and determine that localism is *not* served by ever greater media concentration?" See Federal Communication Commission, *Notice of Inquiry in the Matter of Broadcast Localism* (Washington, DC: GPO, 1 July 2004).

64. See, for example, Lawrence L. Knutson, "President of Cyberspace," *Chicago Sun Times* (10 March 1996): 28 on the occasion of President William Jefferson Clinton's opening of a statewide effort in California to link classrooms to the internet. Clinton called the event the "modern-day equivalent of an 'old-fashioned barn-raising'" and furthered the frontier analogies by calling volunteers and students "pioneers" of cyberspace. Reference to Middle American and, specifically, midwestern "sensibilities" as different from those on the coasts is a consistent feature of trade-industry publications and discussions. See, for example, Doug Halonen, "FCC Is Now 'Pvt. Ryan's' Battleground," *Television Week* (15 November 2004): 22.

65. Andrew Ross, *No Respect*, 59.

66. Janice Radway, *A Feeling for Books: The Book-of-the-Month Club, Literary Taste, and Middle-Class Desire* (Chapel Hill: University of North Carolina Press, 1997).

67. William Zinsser, "Out Where the Tall Antennas Grow," *Harpers Magazine* (April 1956): 37.

NOTES TO CHAPTER 2

1. *Jubilee, U.S.A.* co-producer, Si Siman, on his meetings with national sponsors, quoted in Reta Spears-Stewart, *Remembering The Ozark Jubilee* (Springfield, MO: Stewart, Dillbeck & White Productions, 1993), 8.

2. Gary A. Steiner, *The People Look at Television: A Study of Audience Attitudes* (New York: Alfred A. Knopf, 1963), 235.

3. Erika Doss, *Benton, Pollock, and the Politics of Modernism: From Regionalism to Abstract Expressionism* (Chicago: University of Chicago Press, 1991), 137, and, quoting Thomas Hart Benton, 111–112.

4. Michael C. Steiner, "Regionalism in the Great Depression," *Geographical Review* 73 (1983): 432.

5. Andrew Cayton and Peter S. Onuf, *The Midwest and the Nation: Rethinking the History of an American Region* (Bloomington: Indiana University Press, 1990), xv.

6. Warren Susman, *Culture as History: The Transformation of American Society in the Twentieth Century* (New York: Pantheon Books, 1984), 29, 31.

7. Ibid., 31, 35.

8. Ibid., 31, 33, 36–37.

9. William Boddy, *Fifties Television: The Industry and Its Critics* (Urbana: University of Illinois Press, 1993), 101, 235.

10. James R. Shortridge, *The Middle West: Its Meaning in American Culture* (Lawrence, Kansas: University Press of Kansas, 1989), 67.

11. Serge Guilbaut, *How New York Stole the Idea of Modern Art: Abstract Expressionism, Freedom, and the Cold War,* trans. Arthur Goldhammer (Chicago: University of Chicago Press, 1983), 4.

12. Doss, *Benton, Pollock, And the Politics of Modernism,* 4.

13. Guilbaut, *How New York Stole the Idea of Modern Art,* 3–4.

14. See, especially, James Baughman, *Television's Guardians: The FCC and the Politics of Programming, 1958–1967* (Knoxville: University of Tennessee Press, 1985); Boddy, *Fifties Television*; Michael Curtin, *Redeeming the Wasteland: Television Documentary and Cold War Politics* (New Brunswick: Rutgers University Press, 1995); Laurie Ouellette, *Viewers Like You? How Public TV Failed the People* (New York: Columbia University Press, 2002).

15. William S. White, "The 'Midwest Mind' in Congress," *The New York Times Magazine* (1 March 1953): 10; "Grant," *Variety Television Reviews* (6 July 1955); Hugh Sidey, "At the Heart of the Land Ocean," *Life* 66 (13 June 1969): 4.

16. Raymond Williams, *Marxism and Literature* (New York: Oxford University Press, 1977), 122.

17. Ibid., 124.

18. Christopher Anderson and Michael Curtin, "Mapping the Ethereal City: Chicago Television, the FCC, and the Politics of Place," *Quarterly Review of Film and Video* 16.3–4 (1999): 296.

19. Peter Guralnick, *Last Train to Memphis: The Rise and Fall of Elvis Presley* (Boston: Little, Brown & Co., 1994), 286.

20. Oliver Treyz, quoted in "The New ABC of It," *Newsweek* (10 December 1956): 48. This counter-programming and audience-development strategy anticipates the Fox network of the 1980s or UPN in the 1990s, both of which staked their identity as new networks on otherwise under-served audiences. Fox and UPN explicitly counter-programmed to urban African American and youth audiences to build an audience base from which each could gain enough viable

capital to later focus on more "traditional" audiences, arguably abandoning this viewer base.

21. Baughman, *Television's Guardians,* 88. See also Christopher H. Sterling and John M. Kittross, *Stay Tuned: A Concise History of American Broadcasting,* 2nd ed. (Belmont, CA: Wadsworth Publishing Company, 1990), 261, and 385 on ABC's network composition—dependent upon affiliates that "usually were smaller and rural stations," as well as on the relative aesthetic impoverishment of the network's programs.

22. Christopher Anderson, *Hollywood TV: The Studio System in the Fifties* (Austin: University of Texas Press, 1994), 12, emphasis mine.

23. SHSW. Statement of Oliver Treyz, President, ABC-TV Network, before the FCC (5 February 1962). Newton Minow Collection, Correspondence, Box 2, Folder entitled American Broadcasting Company (May 1961–May 1963). Folders in Minow collection are alphabetical within boxes, not numeric.

24. SHSW. Testimony of Sylvester "Pat" Weaver in Network Hearings, as noted in Newton Minow Collection, Box 42, Folder entitled Television Shows, Letters from Viewers and Producers (August 1961–February 1963).

25. Ouellette, *Viewers Like You?,* 37.

26. Ibid.

27. Anderson, *Hollywood TV,* 169.

28. John Thornton Caldwell, *Televisuality: Style, Crisis, and Authority in American Television* (New Brunswick: Rutgers University Press, 1995), 34, 56.

29. Interdepartment Correspondence to Mr. David Adams from Peter M. Tintle, dated 13 October 1958. Harry R. Bannister Collection, Box 6, Folder 7, Affiliates, TV, General Correspondence, Folder 21—Stations (1953–54, 1956–58).

30. Caldwell, *Televisuality,* 36–37. It should be noted that *Ted Mack's Original Amateur Hour* ran on the ABC network during the 1955–1957 and 1960 seasons. It spent time, from 1948 through 1970 on *each* of the "Big Three" networks and its first season home was with DuMont.

31. Charlotte Brunsdon and David Morley, *Everyday Television: Nationwide* (London: British Film Institute, 1978), 82.

32. Ibid., 9.

33. Quoted by Reta Spears-Stewart in her *Remembering the Ozark Jubilee,* 7.

34. "Tain't Hillbilly, Neighbor! It's Country Music That's Making a Splash on TV," *TV Guide* (27 August 1955): 10–12. The series' title changed from *Ozark Jubilee* to *Jubilee, U.S.A.* in the program's second season—reflecting the program's broadly national audience. I have used this last title, throughout, for consistency.

35. "Hillbilly TV Show Hits the Big Time," *Business Week* (10 March 1956): 31.

36. "They Love Mountain Music," *Time* (7 May 1956): 60.

37. "She'd Druther Ketch Frogs," *TV Guide* (22 December 1956): 20–21, and "They Love Mountain Music," 60.

38. William K. Schweinher, *Lawrence Welk: An American Institution* (Chicago: Nelson-Hall, 1980), 53.

39. Ibid., 15.

40. Mark Williams, "Televising Postwar Los Angeles: 'Remote' Possibilites in a 'City at Night,'" *Velvet Light Trap* 33 (Spring 1994): 27.

41. Schweinher quoting producer Don Fedderson, *Lawrence Welk*, 16.

42. Lawrence Welk, "Television Places Unique Burden on Bands," *Downbeat* (18 April 1956): 71.

43. SHSW. NBC Collection, Advertising Files, National Audience Promotion Division Files, Box 135c, Folder 12, CBS and ABC Advertising Plans, 1958–1959.

44. "A Good Time for Mother: That's the Philosophy Behind Lawrence Welk's Tremendous Success," *TV Guide* (21 January 1956): 14. Two scholars' work on "low" TV programming and audience interactivity in particular helps to theorize Welk's understanding of the gendered and generational pleasures of his show and the accompanying critical disdain for these same qualities. See Marsha F. Cassidy, "Sob Stories, Merriment, and Surprises: The 1950s Audience Participation Show on Network Television," *Velvet Light Trap* (Fall 1998): 48–62; and, John Fiske, "Quizzical Pleasures," in *Television Culture* (New York: Routledge, 1987), 265–280.

45. David Marc, *Comic Visions: Television Comedy and American Culture* (Boston: Unwin Hyman, 1989), 43.

46. Schweinher, *Lawrence Welk*, 151.

47. These assertions and all that follow are based upon screenings of five to six episodes of *The Lawrence Welk Show* (including *The Dodge Dancing Party*) from each decade of its network (1955–1960, 1961–1971) and syndicated (1972–1982) run—approximately twenty episodes in all, plus each "reunion" special of the 1980s and 1990s (which now run weekly on PBS stations across the country in themed, cut-down episodes), and the guest appearance Welk made on *The Jack Benny Program* in 1964.

48. "Champagne with Welk," *Newsweek* (21 May 1956): 75.

49. Quoted in Schweinher, *Lawrence Welk*, 163.

50. Ibid., 164.

51. Ibid., 111, x.

52. Susman, *Culture as History*, 244.

53. Bernice McGeehan, "Champagne and Grace Notes," *The Saturday Evening Post* (March 1980): 52.

54. Lawrence Welk, "The American Spirit—as Lawrence Welk Sees It," *U.S. News and World Report* (24 January 1977): 69.

55. "Some Champagne for the Folks," *Life* (6 May 1957): 127.

56. Schweinher, *Lawrence Welk,* 56, 73.

57. Ibid., 175.

58. Quoted in Schweinher, *Lawrence Welk,* 178.

59. Jay Joslyn, "Now They're Screaming for Welk," *Milwaukee Sentinel* (31 August 1970): TV 7.

60. George Lipsitz, "The Meaning of Memory: Family, Class, and Ethnicity in Early Network Television Programs," *Camera Obscura* 16 (January 1988): 80–81.

61. Ibid., 83.

62. Ibid., 85.

63. Ibid., 108.

64. Elting Morrison, "Wunnerful, Wunnerful: A Wooden Baton and an Iron Rod," *The New York Times Book Review* (17 October 1971): 39.

65. Ibid., 39.

66. Pete Rahn, "Red, White and Blue 'Special': Welk's 'Thank You America,' " *St. Louis Globe-Democrat* (20 November 1970): 13C.

67. A sentiment clearly expressed in television documentary coverage of the period, including, for example, *CBS Reports: The New Left* (1968).

68. Lawrence Welk, *My America, Your America* (Englewood Cliffs, NJ: Prentice-Hall, Inc., 1976), 133, 135.

69. Quoted in Schweinher, *Lawrence Welk,* 170–171.

70. This program illustrates Denise Mann's analysis of Benny's show as one of several in the 1950s and 1960s which "reworked the middle-class housewife's relationship" to celebrities "by foregrounding the position of the female fan." Uniquely, here, however, "Benny undermined his own status as a star by pitting himself against" a broadcast television star rather than a "glamorous movie" star. See Denise Mann, "The Spectacularization of Everyday Life: Recycling Hollywood Stars and Fans in Early Television Variety Shows," in *Private Screenings: Television and the Female Consumer,* eds. Lynn Spigel and Denise Mann (Minneapolis: University of Minnesota Press, 1992), 41–70.

71. Joslyn, "Now They're Screaming for Welk," 1.

72. Lawrence Welk with Bernice McGeehan, *My America, Your America,* 109.

73. Quoted by Rahn, "Red, White and Blue 'Special.' "

74. Welk, *My America, Your America,* 133.

75. Michael Miller, "Polkas, Waltzes, and Champagne Music," *North Dakota Horizons* (Winter, 1994), 28.

76. Cited in James W. Carey, *Communication as Culture: Essays on Media and Society* (New York: Routledge, 1992), 179.

77. Arthur Schlesinger, Jr., "The Amazing Success Story of 'Spiro *Who?*' " *The New York Times* (26 July 1970).

78. John Leland, "Old Fans Still Bubble Along to Lawrence Welk," *The New*

York Times (11 September 2004) notes that: "Twelve years after Welk's death *The Lawrence Welk Show* is the highest-rated syndicated show on public television, . . . His viewers outnumber those for MTV, VH1 and BET on Saturday nights."

79. President George Herbert Walker Bush, quoted in Joe Queenan, "The Pork Barrel Polka: Does the President Now Risk Losing the Lawrence Welk Vote?" *The Washington Post* (2 February 1992): C5.

80. *People Weekly* (19 November 1990): 68, and Steven Stark, "A Wunnerful, Wunnerful Idea," *The Washington Post* (23 June 1991): B5.

81. Frank Morgan, "Report from the Heartland," *Newsweek* (11 September 1972): 27.

NOTES TO CHAPTER 3

1. *Webster Groves Revisited* aired on CBS on April 8, 1966.

2. This chapter's approach to reading public responses is particularly indebted to methodology developed and exemplified by Aniko Bodroghkozy, "Is This What You Mean by Color TV?" in *Private Screenings: Television and the Female Consumer,* eds. Lynn Spigel and Denise Mann (Minneapolis: University of Minnesota Press, 1992), 142–168, and Steven D. Classen, *Watching Jim Crow: The Struggles Over Mississippi TV, 1955–1969* (Durham: Duke University Press, 2004).

3. Michael Curtin, *Redeeming the Wasteland: Television Documentary and Cold War Politics* (New Brunswick: Rutgers University Press, 1995), 3.

4. James Baughman, *Television's Guardians: The FCC and the Politics of Programming, 1958–1967* (Knoxville: University of Tennessee Press, 1985), 114.

5. Laurie Ouellette, *Viewers Like You? How Public TV Failed the People* (New York: Columbia University Press, 2002), 30.

6. Curtin, *Redeeming the Wasteland,* 2.

7. Chapter 5 examines a more recent iteration of this "aspirational" viewer identification, through what Ron Becker has termed the "slumpy" viewer/market and what Jon Kraszewski has called the "urban aspirant." See Ron Becker, *Gay TV and Straight America* (New Brunswick: Rutgers University Press, 2006), and Jon Kraszewski, "Country Hicks and Urban Cliques: Mediating Race, Reality and Liberalism on MTV's *The Real World,*" in *Reality TV: Remaking Television Culture,* eds. Susan Murray and Laurie Ouellette (New York: New York University Press, 2004), 179–196.

8. Gary A. Steiner, *The People Look at Television: A Study of Audience Attitudes* (New York: Alfred A. Knopf, 1963), 233, emphases mine.

9. Curtin, *Redeeming the Wasteland,* 260, 14.

10. John F. Kennedy, "We Must Climb to the Hilltop," *Life* (22 August 1960): 72.

11. Newton Minow, "The Vast Wasteland," *Equal Time: The Private Broad-caster and the Public Interest,* ed. Laurence Laurent (New York: Atheneum, 1964), 55.

12. Ibid., 53.

13. Ibid., 54.

14. Ibid., 48.

15. Ibid., 57–58.

16. SHSW. "Analysis of Letters Received in Response to Chairman Minow's Address to the National Association of Broadcasters, May 9, 1961." Newton Minow Collection.

17. "An Open Letter to Chairman Minow," *Sponsor* (2 April 1962): 65, and SHSW. "Editorial: Minow—Another Bigot at the Spigot?" *Peoria Journal Star* (17 May 1961). Newton Minow Collection, Box 29, Speech of May 9, 1961, responses.

18. SHSW. Letter from Mrs. Paul Appel, East Lansing, Michigan (5 June 1961). Newton Minow Collection.

19. SHSW. Letter from Mrs. J.M. Stillwell, Jr., Upper Marlboro, Maryland (17 May 1961). Newton Minow Collection.

20. SHSW. Letter from Joanne Spencer Kantrowitz of Chicago, Illinois (no date). Newton Minow Collection.

21. Baughman, *Television's Guardians,* 114.

22. According to Curtin's analysis (which focuses on the years 1959–1964, pre–*Webster Groves*), internationally focused documentaries made up eighty-one percent of all such programs in the 1959–1960 season, and remained the majority focus of documentaries until the 1962–1963 season, when seventeen of the forty-four network-produced documentaries fell into this category. Other key examples of "home front" documentaries of the period include: *Bell & Howell Close-Up! Cast the First Stone* (ABC, March 28, 1961), *Bell & Howell Close-Up! Walk in My Shoes* (ABC, September 19, 1961), *David Brinkley's Journal: Our Man on the Mississippi* (NBC, February 5, 1964), *Smalltown, USA* (NBC, September 23, 1964), *CBS Reports: Watts—Riot or Revolt?* (CBS, December 7, 1965), and *Newark: Anatomy of a Riot* (ABC, July 14, 1968). See Curtin, *Redeeming the Wasteland,* 261–266.

23. Ibid., 13.

24. Jack Gould, "TV: Integration Problem," *The New York Times* (28 May 1960): 45.

25. Curtin, *Redeeming the Wasteland,* 181.

26. Ibid., 183.

27. Ibid., 153.

28. Anna McCarthy, "'Stanley Milgram, Allen Funt, and Me,' Postwar Social Science and the 'First Wave' of Reality TV," in *Reality TV: Remaking Television*

Culture, eds. Susan Murray and Laurie Ouellette (New York: New York University Press, 2004), 23.

29. Curtin, *Redeeming the Wasteland,* 9.

30. SHSW. Letter from Kermit McMeans, Jr., Newark, Delaware (5 February 1964). David Brinkley Collection.

31. SHSW. Letter from Victor W. Take, Kirkwood, Missouri (2 February 1964). David Brinkley Collection.

32. "Bill," "Review: Our Man on the Mississippi," *Variety Television Reviews* (5 February 1964).

33. SHSW. Letter from Ted McElhiney, Bettendorf, Iowa (3 February 1964). David Brinkley Collection.

34. Thirty three years later, *Time* magazine returned to Webster Groves to study "A Week in the Life of a High School," arguing that, "*Time* picked this school for the same reason marketing experts and sociologists like to wander this way when they are taking the country's temperature: the state of Missouri, especially the regions around St. Louis, are bellwether communities, not cutting edge, not lagging indicators, but the middle of the country, middle of the road, middle of the sky." See, Nancy Gibbs, "A Week in the Life of a High School," *Time Magazine* (25 October 1999), accessed at http://www.time.com/time/magazine/printout/9,8816,992319,00.html.

35. "Sociologist Declares Students Work Hard for the Wrong Reasons," *The Los Angeles Times* (25 February 1966): 16.

36. "Pressures on Webster Groves Students Cause Cheating," *St. Louis Globe-Democrat* (24 February 1966): 5A.

37. Rick DuBrow, "Follow-Up by CBS Called Effective," *St. Louis Post-Dispatch* (12 April 1966): 3D.

38. Pit, *"Sixteen in Webster Groves,"* Variety Television Reviews (2 March 1966).

39. DuBrow, "Follow-Up by CBS Called Effective," 3D.

40. Quoting Mrs. Richard K. Morse and Mr. Edward E. Kice, Jr., respectively, in "TV Program on Teen-Agers Stirs Anger and Soul Searching," *St. Louis Post-Dispatch* (26 February 1966): 3A.

41. Shortly after the Webster Groves documentaries aired, Kuralt embraced a new journalistic persona and investment in stories of Americana, filing his "On the Road" reports for CBS News and specials. According to Kuralt, his idea was to produce and promote awareness that "stories do exist in places where we hadn't looked for them before." See "Into the Heartland," *Newsweek* (1 January 1968): 54.

42. Thomas J. Sugrue, *The Origins of the Urban Crisis: Race and Inequality in Postwar Detroit* (Princeton: Princeton University Press, 1996), 268.

43. Harry C. Boyte, "Beyond Politics as Usual," in *The New Populism: The*

Politics of Empowerment, eds. Harry C. Boyte and Frank Riessman (Philadelphia: Temple University Press, 1996), quoting George Will, 4.

44. Jonathan Reider, "The Rise and Fall of the 'Silent Majority,' " in *The Rise and Fall of the New Deal Order, 1930–1980,* eds. Steven Fraser and Gary Gertle (Princeton: Princeton University Press, 1989), 262.

45. Lizabeth Cohen, *A Consumer's Republic: The Politics of Mass Consumption in Postwar America* (New York: Alfred A. Knopf, 2003), 309.

46. Agnew is here responding to the network coverage of President Nixon's speech on "Vietnamization" and the rebuttals following the address. Agnew's speech was written by Pat Buchanan, and his address was delivered to the Midwest Regional Republican Committee Meeting on November 13, 1969. See, John R. Coyne, *The Impudent Snobs: Agnew vs. the Intellectual Establishment* (New Rochelle: Arlington House, 1972), 267.

47. James Gerstenzang, "Quayle Attacks 'Cultural Elite' on Moral Values," *The Los Angeles Times* (10 June 1992): A1.

48. Laurie Ouellette, *Viewers Like You?,* 176, emphasis mine.

NOTES TO CHAPTER 4

1. Pierre Bourdieu, *Distinction: A Social Critique of the Judgement of Taste,* trans. Richard Nice (Cambridge: Harvard University Press, 1984), 266.

2. Tracy Johnson, "Why 30 Million Are Mad about Mary," *New York Times Magazine* (7 April 1974): 98.

3. David Halberstam, "The Coming of Carter," *Newsweek* (19 July 1976): 11.

4. James R. Shortridge, *The Middle West: Its Meaning in American Culture* (Lawrence: University Press of Kansas, 1989), 6, 9.

5. James R. Shortridge, "The Persistence of Regional Labels in the United States: Reflections from a Midwestern Perspective," *The New Regionalism,* ed. Charles Reagan Wilson (Oxford: University Press of Mississippi, 1998), 58.

6. Shortridge, *The Middle West,* 67.

7. Ibid.

8. Editors of *Time,* "Man and Woman of the Year: The Middle Americans," *Time* (5 January 1970): 10.

9. Henry Luce, "A Letter from the Publisher," *Time* (5 January 1970): 3.

10. "Man and Woman of the Year," 10.

11. Frank Morgan, "Report from the Heartland," *Newsweek* (11 September 1972): 24, 27.

12. Editors of *Time,* "The Good Life in Minnesota," *Time* (13 August 1973): 24.

13. Ibid.

14. Ibid., 34.

15. Quoting Frank Barth, Minneapolis resident and transplanted Chicagoan, ibid., 24.

16. Ibid., 31.

17. Ibid., 34.

18. "The Heartland: America Rediscovered, Part 4," *Better Homes and Gardens* (July 1976): 113.

19. Judah Stampfer, "Midwest Taste & Eastern Critics," *The Nation* (9 November 1974): 473.

20. "The Heartland: America Rediscovered," 115, 116.

21. Thomas D. Anderson, "The Liberal Midwest," *The Nation* (13 December 1975): 625–626.

22. Jack Gould, "Here's to Relevance—But Will It Sell?" *The New York Times* (1 March 1970): 109.

23. The 1968 Court of Appeals ruling was in the case of *John Banzhaf III v. GCC*. In 1969, the Public Health Cigarette Smoking Act was passed, which also encouraged networks to remove cigarette advertising from the air.

24. As told to interviewer Morrie Gelman, Archive of American Television Interview with Grant Tinker, part five of ten. Accessed at http://video.google.com/videosearch?q=Archive+of+American+television+interview+grant+tinker&he=en.

25. Todd Gitlin, *Watching Television* (New York: Pantheon, 1986), 207.

26. For excellent histories of this period, see also Sydney W. Head, Christopher Sterling and Lemuel B. Schofield, *Broadcasting in America: A Survey of Electronic Media*, 7th ed. (Boston: Houghton Mifflin Company, 1994), and Michele Hilmes, *Only Connect: A Cultural History of Broadcasting in the United States* (Belmont, CA: Wadsworth/Thomson Learning, 2002), 218–254.

27. Aniko Bodroghkozy, *Groove Tube: Sixties Television and the Youth Rebellion* (Durham: Duke University Press, 2001), 65.

28. Ibid., 129, and Jeffrey Miller, " 'And Then There Was Bloomington': Quality and the Cultural Geography of M*A*S*H," presented at the Society for Cinema and Media Studies Annual Conference, Denver, CO, 2002.

29. Gitlin, *Watching Television,* 216.

30. Kirsten Marthe Lentz, "Quality Versus Relevance: Feminism, Race, and the Politics of the Sign in 1970s Television," *Camera Obscura* 43, 15.1 (2000): 68. See also, on "whiteness' " association with the "intellect" and "sexual modesty," Richard Dyer, "White," *Screen* 29.4 (Autumn 1988): 44–65.

31. Lentz, "Quality Versus Relevance," 67.

32. Mary Richards poses this question to Mr. Grant in "Best of Enemies," *The Mary Tyler Moore Show* (CBS, January 26, 1974).

33. Lance Morrow, "Goodbye to Our Mary," *Time* (14 March 1977): 37.

34. Karl E. Meyer, "A Farewell Bouquet for Mary Tyler Moore," *Saturday Review* (19 March 1977): 49.

35. Ibid., 49.

36. Rowland Barber, "We Are All Pussycats Here," *TV Guide* (8–14 February 1975). Accessed at http://www.mtmshow.com/tvg1975art.shtml.

37. Johnson, "Why 30 Million Are Mad about Mary," 31, 98.

38. Quoting Don Rickles in Dwight Whitney, "Still Button-Down, But No Longer Buttoned Up," *TV Guide* (20 January 1973): 22.

39. Karen Stabiner, "For Bob Newhart, Affection Is Still the Essence of Successful Comedy," *The New York Times* (26 December 1982): H25.

40. Ernest Pascucci, "Intimate (Tele)visions," in *Architecture of the Everyday,* eds. Steven Harris and Deborah Berke (Princeton: Princeton Architectural Press, 1997), 39.

41. Moore quoted from "The Making of *The Mary Tyler Moore Show,*" on *The Mary Tyler Moore Show: The Complete First Season* DVD (Twentieth Century Fox, 2002).

42. Ibid.

43. Quoting David Davis and then Allan Burns, ibid.

44. John Thornton Caldwell, *Televisuality: Style, Crisis, and Authority in American Television* (New Brunswick: Rutgers University Press, 1995), 18.

45. James L. Brooks quoted by Robert S. Alley and Irby B. Brown in *Love Is All Around: The Making of the Mary Tyler Moore Show* (New York: Dell Publishing, 1989), 6.

46. Quoting Lorenzo Music in Whitney, "Still Button-Down, But No Longer Buttoned Up," 23.

47. As told to interviewer Karen Hermann, Archive of American Television Interview with Jay Sandrich, part one of ten. Accessed at http://video.google.com/videosearch?q=Archive+of+American+television+interview+jay+sandrich&he=en.

48. Bob Newhart quoted in Don Oldenburg, "Bob Newhart Gets Call for Twain Prize," *The Washington Post* (4 April 2002): C1. On Newhart's subversiveness, see also Stephen E. Kercher, *Revel with a Cause: Liberal Satire in Postwar America* (Chicago: University of Chicago Press, 2006).

49. Silverman quoted from Moore quoted from "The Making of *The Mary Tyler Moore Show.*"

50. M. MacPherson, "MTM and Her All-Star Team," *Newsweek* (29 March 1973): 60.

51. "Have I Found a Guy for You," *The Mary Tyler Moore Show* (CBS, November 18, 1972).

52. As told to Joseph N. Bell, "My Friend, Valerie Harper," *Good Housekeeping* (February 1974): 141.

53. Quotes taken, respectively, from "Hi There, Sports Fans!" (CBS, October 13,1973); "Divorce Isn't Everything" (CBS, October 10, 1970); "He's No Heavy, He's My Brother" (CBS, October 2, 1971); "I Am Curious Cooper" (CBS, September 25,1971); and "Cover Boy" (CBS, October 23, 1971).

54. Constance Penley has theorized this appeal through the idea of "represen-

tative mediocrity," in her analysis of Christa McAuliffe's persona at NASA, as "the all-American girl next door, pretty but not too pretty, competent but not overly intellectual, a traditional mother and teacher whose lawyer husband was her high school sweetheart." These were appeals that reveled in and promoted, as exceptional, McAuliffe's very "ordinariness." See Constance Penley, "Spaced Out: Remembering Christa McAuliffe," *Camera Obscura* 29 (Winter 1992): 180, 183.

55. Serafina Bathrick, "*The Mary Tyler Moore Show*: Women at Home and at Work," in *MTM: 'Quality Television,'* eds. Jane Feuer, Paul Kerr and Tise Vahimagi (London: BFI Publishing, 1984), 112. Bathrick notes that Mary "remains a Midwestern middle-class woman who lives alone on the middle floor of her apartment house" between Rhoda upstairs and Phyllis downstairs.

56. James L. Brooks quoted in Alley and Brown, *Love Is All Around*, 7.

57. Laura Koss, "International Appeal," *Hotel & Motel Management* (1 November 1993): 59.

58. Eric Ringham, "Minneapple Rolls Over the Red Carpet," *Star Tribune* (12 April 1982): 1A.

59. Jeffrey Zaslow, "Tam-Tossing TV Girl Makes a City Debate Limitations of Statue," *Wall Street Journal* (19 June 2001): A1.

60. Jerry Haines, "Hip in the Heartland," *St. Petersburg Times* (1 July 2001): E1.

61. Bourdieu, *Distinction* 479.

NOTES TO CHAPTER 5

1. Paul Rudnick, "Will Ellen Still Wear Pants?" *Newsweek* (14 April 1997): 70.

2. Andrew Ross, *No Respect: Intellectuals & Popular Culture* (New York: Routledge, 1989), 61.

3. Pierre Bourdieu, *Distinction: A Social Critique of the Judgement of Taste,* trans. Richard Nice (Cambridge: Harvard University Press, 1984), 124.

4. Ron Becker, *Gay TV and Straight America* (New Brunswick: Rutgers University Press, 2006), 80–81.

5. Ibid., 81.

6. Ibid., 90.

7. Ibid., 90.

8. Becker and Alexandra Chasin call attention, though, to the fact that this advertiser-driven rhetoric regarding the affluent gay and lesbian demographic was largely promotional, rather than actual, and experienced unevenly where true. See Alexandra Chasin, *Selling Out: The Gay and Lesbian Movement Goes to Market* (New York: St. Martin's Press, 2000), 34.

9. Danae Clark, "Commodity Lesbianism," *Camera Obscura* 25/26 (1991):

194. John Caldwell also argues that this strategy historically has been critical to television's operation, noting the medium's "serious investment in American racial and class politics." "Historically, television did not simply define and leave the aesthetic threat out there on the margins. It also actively worked to turn the aura" of "dangerous forms of race and sexuality" "into practical behaviors and commodities that 'you too could own.'" See, John Thornton Caldwell, *Televisuality: Style, Crisis, and Authority in American Television* (New Brunswick: Rutgers University Press, 1995), 68, 70.

10. Joe Mandese, "Beyond the Top 25 Markets," *Television Week* (29 January 2004): 10.

11. Ibid.

12. Michael Novak, "You Can Go Home Again," *Forbes* (3 September 1990): 86.

13. Ralph Keyes, "The Flyover People," *Newsweek* (3 August 1998): 14.

14. Susan Chandler, "Lately, Target Just Can't Miss," *News & Observer (Raleigh)* (31 August 2001): D1, 6.

15. Herman S. Gray, *Cultural Moves: African Americans and the Politics of Representation* (Berkeley: University of California Press, 2005), 92.

16. Ibid.

17. Anna McCarthy, "'Must See' Queer TV: History and Serial Form in *Ellen*," in *Quality Popular Television*, eds. Mark Jancovich and James Lyons (London: BFI Press, 2003), 88.

18. Alexander Doty, *Making Things Perfectly Queer: Interpreting Mass Culture* (Minneapolis: University of Minnesota Press, 1993), 61, 103, 122–123n27; Kathleen Rowe, *The Unruly Woman: Gender and the Genres of Laughter* (Austin: University of Texas Press, 1995), 219; Pamela Robertson, "What Makes the Feminist Camp?" in *Queer Aesthetics and the Performing Subject*, ed. Fabio Cleto (Ann Arbor: University of Michigan Press, 1999), 271.

19. Judy Rose, "Ordinary People, Extraordinary Love," *Detroit Free Press* (23 December 1988): 1B.

20. Joy Horowitz, "June Cleaver Without Pearls," *The New York Times* (16 October 1988): 2, 1.

21. Caryn James, "Roseanne and the Risks of Upward Mobility," *The New York Times* (18 May 1997): Arts 37; Jeff Borden, "Funny, Not Pretty," *The Charlotte Observer* (16 October 1988): 1F.

22. Rick DuBrow quoting Harbert in "TV Academy Is Snubbing Roseanne," *Los Angeles Times* (23 July 1994): F16.

23. The term "cultural forum" is from Horace Newcomb and Paul M. Hirsch, "Television as a Cultural Forum," in *Television: The Critical View*, 5th ed., ed. Horace Newcomb (New York: Oxford University Press, 1994): 503-515.

24. Rick Marin and Sue Miller, "Ellen Steps Out," *Newsweek* (14 April 1997): 67.

25. See, respectively, quoting Terry Rakolta of Americans for Responsible TV in Greg Braxton, "Roseanne's Kiss: And Now the Aftermath," *Los Angeles Times* (3 March 1994): F1, and Mark Steyn, "Everybody Out! Ellen DeGeneres Ignites Lesbian Fever," *The American Spectator* (June 1997): 50.

26. Matthew Gilbert, " 'Ellen' Was Gay, But Just Not That Humorous," *Boston Globe* (13 May 1998): C1. *Ellen,* on the other hand, now received more attention than it had garnered previously, as a top-twenty show that was generally under the critical radar. Now it was alternately praised—for awakening to a political voice and "niche" appeal, "suddenly mobilized by a newfound reason to exist"—*and* criticized for being "political" instead of funny.

27. Roseanne's comments in an interview by Alex Ben Block at The Museum of Television and Radio's "She Made It!" speaker's series, featuring "Roseanne Uncensored" (16 October 2006, Los Angeles).

28. Drew Jubera, "ABC Won't Show 'Roseanne' Kiss," *Atlanta Constitution* (8 February 1994): E10. Here, Jubera is quoting Tom Arnold, then a producer and periodic guest star on *Roseanne,* as well as Roseanne's husband.

29. Marin and Miller, "Ellen Steps Out," 67.

30. Matt Roush, " 'Roseanne' Boldly Refusing to Kiss Up," *USA Today* (1 March 1994): 3D.

31. Mary McNamara, "What Ever Happened to Hip?" *Los Angeles Times* (22 February 2000): E1.

32. Dana Canedy, "As the Main Character in 'Ellen' Comes Out, Some Companies See an Opportunity, Others Steer Clear," *The New York Times* (30 April 1997): D8.

33. Steyn, "Everybody Out!" 50.

34. Rowe theorizes Roseanne's "unruliness" in *The Unruly Woman.*

35. Elayne Rapping, "In Praise of Roseanne," *The Progressive* (July 1994): 36.

36. McCarthy, " 'Must See' Queer TV," 96, 95.

37. David Zurawik, " 'Ellen' a Nice, Smart Sitcom," *The Baltimore Sun* (24 September 2001): 1E, and Mark Dawidziak, " 'Ellen Show' Lacking Only in Funny Lines," *The Plain Dealer* (24 September 2001): E1.

38. Gilbert, " 'Ellen' Was Gay," B7.

39. Diane Werts, "Dot-Com Dropout Drops Back In," *Newsday* (24 September 2001): B27.

40. "Yeah, She's Gay, But So What?" *Electronic Media* (13 August 2001): 22.

41. See, for example: Gilbert, " 'Ellen' Was Gay," B7; Ken Parish Perkins, "Ellen DeGeneres Is Back, But the Laughs Aren't," *Fort Worth Star Telegram* (24 September 2001): Arts 1; Werts, "Dot-Com Dropout," B27; and Zurawik, " 'Ellen' a Nice, Smart Sitcom," 1E.

42. "CBS Gives 'Ellen' Full Season Order," *Electronic Media* (19 November 2001): 21.

43. Dwight A. McBride, "Ellen's Coming Out," in *Why I Hate Abercrombie & Fitch: Essays on Race and Sexuality* (New York: New York University Press, 2005), 151. DeGeneres herself attempted to simultaneously analogize *and* hierarchize sexual and racial oppression in this sense when, in her *Time* magazine cover-story interview she said (regarding the controversy surrounding her coming out): "But, let's get beyond this, and let me get back to what I do. Maybe I'll find something even bigger to do later on. Maybe I'll become black." Quoted in Bruce Handy, "He Called Me 'Degenerate'? Interview with Ellen DeGeneres," *Time* (14 April 1997): 86.

44. Becker, *Gay TV and Straight America*, 5.

45. Ibid., 214.

46. Samantha King, *Pink Ribbons, Inc.: Breast Cancer and the Politics of Philanthropy* (Minneapolis: University of Minnesota Press, 2006), 38, 30. See also Laurie Ouellette, quoting Toby Miller, in her *Viewers Like You? How Public TV Failed the People* (New York: Columbia University Press, 2002), 38.

47. Amanda Lotz quoting Michael Curtin and Thomas Streeter in her *Redesigning Women: Television After the Network Era* (Urbana: University of Illinois Press, 2006), 26–27.

48. Chasin, *Selling Out*, 142–143.

49. Becker, *Gay TV and Straight America*, 1.

50. Jon Kraszewski, "Country Hicks and Urban Cliques: Mediating Race, Reality and Liberalism on MTV's *The Real World*," in *Reality TV: Remaking Television Culture*, eds. Susan Murray and Laurie Ouellette (New York: New York University Press, 2004), 182–183.

51. Further, as Becker points out, in the immediate aftermath of the events of September 11, 2001, a "politics of social unity" momentarily encouraged a setting aside of such culture-based rhetorics of difference; *Gay TV and Straight America*, 214.

NOTES TO CHAPTER 6

1. Barbie Zelizer, *Covering the Body: The Kennedy Assassination, the Media, and the Shaping of Collective Memory* (Chicago: University of Chicago Press, 1992), 151, 152.

2. Personal correspondence, Edward T. Linenthal to author, January 2002. I would like to extend deepest gratitude to Dr. Linenthal for his conversations with me about this chapter and about Oklahoma City's residents and anniversary and memorial events.

3. Edward T. Linenthal, *The Unfinished Bombing: Oklahoma City in American Memory* (New York: Oxford University Press, 2003), 21.

4. Personal correspondence from Linenthal to author.

5. Mary Ann Doane, "Information, Crisis, Catastrophe," in *Logics of Televi-*

sion: Essays in Cultural Criticism, ed. Patricia Mellencamp (Bloomington: Indiana University Press, 1990), 222.

6. The programs analyzed for this chapter include, chronologically: *CNN Special Report: Oklahoma City—One Year After the Bombing* (CNN, April 14, 1996); *CNN Presents: Legacy of Terror* (CNN, April 14, 1996); *ABC News Turning Point: Rebirth—The Untold Stories of Oklahoma City* (ABC, April 18, 1996); *The Today Show* (NBC, April 19, 1996); *CNN Saturday Morning* (CNN, April 19, 1997); the fictional prime time CBS series, *Promised Land* (CBS, May 7, 1998 and May 14, 1998); and, *The Today Show* (NBC, April 19, 2000).

7. Charlotte Brunsdon and David Morley, *Everyday Television: 'Nationwide'* (London: British Film Institute, 1978), 82.

8. James Carey and John Quirk, "The Mythos of the Electronic Revolution," *American Scholar* 39 (1970): 420.

9. Ibid., 420–421.

10. "President Clinton's Remarks at Memorial Service," *The New York Times* (24 April 1995): A2.

11. Serge Schmemann, "New Images of Terror: Extremists in the Heartland," *The New York Times* (24 April 1995): A12.

12. Quoted in ibid.

13. Nancy Gibbs, "The Blood of Innocents," *Time* (1 May 1995): 57.

14. Barry Tramel, "Oklahomans See World in One Day," *Daily Oklahoman* (20 April 1995): 29. Please see, also, for all *Oklahoman* citations, the newspaper's memorial site and archive of the bombing and its impact on the community and its citizens. http://newsok.com/bombing.

15. This is in contrast to coverage of the Los Angeles uprisings, for example, which typically represented "unthinking mobs" victimizing "rational citizens."

16. Kathleen Treanor, "An Appeal from the Heart," *Daily Oklahoman* (16 October 1998): editorial.

17. Kenneth Foote, *Shadowed Ground: America's Landscapes of Violence and Tragedy* (Austin: University of Texas Press, 1997), 166.

18. Ibid., 15–16.

19. Ibid., 89–90.

20. This requires active work in the sense that current statistics indicate that Oklahoma City's metro population is just under one million residents, while the population within the city limits (506,132 residents, according to 2000 Census data) places the city between St. Louis, Missouri and Nashville, Tennessee in size; Oklahoma is also considered to be a metropolitan state, with over sixty percent of its land mass defined as metropolitan.

21. Zelizer, *Covering the Body*, 5.

22. "Praise God from whom all blessings flow . . ."

23. Cited on the note as Psalm 122:7-8, "Peace within thy walls, and pros-

perity within thy palaces. For my brethren and companions' sakes, I will now say, 'Peace be within thee.' " *The Holy Bible*. Authorized King James Version (New York: Collins' Clear-Type Press, 1954), 737.

24. "A Strike at the Very Heart of America," *U.S. News and World Report* (1 May 1995): 53.

25. John Thornton Caldwell, *Televisuality: Style, Crisis, and Authority in American Television* (New Brunswick: Rutgers University Press, 1995), 4.

26. In reference, particularly, to news broadcasting and to CNN as a cable outlet, Caldwell has argued that post-1980s television has been marked by an "excessive style"—a shift "from a framework that approached broadcasting primarily as a form of word-based rhetoric and transmission . . . to a visually-based mythology, framework, and aesthetic based on an extreme self-consciousness of style." Ibid.

27. Quoting survivor Jim Denny, father of victim Rebecca Denny.

28. Lauren Berlant, "The Face of America and the State of Emergency," in *Disciplinarity and Dissent*, eds. Cary Nelson and Dilip Gaonkar (New York: Routledge, 1996), 399.

29. Leo Marx has outlined this conception of the "American Pastoral" throughout the nation's history in his *The Machine in the Garden: Technology and the Pastoral Ideal in America* (New York: Oxford University Press, 1964). This understanding is echoed in James Shortridge's work, as cited previously.

30. And all with a decidedly unhappy ending. According to *The Daily Oklahoman*, in a report published September 7, 1996, Edye and Tony Smith had filed for divorce.

31. "A Hand Up Is Not a Hand Out, Part One" (CBS, May 7, 1998), and "A Hand Up Is Not a Hand Out, Part Two" (CBS, May 14, 1998). Series creator and executive producer, Martha Williamson, was also the executive producer of *Touched by an Angel* (CBS, 1994–2003) from which the Greenes were spun-off for their own series.

32. Penny Owen, "Coloradans Take Role in Murrah Bombing Trial Seriously," *Daily Oklahoman* (24 March 1997): 8.

33. Jacqueline Mitchard, "TV Heads for the Heartland," *TV Guide* (8–14 April 1995): 28, 30.

34. On the work of the National Memorial Institute for the Prevention of Terrorism and its findings, see Gail Gibson, "War on Homegrown Terrorism Proceeding with Quiet Urgency," *The Baltimore Sun* (17 April 2005): 1A.

35. Kevin Helliker, "In These Tense Times, the Heartland Is Comforting," *The Wall Street Journal* (2 January 2002): A2.

36. Stephanie Simon, "Fargo Hip? You Betcha," *The Los Angeles Times* (10 March 2004): A16.

37. Joel Kotkin, "American Dream Finds a New Home," *The Los Angeles Times* (18 January 2004): M1, M6.

38. Helliker, quoting Matt Karst, "In These Tense Times," A2.

39. Berlant, "The Face of America and the State of Emergency," 398.

NOTES TO THE EPILOGUE

1. See, respectively, Paul Krugman, "Those Farm Subsidy Blues: Blame It on the Red States," *Milwaukee Journal Sentinel* (9 May 2002): 19A; Ann Patchett, "The Country of Country," *New York Times Magazine* (11 May 2003): 15; Ronald Brownstein, "A Red-Blue Stalemate?" *The American Prospect* (18 November 2002): 37.

2. Carolyn Marvin, *When Old Technologies Were New: Thinking About Electric Communication in the Late Nineteenth Century* (New York: Oxford University Press, 1988), 4.

3. David Morley, *Home Territories: Media, Mobility, and Identity* (London: Routledge, 2000), 109. According to the Pew Internet & American Life Project data from the end of 2005, only "24% of adult rural Americans used broadband at home, vs. 39% of those in urban and suburban areas," both figures of which indicate a gradual and relatively uneven dispersal of new media platforms beyond television and cell phone technology (where tri-modal phones are still available). See Paul Davidson, "Plan Would Widen Rural Areas' Access to High-Speed Service," *USA Today* (14 March 2006): 2B.

4. Joe Mandese, "Beyond the Top 25 Markets," *Television Week* (29 January 2004): 10.

5. On housing and economic conditions in the Midwest circa 2004, see Joel Kotkin, "American Dream Finds New Home," *The Los Angeles Times* (18 January 2004): M1. And, on television market revaluing, see Mandese, "Beyond the Top 25 Markets," and, Wayne Friedman, "Broadcast Networks Lose Upscale Viewers," *Television Week* (8 December 2003): 16.

6. Elizabeth Jensen, "ABC Shoots Not at Hip but at Heartland," *The Los Angeles Times* (8 December 2003): E1.

7. Patricia Aufderheide, *Communications Policy and the Public Interest: The Telecommunications Act of 1996* (New York: Guilford Press, 1999), 6.

8. Morley, *Home Territories,* 14–15.

9. Aufderheide has recently pointed out the paradox (and no small disingenuousness) inherent in the networks' attempts, as arms of major media conglomerations, to position themselves in these "lowly" terms, noting that traditional over-air broadcasters fight the encroachment of telecommunication providers and others into digital broadcasting by casting "themselves as the endangered species of the networked era, as old-fashioned over-the-air mass media. . . . the video medium of the poor, the immigrant, the uncabled." Aufderheide, 48.

10. Mandese, "Beyond the Top 25 Markets," 10. During the 2005–2006 season, TV Land used a promotional campaign with the slogan, "TV Land: TV

You Can Watch" which pitted the network's family-friendly, multi-generational program appeal explicitly against the critically acclaimed, "edgy" appeals of Home Box Office (HBO).

11. Diane Mermigas, "PAX-Net Faces Its Doubters," *Electronic Media* (August 1998): 16.

12. Michael Schneider, "Paxon Learns Politically Correct Lesson," *Electronic Media* (27 July 1998): 31.

13. UPN and WB have since joined to form CW, while MyNetworkTV and Univision are each now also considered over-air broadcasters. The stations that made up the PAX network, as of June 2007, operate under the moniker, "ION."

14. Wayne Friedman, "Broadcast Networks Losing Upscale Viewers," *Television Week* (8 December 2003): 16.

15. Tom Shales, "Uncovering the True 'American Idol,'" *Television Week* (26 May 2003): 27.

16. Mandese, "Beyond the Top 25 Markets,"10.

17. Quoted in Christopher Lisotta, "How Moonves Transformed a Network," *Television Week* (20 June 2005): 18.

18. Jensen, "ABC Shoots Not at Hip but at Heartland," E16.

19. Cheryl Lu-Lien Tan, "'Reality' Turns Its Back on Big Cities," *The Los Angeles Times* (19 March 2003): E12.

20. Quoted in A.J. Fruitkin, "Enough with the Fancy Urban Singles: Networks Head for the Heartland," *The New York Times* (22 August 2004): Culture 15.

21. Dee Davis and Tim Marema, "A Rural Perspective," *Center for Rural Strategies Reports,* accessed at http://www.ruralstrategies.org/issues/perspective1.html.

22. Herman Gray, "Television, Black Americans, and the American Dream," in *Television: The Critical View,* 5th ed. (New York: Oxford University Press, 1994), 177 and 186, quoting Bill Nichols on ideology.

23. As seen in the data and visual provided in the map, "2004 Presidential Election: Purple America," and for the 2006 midterm elections, as realized by Robert J. Vanderbei at Princeton University. Accessed at http://www.princeton.edu/~rvdb/JAVA/election2004/.

24. "Ideopolis" is a term used by John Judis and Ruy Teixera in their *The Emerging Democratic Majority* (New York: Scribner, 2002), 71.

25. Erika Doss, *Benton, Pollack, and the Politics of Modernism: From Regionalism to Abstract Expressionism* (Chicago: University of Chicago Press, 1991), and Serge Guilbaut, *How New York Stole the Idea of Modern Art: Abstract Expressionism, Freedom, and the Cold War,* trans. Arthur Goldhammer (Chicago: University of Chicago Press, 1983).

Index

The dates of shows/series are the dates of their original run on the indicated network. Some shows, such as *Supermarket Sweep,* are reincarnations of series that aired previously on other networks.

hip, 152; *Lawrence Welk Show,* 80–81; lesbianism, 159, 161; *Mary Tyler Moore Show,* 112, 136; Midwest's association with, 16–18, 28; MTM Productions, 125, 139; "nerd" compared to, 217n37; populism, 17; sanity in an insane world, 140; self-actualized citizenship, 170; "Silent Majority," 85; urbane squares, 112; values associated with, 17–18; Welk, Lawrence, on, 80–81; whiteness, 18–19; *WKRP in Cincinnati,* 112, 140

Staiger, Janet, 22, 215n17, 219n53
Steiner, Gary A., *People Look at Television,* 92
Stillwell, Mrs. J. M., Jr., 97
Streeter, Thomas, 44
Subaru Forrester campaigns, 151
suburban affluence, 108
suburban conformity, 108
Sugrue, Thomas, 109
Super Bowl XXXVIII (2004) scandal, 214n12
Supermarket Sweep (PAX, 2000–2003), 205
Susman, Warren, 61, 75
syndication, 122

Tandem Productions, 122, 124
Target Corporation, *153,* 153–154, 156, 172
Tassler, Nina, 206
"taste" markets, 33
Ted Mack's Original Amateur Hour (various networks, 1948–1970), 67, 226n30
Telecommunications Act (1996), 9, 24, 201
television: 1920s–1950s, 37; 1950s, 67; 1961–1966, 89; 1970 season, 123; post-1980s, 240n26; 1990s, 149; access to, 7; aesthetic style, 6; as aspirational site of identification, 91–92; association of geography and political allegiance, 208–209; attention to, 201; audience for, 122–123; ball games on, 96–97; branding/promotional appeal, 6; broadband usage, 241n3; broadcast policy (*see* broadcast law/policy); cable television, 37, 220n13; centrality of, 9–10; "class" *vs.* "mass" programming, 66; consumerism, 78, 99; content delivery platforms, 201; core audience, 4–5; cultural pro-

duction, shared site of, 10; "daypart" of, 10; digital television, 223n63, 241n41; "elite" *vs.* "populist" perceptions of, 110; equality of service, geographically defined, 45, 46–47; genres of, 10–11; "Golden Age" programming, 25; good programming, 90; histories of American television, 25; liberal bias of television news, 110; locally affiliated stations, 33; market development strategy, 6; mass-market periodicals, 20–21; multi-generational family audience, 203; national network development (*see* national network development); national programming (*see* national programming); "neo-network" period (late 1990s on), 9, 24, 201–202; New York World's Fair (1939), 1–3, 40; news on, 110; parochialism of American, 9; pedagogy/public education, 91; place-bound ideals, 3; populism, 4; populist tastes and values, 8; profit structure, 122; promotional rhetoric, 37, 57; quiz programs, 63, 101; reform of, 89, 110; regionalism, 4, 6, 25; regulatory policy (*see* regulatory policy); rise to prominence, 25; self-conscious style, 240n26; service in the public interest (*see* service in the public interest); significance of, 9–10; sitcoms, 149, 166, 215n17; sponsorship models, 122; standardization, 3; three-network era (1940s–1980s), 8–9, 10; time spent viewing, 213n1, 214n12; usage, 213n1; values, transformations in, 78; viewership, 205; westerns, 63
television history, 209
television studies, 209
"television tourism," 142–143
"televisuality," 66
terrorism, representations of, 174–175
Texas, 208
"TGIF" line-up, 206
Thompson, Emma, 147, 162–164, *163*
Thompson-Hajdik, Anna, 23
Timberlake, Justin, 214n12
Time (magazine): 1970 Man and Woman of the Year, 115–116; "Blood of Innocents," 178; DeGeneres, Ellen, interview of, 238n43; *Jubilee,* 68; *Mary Tyler Moore Show,* 127; Minneapolis, 143; Minnesota, 117–119; Webster Groves,